Barfrestone

ISBN: 978-1-9993680-9-8 (hardback)
ISBN: 978-1-9993680-6-7 (paperback)

Published by the Orage Press
16A Heaton Road
Mitcham
Surrey
CR4 2BU
England

© MMXXIV All rights reserved. No part of this publication may be reproduced, performed, distributed, or transmitted in any form or by any means, including photocopying, recording, or other electronic or mechanical methods, without the prior written permission of the publisher, except as permitted by law. Michael Paraskos has asserted his right under the Copyright, Designs and Patents Act 1988 to be identified as the author of this work. The poem 'Like A Desolate Moon Skinned' © Ronnie McGrath (aka ronsurreal), used by kind permission.

This is an art history book, but it includes fictionalised elements that are intended to interact with the art theory and history discussed. Where fictionalised elements are included, no identification with actual persons (living or deceased), locations, organisations or products is intended or should be inferred.

Michael Paraskos

Barfrestone

**This edition includes the
Art-Art History Manifesto**

The **Orage** Press

For Ben

§1 The headmaster's ritual

'Boy! Boy! What are you doing boy?'

'Woh?'

'I said what are you doing boy?'

'Nuffin' sir.'

'I can see that boy. But what are you meant to be doing?'

'Gardnin' sir. Birdy said we should pick up weeds, sir.'

'Birdy? Do you mean Mr Partridge?'

'Yes, sir, sorry sir. Partridge said we should pick up weeds, sir.'

'It's Mr Partridge, boy. So why are you standing around doing nuffin'? I mean nothing.'

'Dunno, sir.'

'Don't know, boy. Not dunno. I don't know.'

'Me neither, sir.'

'You neither what, boy?'

'I dunno either, sir.'

'If Mr Partridge asked you to pull out all the weeds in the flower bed why are you not doing what he asked you to do?'

'Can't, sir.'

'Cannot. Not can't. I cannot.'

'Me neither, sir.'

'You neither what, boy?'

'I can't pick up the weeds, sir.'

'Forget the weeds. Say I cannot, not I can't. And certainly not me neither. How do you expect to get on in the world if you speak like that?'

'That's me bruvver, sir.'

'What's your brother, boy?'

'Ge'in on in the world. That's his job. Not mine, sir. He went to gramma. I'm just passing time. You know — gardnin', sir.'

'Except you are not, are you boy?'

'Noh woh, sir?'

'Gardening. You are not gardening boy. You are doing nothing.'

'Yes, sir. 'Cos I can't, sir.'

'I cannot!'

'Me neither, sir.'

'Oh don't start that again you stupid boy. Why can you not do the gardening?'

'It's the weeds, sir.'

'What about them?'

'Can't tell the diff'rence, sir. I mean, I cannot tell the diff'rence, sir.'

'Difference? I don't understand.'

'Me neither, sir. They all look the same. It's like they're all plants init. Or they're all weeds. I mean how do I know if it's a plant or a weed? It's like the weeds are pretending to be plants so people don't pick 'em. Some of 'em even have flowers, sir.'

'Oh. I see. Well go and ask Birdy — I mean Mr Partridge, how to tell the difference?'

'Can't sir.'

'Cannot boy! I cannot.'

'Me neither, sir. I can-not.'

'Why not you stupid boy?'

'Cos when I was weeding over there I asked him and he told me not to be such a stupid boy. So he sent me over here, sir. Said I was in the solent, sir. But I was just asking.'

'Well in that case, go and stand outside my office boy.'

'Sir? But why, sir?'

'Because I say so. Now boy!'

* * *

Sir? But why sir?

Because that is what we do, boy.
We empty you of all we see
And fill you up with what we need.

What do we do?

You empty me of all you see
And fill me up until I bleed.

Thank you, sir.

§2 Angel, angel, down we go together

Professor Geroud stood at the window of his office on the third floor of the bow-bay-windowed Georgian building that flanked one side of the pretty courtyard garden and saw the students gathering below. They were getting ready for the lecture he had scheduled that morning, to be delivered amongst the living acanthus leaves growing in the garden, and half formed acanthus leaves that seemed to grow from the rocks being carved by the students into Corinthian capitals. Strike them with your chisel and you have a literal egg and dart. It's oolitic stone you see? *Get it?* Oolitic — egg-like. And chisel — like a dart! Egg and dart.

> **Oh how we laughed at that one!**

Not Professor Geroud though. He didn't get it. And yet, there he was, a man who should have got it, being a professor and all, especially a professor about to give a lecture to the art school's carving students, many of them already seated on the hard blocks of billions of ooliths, like chickens incubating unhatched broods.

Guffaw, guffaw!

No, Geroud didn't get that one either.

Did I say *his* lecture? Yes, of course I did, and to the tiny crowd in the garden below there might have been an assumption Professor Geroud did write his own lectures. But he didn't. I don't mean they weren't written — of course they were written. It is just that Professor Geroud didn't write them. How could he? Despite being the art school's only Professor of Art History, Professor Geroud knew nothing about art, or history, or even art history. As he would put it, he was an imposter.

As the Professor looked down on the students below, resembling a figure in a Caillebotte painting — *something he could not have known either* — he saw the real author of the words he was about to speak walk across the garden. Well-dressed, with a handsome if slightly doggy face, like Charles Boyer, he mingled effortlessly with the dusty students below, in a way Geroud could only dream of doing. 'Trust me, Lonely Heart,' he'd say. 'They're going to love you.' *Trust me.* He was always saying that, but the more he said it, the less Professor Geroud did. Experience should have taught Professor Geroud, *the doggy-faced man's Lonely Heart,* the limits of trust. But what was the alternative? There was too much sunk cost to back out now.

A short while later the strange doggy-faced man was in Professor Geroud's office, sitting in a large leather library chair, his feet on the professor's desk, smoking a cigarette. 'You're going to make them think,' the doggy-faced man said. 'They're going to think about what the world could be like, rather than accepting it for what it is. You're going to start a revolution.' Professor Geroud looked doubtful. 'You know, it's the one thing I don't understood about carvers these days. They used to be such radical chaps. Now they seem so resigned to their fate. Victims of fate you might even say.' The strange doggy-faced man took his feet off the desk suddenly and leaned forward. 'You're going to be a firework right up their —' As he spoke, a lorry or bus screeched to a sudden halt somewhere on the road outside, its brakes howling so loud Professor Geroud never heard where the firework was destined. But he knew the doggy-faced man had done that on purpose, just to play up the Ealing Comedy effect, even if it meant some poor sod had to be hit by a bus outside. 'Tell them it's a thought experiment in utopian thinking and follow the script.'

'And when they go off script?' mumbled Professor Geroud, looking at the typed manuscript he was holding in his hand.

'My dear Lonely Heart, that's the point of a thought experiment. They're meant to go off script. Trust me, you won't be alone. I've made the usual arrangements.'

On this point, the doggy-faced man was as good as his word. He always ensured Professor Geroud was never left alone to give his lectures. That would be foolish when the good professor knew so little about his subject. Geroud was no academic. He had no O' Levels (a statement that might help to date when these events are supposed to have taken place). He had no A' Levels either, and he had never been to university. Until recently he hadn't even heard of a subject called art history. And so, despite Geroud's rapid and some might say inexplicable elevation to the chair of art history in this little art school, the doggy-faced man knew Geroud couldn't give a lecture on his own. To remedy this flaw in the arrangements, every time Geroud was due to speak the doggy-faced man sent an assistant to help him — someone, or some thing, able to deliver a little talk as the professor should have been able to deliver it. It was clear the doggy-faced man was pleased with this particular ruse.

So it was on that day, with the sun shining, someone called Professor Geroud, somewhere in his late thirties, a second generation immigrant from some former British colony, descended the narrow staircase from his office, walked into a garden and faced a group of carving students, all now seated on a ragtag assortment of wooden, metal and plastic chairs and half carved limestone blocks set amongst the plants. And, as the strange doggy-faced man had predicted, they did seem to like him. They greeted him, casually, one by one, as he moved through them like a prosaic guru. But perhaps that was Geroud's skill. By not knowing anything on his subject he avoided intimidating students who knew just as little.

Reaching the front of the crowd Geroud found the doggy-faced man was already waiting for him. 'There you are! I was wondering if you'd run away.'

'Where would I run to?' replied Geroud. His voice might have sounded bitter if it wasn't so colourless. The doggy-faced man just smiled, before moving away to leave Geroud alone to give his lecture. Except, he wasn't alone. Standing to his side was another familiar figure, a handsome creature that might have passed for one of the young students, except for being too well-dressed, in a slightly old-fashioned and crisply-pressed grey suit. The creature's white shirt was buttoned tightly under its neck, and its crimson tie was probably the only neckwear being worn in the building. Moving forward, the creature stood behind Geroud, took hold of his hands, one in each of its own, and pressed its body against Geroud's back. It seemed to exert only the slightest of pressure, little more than a quiver, before vanishing, as though it had pushed itself inside Geroud's body. That the students never seemed to notice any of this always amazed Geroud, but he had come to accept it as one of life's mysteries, a secret riddle never to be solved.

With the creature now inside him, Geroud was relegated to the role of spectator of his own life, the Caillebotte figure now looking out of his own eyes as if they were just windows, watching as the creature give one of its invariably popular lectures. Geroud wished he really had the knowledge, confidence and wit of the creature to do this himself. But that was impossible. Geroud did not suffer from Imposter Syndrome. He was an imposter, living a life that his background, ambition and schooling had never intended him to live.

§3 Earth is the loneliest planet

'Today, I want to talk to you about utopianism. I want to talk to you about utopianism as a kind of thought experiment in which you might become utopian in your own thinking. To me this is important. It relates to the idea of transcendence, the desire to transcend a broken reality and replace it with a reality that is whole and in some way reconciled.

'One of the most remarkable features of the early history of America is the degree to which the early European settlers there saw it as a place in which to create utopia. We might disagree with what many of those early settlers thought was utopia, and the establishment of European settlements was rarely a utopian experience for the native inhabitants of the continent. But the fact is that many of those who left Europe for America were idealists who believed they were swapping the dystopia of the old world for the potential to create utopia in the new.

'For many of those European settlers the utopia they sought was religious, motivated by a desire to escape from the religious persecution they faced in much of Europe. Such was the draw of this utopian vision in the seventeenth century it led to mass emigration by Protestant Christians from Europe to New England, where groups like the Puritans created what were called Bible Commonwealths in which life was regulated by their interpretation of the Christian Bible. Similarly in Pennsylvania, the Quakers, Mennonites, Dunkers, Schwenkfelders, Moravians and other radial religious groups set up communities, creating what a contemporary Dutch settler, Esther Werndtlin, called 'an asylum for banished sects'. Mind you, she also called it 'a sanctuary for all evil-doers from Europe, a confused Babel, a receptacle for all unclean spirits, an abode of the devil.'

'It is interesting that many of those early European settlers saw America as a new Garden of Eden. Of course this tied nicely into their religious beliefs, but it was not only the religiously-minded who sought a new Eden on the other side of the Atlantic. In the wake of the Christian dissenters there were numerous examples of radical socialist, or at least proto-socialist, groups trying to establish utopian communities in America. This included Etienne Cabet, the leader of the Icarians, a French group, who sought to establish a utopian socialist community in the still independent nation of Texas in the 1840s. Later Cabet succeeded in starting a community in Illinois and again later in Missouri.[1] Another French radical, influential on both socialism and anarchism, Charles Fourier, was the inspiration behind the founding of Brook Farm in Massachusetts in 1841, a community which included the novelist Nathaniel Hawthorne.[2] However, it was not only in America that utopian communities were established. Robert Owen, an early British socialist and founder of the co-operative movement, helped turn the Scottish mill village of New Lanark into an early socialist co-operative community from 1800 onwards.

---

[1] See Donald Drew Egbert, *Social Radicalism and the Arts* (London: Duckworth, 1970) 143f

[2] See Donald Drew Egbert, *Social Radicalism and the Arts* (London: Duckworth, 1970) 133f

Later he too tried to establish a utopian community in America, this time in Indiana in 1825.

'As with the religious utopian communities, we might not agree with the principles under which these early socialists, co-operators and anarchists sought to live, but there is an important lesson to be learned from them. It is the lesson that sometimes it is necessary to abandon the mainstream arena in order to be permitted to practice one's beliefs. Perhaps we could go so far as to say it is impossible to achieve utopia within a mainstream location or society, just as it is impossible to achieve utopia with a mainstream mindset. Maybe to join the mainstream is to become the very thing you are fighting against. If so, a utopian community outside of the mainstream is the only serious option for people who are serious in what they claim to believe, a view that has potential implications for all of those who seek social change.

'Artists have long accepted this principle to be true. Even august institutions such as the Royal Academy of Arts in London started life as a utopian artists' group — utopian in the sense that it was set up to raise the status of art and artists in England through the rejection of what was the normative life for an artist by gathering together into a radical new mutual aid organisation. Entering the imposing classical building on Piccadilly that is the home of the Royal Academy in London today it is hard to believe the Royal Academy is in fact an artists' co-op. That might suggest a similarity between the establishment of artists' groups and radical political and religious groups, but it is possible to make that connection much closer. In the nineteenth century some dissenting artists' groups even began to resemble dissenting religious and socialist communities. One of the most well known of these was the Nazarenes who set up an artists' commune in Rome in 1809 in a former monastery, and began to live a semi-religious life. Their example was followed by the Pre-Raphaelite Brotherhood in England in 1848, which led in turn to the socialist artists' communities founded by William Morris, and the Secessionist art groups in various European cities in the late nineteenth and early twentieth centuries. One of my favourite of these groups was the Russian group, the Peredvizhniki, or

Wanderers, who literally set up an artists' co-op in St Petersburg in 1863, and who were close to writers like Dostoevsky and Tolstoy.[3]

'There are numerous other examples I could give, but the point is that in each case there is radical dissatisfaction with the mainstream art world and the radical solution is to establish an alternative art world to take its place. This is a political as much as an artistic agenda.

'To some extent this has happened in our own time by default. Living in a culture that tends to elevate immaterial thought above physical experience has given conceptualist artists an advantage in colonising many of the main art institutions in Western societies. As a result material art has been driven out of many of those institutions — and is misrepresented by those who remain — as intellectually inadequate. Some even call it nothing more than 'blind practice'. This in turn has given the corporate capitalists who run most universities a fig-leaf to justify cutting art courses,

---

[3] Elizabeth Kridl Valkenier, 'The Peredvizhniki and the Spirit of the 1860s' in *The Russian Review* vol. 34, no. 3 (Jul., 1975) 247-265

particularly space and facility hungry practices, such as ceramics and sculpture, diminishing the practice and teaching of art as a material activity. As a result, art as it is taught in most Western universities has come to resemble an act of capitalist-conceptualism and this fact has led many non-conceptual artists to distance themselves from the mainstream art world as much as possible. It would be tempting to suggest there is a kind of secessionism in that distancing, but unlike earlier 'secessions' it has not really resulted in the setting up of alternative meeting, exhibiting and debating spaces. There have been a few — I think of Turps Banana for example — but not quite to the same extent that the dismay with mainstream art in the nineteenth century led to an explosion of alternative spaces for artists, from cafes that were associated with particular art groups, to magazines that pushed particular lines, to *ad hoc* exhibiting societies dedicated to specific forms of dissenting art. Or indeed in the late 1960s and early 1970s when radical feminist art activity had very little to do with university art institutions.[4] Instead, withdrawal from the mainstream art world in recent history has resembled something more like giving up. Many artists who have not fitted-in with the late twentieth-century mainstream conception of art have simply left the field of battle and found a quiet corner in which to eek out their lives in often bitter obscurity.

'Perhaps that is unfair and I exaggerate. Hyperbole is the right of the polemicist, but it risks missing details that could tell a different story. For example, in North America there has been a revival of interest in the type of salon or academic art that was displaced in the 1870s and 1880s by modernism. But this strikes me as a curious route to follow, rather like pretending the British Empire never existed because one doesn't like imperialism. I am not sure withdrawing from reality is quite the same thing as setting up alternative structures, or that living in a fantasy world can ever be a long term solution to a problem. It just

---

[4] I am thinking here of someone like the photographer Jo Spence, amongst many others. See Simon Watney, 'Jo Spence' in *History Workshop,* spring, 1986, no. 21 (spring, 1986) 210-212. Also, Linsey Young (ed.), *Women in Revolt* (London: Tate Publishing, 2023)

seems delusional when what we really need, I would suggest, is a *kind of* new secessionism. If the current art institutions are not fit for purpose then the answer is surely to secede from them and establish new art institutions.

And yet, and yet, and yet, that sounds hideously daunting, or even impossible, especially for anyone with little money or time. *And yet.* And yet, in the lack of money and time so many of us experience maybe there lies the seed of an answer to the problem. If large and well-funded capitalist art institutions are not fit for purpose then the answer is clearly not to go and start another large and well-funded capitalist art institution. By that I mean the answer is clearly not to start yet another structure that does not produce worthwhile art or artists. As a thought experiment, wouldn't it make more sense to stop thinking of an art school as a university at all. What this means is that the true lesson to learn from our failing capitalist university art schools is that a functional art institution needs to be radically different to anything that exists now or else it too will fail in the same way. If dysfunctional art institutions tend to be in well-appointed buildings, with large administrative staffs and predetermined mission statements that appeal to bureaucratic minds, then maybe functional art institutions should not have any of these features, just as those Puritan Christians who settled in their utopian communities in North America did not arrive in their new home and expect or want to find large cathedrals and a church hierarchy, like the one they chose to leave behind, in place to greet them. Maybe for radical new secessionist artists an art school doesn't need to be a building at all. Maybe it could instead be any collection of artists that comes together to talk about art. Such an art school could, in effect, exist as a kitchen table, or a table in a bar or tea shop, or in a Greek restaurant or a curry house. Like the coffeeshops of eighteenth-century London and Paris, some of these new art institutions might not move beyond their humble beginnings — *and good on them for not compromising!* — but others might grow to ever greater things, hopefully taking on new forms unlike anything that exists in the staid world of art education today. But even without that happening, these table top schools of art could reconnect artists with each other, so those who really care about material art would not simply have to withdraw from the field of battle, they could instead stay engaged with art. There are precedents for this, such as the Hackney Flashers in London in the 1970s.[5]

'I like the unpredictable grass roots aspect of this, which appeals to my anarchistic instincts. I also think this bottom-up approach will be stronger and more connected to the flow of life than some grand scheme imposed from above. One of the mistakes people in the art world often make is to assume that if someone would only pay for a new museum, gallery or art centre then things will be alright. In reality, if someone did that then the institution would probably be so overrun with bureaucracy, or worse the ill-informed ego of an ignorant patron, it would kill off any creative spirit those working inside might have.[6] All it takes is a

---

[5] See Na'ama Klorman-Eraqi, 'The Hackney Flashers: Photography as a Socialist Feminist Endeavour' in *Photography & Culture* vol. 10, no.1 March 2017, 1–19

[6] Herbert Read, *To Hell with Culture* (London: Routledge, 1963: 2002) 88

recognition that there is no mystery about institutions. An institution is essentially a group of like-minded people who meet and work together consistently and regularly with a sense of common purpose. This is called a *communitas,*[7] and it is so simple a formula that it suggests there should not be a single serious artist in the land who does not have their own art school, and each of those art schools could easily take a radically different form, from an occasional meeting between fellow artists, to an informal tutorial between a professional and a novice painter or sculptor. Such a situation for the art world would not require unanimity when it comes to what type of art might be made or who has the right to make it. In fact it would encourage genuine diversity. To paraphrase Herbert Read, it would lead to a society in which each type of artist could express themself in the manner which they found most apt, each type of artist living and working side by side in perfect amity. And to quote Read directly: 'I do not suggest that such a community of individuals is too

---

[7] See Edith Turner, *Communitas* (London: Palgrave Macmillan, 2012)

idealistic to contemplate; it is, in fact, the ideal towards which we should aim.'[8]

---

[8] Herbert Read, *The Politics of the Unpolitical* (London: Routledge, 1943) 116-7

§4 You've got everything now

On the 3rd September 1976, some twenty-odd years earlier, a young boy pulled a book from a homemade bookcase. The bookcase was carefully constructed to be integral to the wall, which is to say that without the wall it would not stand up. Or, to put it another way, it had to lean against the wall to stop itself collapsing under the weight of knowledge it held. This young boy was also Geroud.

At his home Geroud found the books were very different to those he saw at school. Few of them had pictures, except the art books, but even those were not like the picture-books at school. They were full of naked bodies. Art seemed to like naked bodies. Geroud had his own book. It had come from school but it was his. It was not a library book. When it arrived his teacher called him to the front of the class and handed it to him. It was wrapped in brown paper with his name hand-written onto a white label stuck to the front. Receiving it felt like winning a prize. Except Geroud didn't win prizes and he hadn't won the book. His mother had bought it for him. He knew that as he'd taken in twenty-five pence each week to hand to the teacher every Monday morning for the past six weeks. But still, as his name was read out, and as he was told to go to the front to collect one of brown paper parcels piled precariously high on the teacher's desk, it felt like a prize.

The book was *The Owl Who Was Afraid of the Dark* by Jill Tomlinson. I often wonder why Tomlinson doesn't have a Wikipedia page. She should, she has an interesting life story. But there's an obvious reason I guess. Anyway, for rather less obvious reasons, *The Owl Who Was Afraid of the Dark* was a book that haunted Geroud's mind long after he ceased to be a young boy. But then, he was a boy often haunted by the memories of his past, and eventually he would become a man haunted in the same way. That might have been a good thing for more elevated people. In later life they might say things like, *I read Homer at an early age and it haunted me forever.* But Geroud never read Homer. He read *The Owl Who Was Afraid of the Dark,* and it was that little Puffin book that haunted him forever. For those of you who have never read this alternative to Homer, the story centres on an owlet, called Plop. Plop doesn't want to be a night-time bird. He calls the dark nasty. Geroud thought the dark was nasty too, but in the book Plop was cured of his fear.[9] That's the point, you see. In a surprising way Geroud would also be cured of his fear of the dark. Or do I mean the darkness? Either way, had he not been cured of his fear he might not have found himself standing, a couple of decades later, in front of a group of students delivering a lecture on a topic he knew nothing about. Mind you, unlike Geroud, Plop had no real choice but to go outside and embrace the darkness. He was an owl after all and so Tomlinson's book is a kind of primer in stoic philosophy, teaching children to accept that which is inevitable with a sense of equanimity. As Epictetus might have said, 'We have no power over external things.' Plop, you have to go outside, otherwise you will starve to death.

---

[9] Jill Tomlinson, *The Owl Who Was Afraid of the Dark* (Harmondsworth: Penguin Books, 1973)

Geroud opened a book he pulled from the tottering bookcase, but it is not *The Owl Who Was Afraid of the Dark*. It was a book of poetry by Ronnie McGrath. He read one of the poems and was changed by it. He didn't know he had been changed. But that's the dangerous thing about good poetry. It changes you when you least expect it. It haunts you for the rest of your life.

Like A Desolate Moon Skinned
by Ronnie Mcgrath

The last dimension of reality is this/the inexorable ageing process into which we are born moves toward the supreme darkness/where the mystery of the womb incubates her planets/the subconscious pit of the mind's being/flowing like a menstrual cycle/like an ontological meandering in search of history books/the grand narrative of some fictitious empiricism/where I am trapped/in cubby holes/in phobic skin/beneath the sea level of an ordovician swim/inside a panoptical gaze/on the surface of the conjurer's screen/ where the director's cut flashes back to the neo-realisms of primordial cave paintings/Plato's republic writ large upon stone/upon eyeball surface/upon a deep structured wall known as introspection/his shadow on my shadow/his graffiti on my graffiti/a ubiquitous illusion known as advertising/the self-conscious narrator of him/turning grand narratives into diegetic Morse encodings/the deconstructed concept that I am/a wombed-man of intertextuality/a fabulated coil without centre or planet to cling to/ anthropocenised/the death of me is the death of cars/the death of cars is the death of road kills/and everything is life and death here/a literary cycle of dead poets/of dead planets and lachrymose/the continental drift of our meaning deferred/our love of crisis/an aesthetically pleasing protest song/a microbial mat poem positioning morning papers/dialectics of a sonnet postmodernised/avantly guarded by the coded verse of beatitude and protest songs/a surrealistic rendition of the flutes embouchure/a diasporic chord progression in the key of spectacle and incarceration/the visual noise of it all/mercurial night of the bewildering darkness/da/da/da/da/da/da/and if art is for the sake of its own sake/a poem will be just as sweet by any other name/

§5 Julie in the weeds

It's another day, maybe early spring, in 1978 this time, and on this occasion the young Geroud is sat on the first floor landing of a tall gothic-revival school house. He is surrounded by dozens of soft toys.

Is? Or was?

It *was* sunny outside, a warm spring day, but Geroud's mother had not yet forced her son to leave the safety of the strange space in which he sat, to play in the bright sunshine outside.

Strange space?

Yes, it was a strange space, where the rise of the staircase was met by the return of a *kind of* balcony, running the length of the staircase, forming a *kind of* corridor that led nowhere in itself except into Geroud's imagination.

> I think you've mentioned this space before.
> But, when you teach your students architectural
> history and they ask, *what do you call that?*,
> and you don't know, what do you say?

I say I don't know, but it's a kind of… It's a *kind of soffit* or a *kind of moulding*, or in this case, *it's* a *kind of gallery*. That kind of thing. Always a kind of thing. Anyway, at the end of this *kind of* gallery a pointed-arched gothic window — *a lancet light no less* — gave a view out onto the small overgrown garden in front of the house, most of it in deep shade from an ancient apple tree. Beyond the garden ran the strangely-named Kake Street, the main road through the village. And beyond that, an open paddock in which horses grazed lazily in the sunshine, and beyond that….

'Geroud!' called Geroud's mother from downstairs. 'Geroud!'

At first Geroud ignored the call, a frown playing across his face as he picked up one of the soft toys and began to pick at its spotted dress.

'Geroud!' came a more insistent call. Geroud put the toy down, stood up and walked to the top of the stairs. Down below he could see his mother looking up from the hallway. 'Why don't you come when I call?'

'I told you,' replied Geroud petulantly. 'I'm extremely busy today.'

'Well whatever you're doing, can you come down? I want you to go to the shop.' Geroud began to descend the staircase, taking each step as though it was the ascent of Everest. The slow progress prompted his mother to try a different tack. 'You can get some sweets if you like.' As if his mother had spoken some magic words in a pantomime, — *issy-wizzy-let's-get-busy* — Geroud ran down the remaining steps, jumping the last two to land at his mother's feet with a thud. To the soft toys, still seated on the balcony, looking through the spindle balustrade at the events below, Geroud probably resembled Alice disappearing down a rabbit-hole.

'Careful!' cried his mother laughing as Geroud landed. 'You almost hit Lewis.' Lewis, the large ginger tom, looked up briefly from the wood and wicker chair on which he lay, smiled broadly at Geroud, and winked, before going back to sleep.

'He doesn't mind!' exclaimed Geroud, tickling Lewis behind the ears. Lewis purred in agreement.

'Are you sure you don't want to change before you go?' asked Geroud's mother, trying to sound casual.

'No!' said Geroud. 'Why?'

His mother paused. 'They're not really outside clothes,' she said. 'But never mind.' She placed a hand on each of Geroud's shoulders and pushed him backwards towards the kitchen like a supermarket trolley. Geroud giggled at being led this way. Once in the kitchen his mother pulled a tatty green pound note from her purse and gave instructions to buy a bottle of bleach and ten *No. 6*. Taking the money, Geroud ran into the back kitchen, stopping only to turn the big brass handle on the back door, which he always struggled to open, and out into the sunshine.

'No more than five-pence on sweets,' his mother shouted as Geroud ran down the driveway that their house shared with the neighbouring primary school. 'I want some change.'

Geroud waved and ran onto Kake Street, and on towards the only shop in the village — *Phippo's as everyone called it* — owned by Mr and Mrs Phipps.

The road was empty of cars. The village was not really between somewhere and anywhere, so few had reason to drive through it, and it wasn't much of a destination in itself. Also, did I mention this was 1978, the last year things were alright, and there weren't so many cars in those days? For a moment Geroud's only company stood in the paddock opposite the house. There he could see three or four horses. He slowed as he passed them, trying to ignore their stares which he took as a sign of their intense hatred of him. He had seen *Black Beauty* so knew the hideous beasts could rear up and trample you to death if they had a mind to. He even had nightmares about it, when the sound of their whinnying would slope through the night air, cross the field, unlatch the gate to the paddock and creep across the street. From there it sidled through Geroud's bedroom window and violated his sleep. Why would anyone with any sense like horses? But Geroud hated these horses more than most. Once a month they met with others of their kind for the local hunt. They gathered outside his house. Being a good little boy, Geroud hated the idea of hunting foxes, both on principle and because foxes looked sweet. Even in his still developing mind, the idea of hunting a small dog with other small dogs seemed cruel and stupid. Poor little blighters! But the gammon-faced men and shrew-faced women he saw on the monstrous horses outside his house each month were particularly cruel and stupid. They were barely human. He wished they'd fall from their saddles and be trampled to death by their own hideous horses. There would be no mourning them.

As he neared Phippo's Geroud slowed again, this time seeing two boys outside the shop. They were older than him, in the uniforms of Maudlin Street Secondary Modern School, and sat swaying on their Grifter bikes, like dull simulacra of their fox-hunting parents. Geroud had an instinctive fear he might be the fox.

'What the fuck's that?' shouted one of the boys as Geroud approached. 'Some bent fucker!' His friend laughed. Geroud tried to ignore them and went inside the shop. There he spent a long time looking for the bleach, even he knew exactly where it was, and once he had found it he was equally long in deciding which bleach to buy, even though the little shop only stocked two types, *Domestos - the Strong One!* Or Maid Marian: 'Don't buy that, it's just water.' He spent even longer choosing his sweets, despite having only five pence to spend. He always chose the same things, ten ha'penny chews, Blackjacks and Fruit Salads, but this time the choice took longer. Occasionally he looked up, to glance out of the window, hoping the two boys had gone away. But he knew they were still there, lying in wait for him.

'Are you alright dear?' asked Mrs Phipps from behind the counter, sparking panic in Geroud that he had stayed longer than was permitted. He did not realise there was a time limit on browsing. Silently Geroud nodded. He chose his usual sweets, placed them on the high counter and stretched up to balance the bottle bleach next to them. 'Mind that bleach,' said Mrs Phipps. 'It's dangerous. Anything else dear?'

'Could—I—have—ten—number—six—please,' said Geroud mechanically as through reading out loud in class.

'Are they for your mother?' asked Mrs Phipps. Geroud nodded as Mrs Phipps turned to the rack of cigarettes behind the counter and pulled out a small green and white box of Players No. 6. 'That'll be 44½p dear.'

Geroud handed Mrs Phipps the pound note he had held in his hand since leaving the safety of the house. It was damp and crumpled from his palm. Mrs Phipps took the note and placed it in front of the till. She stooped, took a plastic carrier bag from under the counter and placed the bleach into it. The sweets went into a paper bag and then they too went into the carrier bag. Finally the cigarettes followed. Mrs Phipps was inexplicably slow, but today Geroud was grateful for it.

The provisions bagged up, Mrs Phipps turned to the till again, pressed three or four of its typewriter-like keys, causing the machine to jump as if surprised at being wakened. She took the pound note, placed it in the now open draw and removed a shiny fifty-pence coin, a dirty old silver shilling and a dull copper halfpenny. Closing the draw she leaned forward and handed Geroud the change, counting it out — forty-four-pence-ha'penny, ha'penny makes forty five, five makes fifty and fifty makes a pound. Geroud never understood this numerical incantation, but accepted it as part of the process. The coins handed over, Mrs Phipps lowered the bag gently over the edge of the counter until Geroud could take it.

'Thank you,' whispered Geroud.

'Mind how you go dear,' said Mrs Phipps.

Outside the two boys were still waiting. 'Oh, it's that fuckin' wop,' one of them said loudly. 'The little one. Hey, you, why you dressed like that? You a fag?' Geroud didn't know what a fag was. He thought it was a cigarette. Did the boys want his mother's cigarettes? He ignored them and started to walk home. He wanted to run, but the weight of the bag forced him to walk. The boys followed him on their bikes, calling him names. He was a 'fuckin' fag' and 'a bent bastard'.

Soon Geroud arrived by the overgrown village pond, located at the side of Kake Street, midway between the shop and his house. No one used the pond any more, except on hunt days, when some of the horses took a drink there. Near it there were no houses to run to. Sensing their advantage, the boys peddled ahead and blocked Geroud's path.

'Oi, fag — you know it's fuckin' rude to ignore people?'

'Sorry,' mumbled Geroud. The boys laughed.

'Why do you dress like that?' one of them asked.

'I don't know,' mumbled Geroud.

'You're a fag. A bender, that's why.'

Geroud stayed silent.

'Maybe it's just an ugly girl,' said the other boy, grabbing at Geroud's tee-shirt. Geroud stepped back and felt his foot sinking into the soft mud at the side of the pond. The boys laughed again.

'What you got there?' one of them said, grabbing the carrier bag from Geroud's hand. The boy looked inside and saw the bag of sweets. 'Thanks, I'll 'av those.' He laughed loudly and looked in the bag again. 'And fags! Fags from a fag. Mine too.' Geroud was too frightened to protest.

The other boy took the bag, presumably hoping to find his own spoils. Visibly disappointed, he took out the bleach. 'Look,' he said. 'Something to clean up a dirty fag.' Maybe it was disappointment that his friend got the sweets and cigarettes that made him vicious, or maybe he was just vicious. Village boys could be vicious to small animals. Not just foxes. Anything. There was no compassion or sentimentality in them. The boy unscrewed the lid of the white plastic bottle, and calling to his friend, *Let's clean the dirty fag,* poured the bleach over Geroud. Instinctively, Geroud turned away, saving his face from the liquid, but his bare left arm was covered in it. He couldn't say it burned him. It felt cold and flowed down his arm like syrup. But later his arm came up in a rash.

'You need some water with that,' said the other boy, pressing his bike forward so the front wheel hit Geroud. Falling back, Geroud landed on his backside in the mud. The boys laughed. 'Pathetic. And still just a dirty fag!' one of them shouted as they rode off, leaving Geroud lying half in the water, half in the mud and horse shit.

Perhaps it was the shock, or maybe he hit his head as he fell, but Geroud knew it was odd that he was not crying. Surely he should be crying. Instead he felt a strange sense of shame. Or rather, he felt a *kind of* shame. It wasn't shame at what the boys had said and done. I mean, it wasn't just that.

I felt a kind of shame at having lost my mother's cigarettes and bleach.

Pathetic really.

And a kind of shame that I had lost my own sweets.

Pathetic.

And a kind of shame that the fifty-five and a half pence

I had clasped in my hand
had fallen somewhere into the mud beside me.

A kind of shame
at what my mother would say.

Pathetic. Really pathetic.

§6 Accept yourself

You could always tell when it was about to start. There was a crackle in the air, a kind of static you could feel on your skin, especially the skin on the back of your neck, that seemed to pervade the entire fabric of Maudlin Street Secondary Modern School. Not everyone felt it, but Geroud, some six years after being left in the mud of the village pond, was sensitised through hard training.

But what caused it? Some glances his way? Heads inclining in conspiracy? The sneering grin of a Tyro?

The Tyro is raw and underdeveloped; his vitality is immense, but purposeless, and hence sometimes malignant.[10]

---

[10] Percy Wyndham Lewis, 'Dean Swift with a Brush. The Tyroist Explains His Art', reproduced in Bernard Lafourcade (ed.), *The Complete Wild Body* (Los Angeles: Black Sparrow Press, 1982) 359

If only it was more specific. If only it was that obvious, Geroud would know then to move away, to run. He would know he had to hide. But it was more subtle.

> **Geroud, why did you never hide when you felt it? It's almost though you were party to your own torment, like you brought it on yourself. Why did you bring it on yourself? Did you think you deserved it?**

Maybe. Of course I knew what it meant, the crackle in the air, the hairs on the back of my neck standing upright, but I never knew where the danger would come from today. Where can you hide if you don't not know what you are hiding from?

Geroud could see the small group of boys moving towards him, beasts encircling their prey.

'Alright Gez,' sneered the Tyro Skinner, grabbing Geroud's arm and pulling it into a half nelson. Geroud winced. 'What you got in your pockets?' The Tyro Skinner put hit his free hand into one of Geroud's coat pockets and pulled out a packet of Handy Andies.

Nothing else of interest there, he tried the other pocket only to find another packet of Handy Andies. And another. 'Why've you got so many? It's disgusting.'

'Maybe he's having an abortion,' shouted the Tyro Scatson. Everyone laughed. Geroud joined in. Better to be in on the joke. But too loud, too artificial. Tyro Skinner yanked his arm sharply.

'Time to find you a girlfriend, you bent bastard.'

'Good luck with that,' sneered the Tyro Scatson. 'Unless there's a blind girl in the school.'

'A blind boy more like.'

Surrounded by the troop of Tyros, Geroud was frogmarched around the playground, from bench to bench, classroom step to classroom step — anywhere where the girls gathered. At each stopping point he was ritualistically offered up. 'D'you wanna go out with gay-boy Gez?' This was hard, but it wasn't the physical pain that bothered Geroud, even if his arm felt it was being wrenched from its socket. Nor was it the indignity of being led like some captive animal. Even that question, asked again and again, until barely a girl in the school was left unasked, was not the worst of it. As he was led around, part of him even wondered if one of the girls might say yes. But that was stupid. He knew it was stupid. He knew they were being bullied by his spectacle almost as much as he was, becoming objects for Tyro Skinner and Tyro Scatson's amusement. What bothered him — *what really bothered him* — was the look on the face of each girl as they were asked the question. Of course they'd say *no.* It was obligatory to say no, sometimes with a *get lost* for added variety. That was all to be expected. What really bothered Geroud was the look of absolute disgust on the girls' faces as they were asked. It was universal. Geroud knew he was ugly. Everyone told him he was ugly. But was he that disgusting? He must have been that disgusting. Their faces said he was that disgusting.

Lying on his bed at home that evening, Geroud opened an exercise book with the words 'Stock Index' written in red felt tip pen on the cover. Inside, the pages were pre-printed as graph paper, and down one side were written, in Geroud's scrawny handwriting, the names of everyone in his class. Across the top were dates and beneath each date, running laterally across the page, a series of numbers. For everyone in his class the first number, dating from when he had started the Stock Index, was 100. But as the days had passed, the daily numbers had gone up or down, depending on how Geroud felt the day had gone. Skinner's name was there, his number falling rapidly as the daily rituals of humiliation or violence played out. Scatson was down too. But others varied, up a few points on one day, for a kind word or simple act of humanity, down a few points on another day, for laughing at his expense or joining in with the ritualistic bullying. None of the names were now above 100. The Geroud Stock Index had been a permanent bear market since the start of the school year, his stock falling with everyone. Or almost everyone. One name did still hover near 100, more as a record of Geroud's hope than any real sign of affection. That name was the Melusine's. When it came to her Geroud was the last of the great romantics, full Petrarch in his love. Today, she had been sat on the steps of one of the classrooms and she too was asked if she'd go out with the captive Geroud, even though she was the Tyro Skinner's girlfriend. 'Oh yeah,' she'd said with a sarcastic drawl. 'If you gouge my eyes out with a compass.' A small fall in stock then, as Geroud realised the Melusine was the only girl in the school who hadn't actually said the word *no.*

§7 Handsome devil

Geroud. Geroud. Are you alright? What are you doing?'

'I'm swimming. *Obviously.* I'm swimming widths.'

'Widths? You mean lengths.'

'Do I look like the sort of man who goes the long way round?'

'But why?'

'Because that's what you do in a pool isn't it? Swim. Up and down, up and down.'

'How would you know?'

'I've seen others do it. I've kept watch and made a careful note.'

'Except people usually swim lengths so they don't get in other people's way. You'll just get in the way. And I'm not sure if it even is up and down if you do widths. It's more like back and forth.'

'Whatever.'

'Well, it's not what *you* do. I mean, it's not what you *usually* do. You usually lurk by the changing rooms or up on the balcony. You cannot swim in a pool. Not with your arm.'

'No, I cannot swim. Not in a bleach-filled pool. But today I wanted to know what it's like. What it's like to swim with her.'

'That's it! You keep looking at something.'

'I'm looking at her, sitting on the edge of the pool, like a goddess. A Melusine!'

'A siren more like. A harpy. Just keep away or she'll snare you with a thread of golden hair.'

'No. Not today. Today is different. She is different and I want to swim in the pool.'

'She's the same. She's cruel. Her friends are cruel. They're rank. And that Skinner boy. He scares me.'

'He scares me too. But not the Melusine. Just look at her. You can see she's different. Beautiful! I'm going to speak to her.'

'What's got into you today?'

'I want to swim. Today I want to swim.'

'But you can't. Your arm. You know you can't. Not here. In the sea it's fine, but not in there. Here there are monsters and you'll drown.'

> **The Melusine.**
> **A nasty piece of work,**
> **but with the face of an angel.**
> ***Quelle surprise!***
> **Male author rears up the sexist trope**
> **of a femme fatale.**[11]

* * *

My apologies, I digress. What I meant to say was that aspects of magic, and what we might term 'witchcraft', are all around us. As you will have seen from reading chapters 1, 9 and 10 of *Cursed Britain* by Thomas Waters,[12] as you were asked to do for this week's

---

[11] See Carola Hilmes, 'Femme Fatale' in Hans-Otto Hügel (ed.), *Handbuch Populäre Kultur Begriffe, Theorien und Diskussionen* (Stuttgart: Metzler, 2003) 172f

[12] Thomas Waters, *Cursed Britain: A History of Witchcraft and Black Magic in Modern Times* (New Haven: Yale University Press, 2019)

lecture, belief in and the practice of magic and witchcraft has survived into the modern world. Indeed there are many manifestations of magic today, not all of them formal, like witchcraft, much of it homespun. Some of its practitioners might not even think of it as magic. Of course, that does not mean any of the alleged præternatural aspects of magic are real. It is simply to say that the performance of acts we might define as the practise of magic stems from a belief in the supranatural which is present even in our modern world. We are, as humans, superstitious creatures, not only in our beliefs and in our unwillingness to perform particular acts in case we provoke negative consequences, but in the surprising frequency with which we permute into spell-casters. In other words, the use of magic to provoke positive acts is still with us, or as we might put it, we still believe in active magic alongside passive superstition.

    I would suggest that most passive superstition takes the form of avoidance practices, such as the disinclination many people have to walk under ladders, even if it means stepping onto a dangerous busy road.

Others will ensure they throw salt over their shoulder when it is spilled, although there seems to be some confusion as to which shoulder one should aim for. *[Pause for laughter]*. And there is still widespread dismay at the unlucky consequences of breaking a mirror, aside from the inconvenience of having to clean up the shattered glass afterwards. *[Pause again for laughter]*. These I term passive practices of magic, in that they seek to ward off a potential effect, rather than cause one. And I must admit I am not, for my part, immune to any of these follies. In attempting to compile a list of my own foolish superstitious fears, and passive acts of magic, I find I have to include:

- **a dislike of walking under ladders**
- **the breaking of mirrors**
- **the spilling of salt**
- **passing someone on a staircase**
- **drinking my morning coffee from the wrong cup**
- **drinking other drinks from my morning coffee cup**
- **damaging a photographic image of a loved one**
- **anything to do with the number thirteen**
- **a less specific dislike of the number four**

- **seeing the morning sun without offering a greeting**
- **taking the Lord and Virgin Mary's names in vain**
- **seeing a single magpie without saluting**
- **other people eating pork at weddings (this does not apply to me personally as I do not eat meat)**
- **changing my cardigan or jumper the right way around if it has first been put on inside out**
- **dropping a book without apologising to it**
- **knocking over a particular sculpture in my house without stroking its head and apologising to it**
- **invoking the devil or any of his legions.**

et cetera.

I guarantee, no good can come from breaking any of these beliefs, for which I offer no rational reason, although I swear to God, I am an absolute atheist.

But, in addition to these, there are still plenty of practices of active magic in the modern world. Things done to precipitate a desired result. For example, at my allotment there are still people who sacrifice, as it were, a bottle or two of cider at the bases of their apple trees each spring…

* * *

'Geroud. Geroud. What are you doing?'

'I'm swimming. *Obviously.* I'm swimming widths.'

'Stop. Get out of the water. Your arm. Look at your arm.'

'I want to look at her. She's a goddess. A Melusine.'

'A siren more like. Something from the depths of the sea. Has she seen you?'

'I think so. She beckons with a stare.'

'Are you sure, Geroud? She might just wonder why you keep looking at her. And why you have blusters on your arm.'

'It's more than that. It's magic. The magic has worked.'

'What magic? I don't understand. Sometimes you set me beating my brains to find the hidden meaning in what you say with all this mysticism.'

'That's right, it is mystical. She stares at me and I am possessed.'

'Misguided. There's no such thing as magic, although she might be a witch in disguise.'

'The magic and the ecstasy!'

'Remember the lines my friend — *A mermaid found a swimming lad, took him for his own, pressed his body to her body, laughed and plunging down, forgot in cruel happiness, that even lovers drown.*'

'I've already drowned in her.'

'There you have it! A word to the wise, Geroud. Turn away. Stop-up your eyes and stop-up your ears.'

'Why? The magic has worked. Why should I fear?'

'It's the chlorine in the water. It's got in your blood. Don't go to her. A moment of hope and a lifetime of despair.'

'I will go to her. I will speak to her. I will.'

* * *

In the good old days Geroud would have been drowned as a witch, or shut in an iron maiden, but he was never into heavy metal. The previous Sunday he had spent much of the afternoon reading a strange book on magic and then constructing a paper pyramid, exactly seven inches by seven inches by seven inches, and open at its base.[13]

He had placed the pyramid on the sill of his bedroom widow and ensured one of the corners pointed north, this direction ascertained with aid of a cheap and possibly unreliable plastic compass from a Christmas cracker.

Taking a sharp pin and another piece of paper, he had pricked the forefinger of his left hand and drawn blood. This had hurt, but he persevered and with the blood flowing, he had dipped the head of a pencil into it and written a name on the paper. It was the name of the girl now seated in front of him, the girl in the pool. The Melusine. Or rather Kaz, as she was more generally known to her friends. Geroud had been more formal, writing the name Karen, even though this meant expressing more blood than was perhaps necessary.

---

[13] Maybe the book was Max Toth et al, *Pyramid Power: The Secret Energy of the Ancients Revealed* (Merrimac: Destiny Books, 1999) No that would have been published too late. Something like that though.

Having done this, he placed the gory paper under the pyramid, being sure to maintain its northern alignment, and left the unnatural laws of nature to do their work.

The following morning Geroud went to school and spent the first half of the day in eager anticipation that something extraordinary would happen. But by late morning it was clear nothing was going to happen. Everything was the same. As usual, he had been mocked for his gawkiness and even kicked in the shin by the Melusine's boyfriend, Skinner, as they walked between classes. As usual Scatson called Geroud a bender, although it was unusually curt this morning, missing its standard sobriquets, *fucking bender,* or *fucking dirty bender.* This gave Geroud some hope that the magic was beginning to work.

But no, the magic hadn't worked. Nothing else remarkable happened, leading Geroud to muse on the failure of his carefully constructed experiment into the unexplained laws of nature and the powers latent in humanity. That lunchtime Geroud sat alone on the steps of one of the Portacabin classrooms, unable to comprehend what had gone wrong. The only possible conclusion, he decided, was that magic needed something else to make it work. A catalyst. Maybe a magic word or phrase, like *izzy-wizzy-let's-get-busy,* or just plain old *abracadabra!* Maybe, it needed enacting with some incantation, like mass at church, with the priest needing to say the right words before the bread and wine would turn into body and blood:

> *Hic est enim Calix Sánguinis mei, novi et ætérni Testaménti, mystérium fídei.*

Mystérium fídei. That was the key thing. It was the enixa of the spell. It was the enactment.

Having worked out what had gone wrong Geroud decided the enactment would be in the swimming pool that afternoon. Despite his inability to bathe in water containing chlorine, today he would have to swim. It would be a kind of blood sacrifice swimming in the bleachy water, up and down, up and down, or back and forth. In the pool he would approach the Melusine. Perhaps the enactment would happen the moment he spoke to her. Perhaps speaking to the object of his desire in a *kind of* holy water would set in train a marvellous, miraculous, transubstantive act. At least it was a plan even if a voice seemed to warn him against being so reckless.

    And so, complete with blistering arm, in the pool that afternoon he swam and while he swam he spoke to her.

* * *

Twenty minutes later Geroud sat alone again, this time outside the pool building, on a low wall separating the canopied footpath from the car park where the school bus would soon arrive to take the class back to Maudlin Street Secondary Modern School. In no time the other children would appear and crowd by the main entrance until a *kind of* responsible adult emerged to tell them not to block the doorway. They would climb onto the bus and it would drive them away. Nothing more remarkable than that would happen. Nothing ever did.

    Except today.

Geroud assumed the Melusine had heard him speak, although she had given him no reply. She had just looked at Geroud blankly. Magic required faith — *the book has said that* — but this was a severe test of faith and for a moment Geroud faltered. From his resting place outside the pool he stood up and began to walk along the path, each step careful and slow, like footfalls on the boundary of another world, until he reached the gentle river Stour that ran by the far edge of the car park. In the water below he could see sinister grey shadow-fish moving amongst the long river weeds which swayed like mermaids' hair. He shuddered.

* * *

Geroud couldn't say why he turned around at that moment, but if pressed on the matter he might have said he felt himself being watched. He might have called it a vague feeling, or even a sixth sense. Something magical. Whatever it was, without explanation he felt compelled to turn around and look back along the path.

He expected to see a crowd of school kids being shouted at by an exasperated teacher. But the car park was empty. Or almost empty. In the distance Geroud could see a single figure, the Melusine, watching him as if mesmerised by him as much as he was by her. At last the Melusine began to walk forward, each step as slow as his own had been, trance-like, until she too stood at the riverside. The Melusine looked different. There was no contempt or sneer in her face, just a smile, broad and welcoming. Geroud smiled back, but neither of them spoke. It was as though the magic that had brought them together wanted to hold them in silence, at least for a moment.

It was the Melusine who broke the spell of silence first. She asked Geroud if he wanted to go into town. She suggested they could skip the school bus and get a chocolate mocha at Poppins, or maybe a bite to eat. Geroud agreed, and they walked the river path from the car park to the centre of town, passing through the cathedral precinct on their way, as if to add a holy benediction to their union. As they walked they talked with ease, without hesitation or embarrassment at expressing their feelings, the boy who barely spoke and the girl who had never spoken kindly to him. They were comfortable together.

At Poppins they shared a mocha, each taking a sip from the same tall glass in which it came as though sharing a eucharist tass. Soon the Melusine suggested they should eat at a restaurant nearby, and there they talked through their food and drinks as though they had always been together, an Adam and Eve in the Cathedral City of Eden. With the evening drawing to a close, and the school bus long gone, Geroud said something about getting home, but the Melusine said she was planning to stay in town that night. She said she had booked a room at Baker's Hotel. She suggested that Geroud might want to join her and soon they found themselves in the hotel bar. The Melusine asked Geroud what he wanted drink. Geroud said he'd like a Coca-Cola, with ice and a slice of lemon, but the barman said they only had Pepsi. Geroud said that was fine and the Melusine said she'd have one too. She suggested they take their drinks to her room. Geroud agreed.

In the room the Melusine took a mouth full of Pepsi from her glass and walked up to Geroud. She put he arms around his neck and kissed him — not a standard kiss, but a magical kiss in which Geroud found his mouth was full of sweet Pepsi, still fizzing as it hit his tongue. He giggled and said the Pepsi had gone up his nose. Then he took a sip of his Pepsi and kissed the Melusine, and this time they did not giggle and their kisses tasted sugar-sweet.

The Melusine sat down on the side of the bed and gestured for Geroud to join her. Geroud sat as instructed. The Melusine laid back, turning a little as she did to look at Geroud, before raising her arm and taking into her hand the school tie Geroud still had hanging from his neck. Like tugging a leash, she pulled it towards her and with it went Geroud.

§8 Sing your life

'With today's talk I want to continue our theme of challenges to standard academia by looking at a specific area of academia, namely academic convention. This will be a *kind of* journey into methodology, my methodology, but it is not intended as a methodology set in stone that either I follow invariably, or that you should follow. That would defeat its purpose and would also be impossible as it includes aspects of the logical and the absurd, the predictable and the unexpected, elements that might be called carnivalesque, fluvial or even matrixial. So let us think of this lecture as another thought experiment.

'In some branches of anarchism there is the principle of what has been called the *communitas.* That is a group that comes together for a specific purpose — let's say the exploration of an idea — and then disbands once that specific purpose is achieved. The communitas has no valid function beyond the achievement of that purpose, and so it cannot, unlike standard academic method, come together again in the same way to be applied to any subsequent purpose, even if those purposes are similar. It is resistant to reification as each exploration is unique and so a unique communitas must be initiated to achieve it. In this case, our exploration is into the possibilities for exploring knowledge and understanding in a way which is open-structured, without pre-determined goals, and more like the creative process. In short, I invite you to join me, as part of my communitas, on a journey into the twilight zone of my matrixial world, or do I mean my hypostatic world, I am not sure.

'As I hope I have indicated, any concept of standard academic methods and standard academic conventions, is to my mind, a straightjacket placed on what we do, and consequently on what we think.'

A question! By all means, why not! The lady in the front row with the Carmen Miranda hat.

Yes, I was just wondering, don't you think it's a good idea

to start your talk at the beginning?

'Ah yes. Of course. I thought I had, but perhaps not. As this is meant to be an academic lecture, we might be expected to start at the beginning. A very good place to start. No, wrong musical. And yet, why should we start at the very beginning? We are by now long used to narratives in fiction playing with the sequence of time, so why do we not accept the same with the non-fiction narratives of academia? It is as if 1910 never happened in academia and the modernist moment of disjuncture never passed beyond the university gate, except as a topic to be dissected like a frog on a dissecting board. Perhaps this is a moment of disjuncture, with the academic starting not with the question asked of himself, but one presented by a member of the audience herself. That alone would challenge the power dynamic of the academic discourse upending the traditional relationship between the speaker and the spoken-to. Suddenly the academic could not operate as if he was a neutral, omniscient and god-like narrator of truth. Instead she would need to acknowledge her position as a partial participant.

'That is a terrifying concept in many ways. To turn up at a conference on — let us say — modernism in art and literature, to discover the communitas wants to discuss mediæval architecture, or medical advances in the treatment of athlete's foot, or the current status of Dr Brown's son-in-law, who has just started an English degree at Trinity College Dublin.

'Terrifying. And yet, exactly what life is really like. Unpredictable and only partially open to preparation. When we engage with people, even if we have an agenda, it is not uncommon to veer off subject. For example, not so long ago, on my way to teach a class at Imperial College on Greek mythology and art, I found myself engaged in conversation by a stranger at West Norwood railway station. He was carrying a ukulele, and he told me he busked for a living, having previously been a road sweeper. He said he had a nervous breakdown, the climax of which came when he was pushing his broom down the street, passing the shops of West Norwood, and found the experience so overwhelming, he just threw his brush into the middle of the road, and walked away, so starting a new life as a busking ukulele player. He told me he had never been happier, and it was true he did seem happy. And then my train arrived, and I left him on the station platform, and I found myself at Imperial College, and there I taught my students about the wanderings of Odysseus, and the Labours of Herakles, and how they had been represented in art over the centuries, but I could not help mentioning to them the man with the ukulele. And somehow, in my mind, the story of the busker at West Norwood station, and the ancient tales of Homer and Peisander of Rhodes seemed connected, if only through the humanity of one random incident of human interaction, set against the humanity of ancient Greek poetry. This in turn makes me think, through a process of free-form thinking, of that wonderful 1957 film *Twelve Angry Men,* starring Henry Fonda. You might remember the question put to the men of the jury in the film is whether a young man is guilty of murder. That's the truth the jury seeks, the purpose of the communitas they have formed. But in the film it is not the cold facts of the case that engage the audience, or which lead to the film's humane conclusion on the nature of truth. Rather it is the human interactions of the characters, in their breaks, when they stop for some coffee or a cigarette, and start talking. It is when they talk not of the murder or the guilt of the accused, but on themselves, their families, and their experiences.'

STOP! STOP!

Yes, what is wrong?

You cannot say that. It's wrong.

Cannot say what?

You cannot say 'the wonderful 1957 film *Twelve Angry Men'*. This is meant to be an academic seminar. Calling the film 'wonderful' is a subjective value judgement and worse, it undermines my right to think it is not a wonderful film.

'Yes, you are right. I should keep my opinions to myself, and certainly not present them up as fact. It is my view that *Twelve Angry Men* is a wonderful film, but I cannot impose that on you without soulless qualifications — *I think, in my humble opinion, I hope I do not cause offence when I say Twelve Angry Men is a wonderful film.* And yet it is a wonderful film. I have always seen that kind of thing as a statement of truth, of human truth. Seeing the interior of Santa Maria Nouvella in Florence for the first time, made me cry. It *should* make you cry. Titian was the greatest painter who ever lived, but the most beautiful painting in the world is by his elder contemporary, Giorgione. The scene in the film *The Dead of Night,* in which the ventriloquist's dummy gets up from the chair and tries to strangle the hapless Michael Redgrave, is bloody terrifying. You should find it terrifying too. I know these to be truths because I experience them, bodily. But I am having to learn how to negotiate the rights and wrongs that go with any assertion of truth, and it is not easy, least of all in a world that can seem unforgiving when I make a mistake.'

Yes, the lady in the Carmen Miranda hat again.

We forgive you, but I think I would like to play a game now. Can we play a game now?

'An excellent idea. Let's play the Game of Exquisite Corpse. The Game of Exquisite Corpse might be familiar to you as a children's game, and as a children's game it comes in two forms. To illustrate the first form, I want you to get together into groups of three people. Each group is now a communitas. In front of you, you will find sheets of paper and coloured pencils. What I would like each of you to do, if you are willing, is fold the paper into four equal horizontal parts. Now, each in turn, draw something in one of the sections, starting at the second section from top, and making sure your colleagues in your communitas do not see what you have drawn. When you have finished your drawing, fold the top flap of paper over your drawing, so it is hidden, and pass the paper onto the next person in your communitas. They should repeat this process until you have each drawn part of the total image.

'This is the first form of the Game of Exquisite Corpse. In this version, the outcomes of the drawings' combinations is, theoretically, infinite, bounded only by the imaginations and technical abilities of those doing the drawings. But there is a second form, sold in book and toy shops, and sometimes called 'Mix and Match' books, with all the images pre-printed. With these pre-printed books, you can still put images together in different combinations, so a sheep's head might be placed on a ballet dancer's body, but the outcomes are very much finite — there are only a limited number of combinations possible.

'I present this to you to illustrate my point about the difference between an open and a closed structure. With the open structure there cannot be a presumption of right or wrong, there can only be the process, the experience and the outcome. With the closed structure of the shop bought version of the game, there is always a presumption that there is a right and a wrong answer. We might enjoy seeing the head of a sheep on the body of a ballet dancer, but we also know that, within the mix and match book, the logically-correct body parts for that sheep and that ballet dancer do exist. In fact, the whole point of the shop bought version of the game is not to elicit a surrealist-like response to the sight of a sheep with a ballet dancer's body, as though that might be as beautiful as the chance meeting on a dissecting-table of a sewing-machine and an umbrella. The point is to train young children to put the right body part with the right creature. It is an unapologetic exercise in Cartesian logic, a first stage training in acceptable academic convention.

'Of course, the fear is always that the academic essay will be too personal and too subjective. But this argument is surely problematic on a number of levels. Surely our responses to culture and, I would argue, our scientific observations, are inevitably subjective. How can they be anything else when we are subjective subjects? To argue otherwise sounds like delusion, even stupidity. Doesn't that then mean it is better to acknowledge our subject position, and accept the statements *I think, we think* and *from our point of view,* as the only legitimate outcomes?

'This kind of thinking might well lead us to the writings of someone like Dorit Amir, a professor of music therapy who stated:

> During the past few years, when I send an original case study article to a refereed journal, I usually get comments concerning the first person writing style. The reviewers usually ask me to be more 'objective', to write in a more 'objective' manner and to bring more 'scientific' sources of information. The main comment I get is that extensive use of first person references greatly reduces the professional tone routinely contained in juried journals.[14]

---

[14] Dorit Amir, 'The Use of "First Person" Writing Style in Academic Writing: An Open Letter to Journal Editors, Reviewers and Readers', Blog post for *Voices: A World Forum for Music Therapy,* <https://voices.no/community/index.html?q=fortnightly-columns%252F2005-use-first-person-writing-style-academic-writing-open-letter-journal-editors> accessed 20 January 2022

'As Nina Lykke, a researcher into gender studies and culture has pointed out, third person narratives are not neutral and transparent agents for presenting in an objective way the world that is 'out there'. The third person voice is a social agent, a story told by the subjective self about the 'out there', and as such it is heavily laden with the social and political positions of patriarchy — the white colonising gaze.[15] So to adopt uncritically the third person apparently objective voice is not politically neutral, it is to adopt by default a patriarchal political position by default. It is to assume the position of an omniscient God.'

Yes, the lady in the Carman Miranda hat, you have a question.?

Yes, could we play another game now?

---

[15] Nina Lykke, *Feminist Studies: A Guide to Intersectional Theory, Methodology and Writing* (London: Routledge, 2010) 5

'An excellent idea! I think I've made my point so let's finish by playing a game in which we write an academic essay.'

That doesn't sound like much of a game.

'Trust me, it is all a game. To make an academic essay.

- **Take an academic journal.**
- **Take some scissors.**
- **Choose from this journal an essay the length you want to make your academic essay.**
- **Cut out the essay.**
- **Next carefully cut out each of the words that make up this essay and put them all in a bag.**
- **Shake gently.**
- **Next take out each cutting one after the other.**
- **Copy conscientiously in the order in which they left the bag.**
- **The essay will contain all the elements of objective thought, including its language and, crucially, its citations.**

'And there you are—a highly original academic author who maintains the dream of academic integrity and is able to say without a hint of irony that you are no more than a diminutive individual perched on the shoulders of giants. And should you find yourself unread by the vulgar herd, you will be comforted by the knowledge that you are well on your way to academic tenure.

'With apologies to Tristan Tzara.'

§9 A rush and a push and the land is ours

Geroud. Geroud. Are you alright? What are you doing?'

'I'm swimming. *Obviously.* I'm swimming widths.'

'Widths? You mean lengths, surely.'

'Do I look like the sort of man who goes the long way round?'

'But why?'

'Because that's what you do in a pool isn't it? Swim. Up and down, up and down.'

'How would you know?'

'Whatever.'

'I mean, it's not what you do. Not what you usually do. You cannot swim in a pool. Not with your arm.'

'No, I cannot swim in a bleach-filled pool. But today I have to.'

'That's it! You're not just swimming. You're looking at something.'

'I'm looking at her, sitting on the edge of the pool, like a goddess. A Melusine!'

'A siren more like. A harpy. Just keep away or she'll snare you with a thread of golden hair.'

'No. Not today. Today is different. Today, she is different.'

'She's the same. Cruel. And look at your arm.'

'Today I'll speak to her.'

* * *

'Hello Karen.'

'What do you want?'

'Just passing.'

'Well pass somewhere else. And what's that on your arm? Urgh! Rank.'

'I just wanted to say, you look very pretty today. Mind you, you always look pretty.'

'Oh piss off, creep.'

* * *

Geroud moves away, trying to let the bleach-filled water of the pool cool his reddening face. The magic hasn't worked. Why hasn't it worked?

      Geroud knows he's being talked about. There is a crackle in the air. He feels the crackle in the air. Someone is swimming towards him. No, not someone, some two, or three. Now by his side in the pool. What's going on? In the water, at his side. One of them seems to be hiding them from the sight of the lifeguard. The other two have grabbed him. They're grabbing at his trunks. He kicks and doesn't know whether to scream or give in. If the water wasn't so deep maybe he could fight. But they are too strong and he has nothing to hold on to. His head goes under. Pushing up he gasps for air and is under again. And now he is free. He spits the bleachy water from his lungs as the boys swim off. They have his trunks and hold them in the air like a trophy. Naked and alone in the crowded pool, Geroud does not know whether he should swim after them. No, that's no use. Too far. They are with the Melusine now and she is brandishing his trunks. She mimes a mock disgust at holding them. Or maybe it's a real disgust.

No time to think about that now. Should he swim to the lifeguard? Humiliation. So should he make a run for it. Humiliation too. But what is the least humiliation? Everyone is looking. Everyone is laughing. He wants to escape, but there is no escape from hell. He swims towards the deep end and then to the shallows. Panic. Steps. Slips. Stands. Runs. Laughter. And all the while the pain of the blistering skin on his arm haunts him like an unlearned lesson from long ago.

* * *

In the changing room Geroud knows he has to dress quickly and escape before the Tyros leave the pool. He opens his locker and grabs his trousers and shirt. That's all he needs to get out. Grabbing his shoes, he runs from the changing rooms into the car park outside. Sitting on the low wall separating the canopied footpath from the car park, where the school bus will soon pull up to take them all back to Maudlin Street Secondary Modern School, he puts on his shoes. No socks. He forgot his socks. Never mind. The others will appear soon and they'll crowd together by the main entrance. Laughter.

Geroud stands and wonders what to do. He could run. But where? A force inside his stomach tells him to run and it doesn't care where. Just run. Geroud knows he has to act on this instinct before it fades. He turns away from the pool building and begins to run. He has to get away. Far away. As far as he can run. He knows if he stays he will be lost.

He reaches the gate of the car park and hurls himself through it. A coach turning into the car park sounds its horn, but he doesn't stop. He just runs, leaving the coach and pool behind.

At first he follows the footpath on Kingsmead Road, turning right into Broad Oak Road, past the houses and warehouses, and the car showrooms and the abattoir, and on and on. It will be miles before he stops running, more a stagger than a sprint by then. But for now it is a real run, fast in case anyone is after him, in case the school catches up with him. Faster and faster, so fast he must seem like little more than a blur to anyone who sees him. Except no one does see him, he is too fast. Broad Oak Road becomes a winding country lane. It leads to overgrown footpaths through wooded copses and fields of corn where no one will ever find him. There his body seems to be possessed with a new spirit, something he hasn't felt in a long time. What is it? Oh, of course. It is joy. He feels free and it fills him with joy. He feels like the first and last man in the world and now it is him laughing. He laughs out loud at nothing except the feeling of freedom. He discovers that freedom makes you happy.

On he goes, letting the ancient country paths lead him on and on and on, until he can go on no more, until he has run out of every breath and can only stumble, pant and walk. Yet even then he goes on, rejoining a country lane somewhere he does no know, back onto footpaths through woods and fields, and from footpaths, back onto country lanes, until he is thoroughly lost.

> *He willed nothing, saw nothing, only before him*
> *Were the free open fields:*

To the fields he ran.[16]

In the sunshine a sense of peace pervades his body. With the birds singing all around him, for once his solitude does not feel like loneliness. He has run away but no one could call it a sin. Freedom is never a sin. It doesn't matter what Skinner and Scatson might do to him when he goes back — if he does go back. For now he feels free in a way that Skinner will never know. They're the real prisoners — prisoners of their own thuggish thoughts.

* * *

Freedom comes to an end when a car passes on some narrow country lane. Geroud is lost, so cannot tell us where. The car comes to a halt a few yards in front of him, and its wheels screech and the gearbox grinds as the car is put into reverse. It stops again, this time beside him. A group of boys he recognises get out of

---

[16] Herbert Read, *Naked Warriors* (London: Art and Letters, 1919) Imperial War Museum facsimile reprint with a new introduction by Michael Paraskos, 2003, 43

the car. And a girl he knows too. Who is the girl? She is waving something in the air. *Did you forget something?* she shrieks. Laughter. One of the boys runs towards him and shoves him. *Want another swim gay boy?* Laughter. He stumbles back, slips and falls into the water-filled ditch by the side of the road. Laughter.

For a moment he wonders if he has been stabbed. And so he has, but not by a blade. It is only a bramble, unhappy at Geroud's intrusion into the roadside pool by which it grows. Geroud tries to move, but a pain in his shoulder is too much. Resigning to his fate, he relaxes, and the bramble resumes its objection, inviting the pool to join in by swallowing Geroud's legs, pulling him into its muddy waters in a grim parody of Waterhouse.

Confused. Maybe he has hit his head. Confused, mind wandering.

> *So why not own your own little bit of paradise in the Kent countryside?*
>
> *And so the lanky spear collapses. Crollalanza!*

The visual noise of it all.

Mind wandering. Maybe just go to sleep. Yes. Just close your eyes, dear Lonely Heart, and go to sleep. If only that nagging bramble will let you sleep.

The voices move away. Laughter. The car doors open and slam shut. Laughter. The car revs its engine as though reaching a wanked-up climax. The wheels screech again. The car is gone. The laughter is gone.

Geroud is alone, with only the bramble, the mud and the leeches to keep him company. A robin, busy feathering his nest, with little time to rest, lands on the ground near his head. It knows Geroud is no threat and robins are brave birds anyway. It looks at him intently to see if it can help. Of course not. You're too small to make a difference my pretty little friend.

Geroud wonders if anyone else will stop to help. Of course not. No one can see him in the ditch and besides, no one ever helps. How cruel. Why are people so cruel?

§10 This charming man

It must be some time later as Geroud is sitting at the top of a gasometer. He has perched himself at the edge of the great metal drum, his legs dangling into the air, with nothing between them and the ground, eighty-three feet and four inches below. Every now and then, he lifts himself up to carry his weight on his arms, like a pommel horse gymnast about to launch himself into the air. Except Geroud doesn't launch himself. Instead he relaxes his arms and rests again on the roof of the gasometer, uncertain how to take the plunge.

      Looking up from the ground, a strange doggy-faced little man can see the iron girders that Geroud must have used to climb up, each a crisscross of metal latticework, studded at points with the crest of the long-defunct Canterbury Gas and Water Company. The pierced girders would have made an ideal ladder for the boy, but there is no way the doggy-faced little man is going to climb them. He doesn't need to. He arrives at the top of the gasometer by his own methods, and strolls casually towards Geroud. 'Keep back,' shouts

Geroud as the doggy-faced little man draws near. 'I'm going to to jump.'

'I know,' replies the doggy-faced little man, ignoring the warning and taking a seat next to Geroud. 'I'm not going to stop you.'

'Don't try those games with me,' shouts Geroud. 'I'm going to jump.'

'Trust me my dear girl,' says the doggy-faced little man, taking a black cigarette from a bright red cigarette case in his breast pocket. 'I have absolutely no intention of stopping you.'

'You haven't?' asks Geroud with a mixture of doubt and disappointment.

The doggy-faced little man pats his jacket in search of a box of Lucifer matches. Finding them he strikes a light and ignites the end of the cigarette. He sucks gently on its gold filter pressed between his lips. 'Nope,' he finally replies. 'I was just passing and I saw you, like. I was curious.'

'You know you shouldn't smoke up here,' says Geroud. 'Gas.'

The doggy-faced little man smiles. 'What do you care?' It'll be better for you anyway. Boom! Much quicker than plunging all the way down there. You know they say in the point-eight of a second it will take you to hit the ground your entire life will flash before your eyes. Like living it all again. Not exactly instant, like.'

'There's other people,' says Geroud. 'They —'

'Like I said,' interrupts the doggy-faced little man. 'What do you care? What good have those other people ever done for you?' Geroud looks at him and for a moment wonders whether he was a man at all. Maybe he's a hallucination. 'Just think of me as a psychic hermaphrodite,' says the doggy-faced little man cryptically as if reading Geroud's mind.

'A what?' asks Geroud.

'It's a ghost category in the construction of sexual inversion. Or so I'm told.'

'A what?'

'A ghost category? Something not real. Apparently.'[17]

---

[17] See Douglas Pretsell, *Queer Voices in the Works of Richard von Krafft-Ebing, 1883–1901* (London: Palgrave Macmillan, 2023) 25 and *passim*

'You're saying you're not real?'

'Do I look real?'

For a moment Geroud is unsure whether to say yes. 'I mean, you look like you're really here.'

'Then I suppose I cannot be saying I am not real, my dear young girl, can I? Unless it's time for the obligatory reference, often found in tales like this, to rabbits wearing waistcoats. Every story has at least one rabbit reference these days. And I think that's two so far in this one. It's positively *de rigueur*. And it papers over any cracks in the narrative.'

'I don't understand,' says Geroud lifting himself up again.

'Books, my dear girl.' says the doggy-faced little man. 'I'm talking about books. You know? The rabbit in a waistcoat?'

'I don't read much,' says Geroud.

'Really?' asks the doggy-faced little man, sounding as though he already knows the answer. 'It's strange, but when I saw you from down there I thought you must be the bookish sort. Sensitive. But maybe I'm making too many assumptions. It's a bit of a cliché isn't it? That books and sensitivity go together. There's plenty of well-read professors screwing their students with the offer of better grades. For all I know you're a book-loving thug who'd throw a soft boy into a roadside pond. Or parade him like a defective sheep around a playground. Or steal his trunks in a public swimming pool.'

Geroud looks at the doggy-faced little man and scowls. He starts to say 'How do you know —' but the doggy-faced little man interrupts again, holding out his hand for Geroud to shake. 'My name's Titivillus.'

Instinctively Geroud takes the doggy-faced little man's hand. It feels soft, almost like a child's, but unnaturally cold. Unclasping, Geroud feels a need to wipe his palm on his trouser leg, albeit surreptitiously so as not to cause offence. 'None taken,' says Titivillus, inexplicably.

'What?' asks Geroud.

'None taken,' repeats Titivillus.

It is Geroud who breaks the brief silence that falls between them. 'That's an odd name,' he says. 'It's like — like something from a fairy tale.'

'So you have read something,' says Titivillus. 'Fairy tales at least. *Alice in Wonderland* is not that different to a fairy tale. Just a bit longer. But you haven't told me your name.'

'Geroud,' says Geroud in little more than a mumble.

'That's a funny name too,' says Titivillus chuckling. 'For a girl anyway.'

'I'm not a girl,' says Geroud, speaking louder this time and sounding confused. 'You can see I am not a girl. Why do you keep calling me a girl?' Titivillus cocks his head slightly. A slight smile plays across his lips.

'To be honest, I hadn't really noticed,' he says. 'I don't really notice things like that. It's a bit — well — superficial isn't it. I'm a girl and your a boy, or your a boy and I'm a girl. Best just ignore the whole thing in my opinion. It can be such a tedious barrier to fun.'

'But I'm not a girl,' repeats Geroud.

'Fine, I'll take your word for it, like. Unless you want to prove it to me.' Geroud finds himself blushing. 'But we're not really here to talk about that are we. So, more to the point — and if you don't mind me asking — why are you about to jump?'

'I don't know,' answers Geroud in a low monotone. He takes a deep breath and for a moment Titivillus wonders if that will be the end of the conversation and the boy sat next to him really will leap into the air. Instead the breath seems to make Geroud want to talk. 'I thought I knew. It was the only thing to do. It was like all the other choices had gone. Or that it was no worse than them. But now I'm not so sure.'

'Oh dear,' says Titivillus, sounding genuinely disappointed. 'I'm afraid that shows something of a wayward character. If you don't mind me saying, like.'

'What?' asks Geroud.

'Wayward,' repeats Titivillus. 'I always think that if you decide to do something you should stick to it. Even if you are wrong, like. Even if you know for certain you are wrong. Almost as if it's a point of principle. Like those gammon-headed men who refuse to turn around even when they know they are driving the wrong way. They just don't want to admit they're wrong. That's the sort of person we should admire. And the sort of person we should emulate. It seems to me — *and I really don't wish to sound rude* — that you give up too easily. If you thought it was a good idea to climb up here and jump, let's say an hour ago, then I think you should stick to that plan now. You should jump. After all you've done the climb. That's the hard part. The next bit is easy. It's always easier to fall.

'What?' says Geroud again.

'I am just saying that I am rather disappointed in people who change their mind so easily. Other people I mean. Of course I have no objection to that trait in myself. In my case it shows I have a flexible and considerate nature.' Geroud tries to stifle a smile. 'But when I book a visit from the gas man I expect — *forsooth* — that the gas man cometh. And when a young woman announces that she is going to jump from a gasometer or other tall structure, and plunge to her almost certain death below, then I expect her to do it.'

'Young man,' exclaims Geroud.

'What young man?' asks Titivillus.

'You called me a young woman again,' says Geroud. 'I'm male. A young man. You're doing it on purpose.'

'I don't think we should fall out over such trifling details,' says Titivillus. 'Especially as we've only just met and this could be your final moment on earth. Besides, when it's all over you'll be neither man nor woman. You'll just be a lump of corned beef splattered on the pavement below. Not a man or a woman, just a bloody thing. An it, like.'

Geroud winces at the image. 'So you meant it when you said you are not going to try to talk me down?' he asks trying to get the image of corned beef out his mind.

'Absolutely,' says Titivillus emphatically. 'I've often thought the best solution to the world's environmental catastrophe is to reduce the world's population. As it's not easy to massacre people any more, att least not in this country, so why not encourage individual enterprise? A kind of privatisation of the environmental conscience through voluntary euthanasia. If we get it right we could even celebrate people's selfless sacrifice with memorial services and plaques — that kind of thing. She threw herself into the swirling waters of the Thames to save the Antarctic penguins. Or he fell under a bus to save Columbian glass frog. Get a few million people to do that each year and the world will soon be a better place.'

Again Geroud finds himself trying to stifle a laugh. He assumes Titivillus is joking.

'The problem for you is that this is a lousy place to jump. At eighty-three feet you cannot guarantee you'll be killed. I'm not saying you won't be. Chances are you will, but there is always a risk you might just be hideously injured. Imagine that, a lifetime of paralysis, unable to walk by yourself, or feed yourself, or even shit for yourself. And no one will step up and put you out of your misery then. *He's so brave* they'll say as they wipe the dribble from your chin. How he carries on, year after year, so so brave.'

Geroud would be forgiven for thinking he has already jumped from the gasometer and is hallucinating as he falls. And, having jumped from the top of the gasometer, perhaps he has failed to hit the ground and is now falling through the earth into a bottomless rabbit hole. He closes his eyes tightly and clutches at the gasometer to make sure he is still there. But, despite feeling its rusting metal surface, he doesn't quite feel he is there. Titivillus seems to sense this and shuffling closer whispers, 'Just imagine, at two-hundred and thirty-six feet and four inches high, as a KGB tourist might say, you'd be guaranteed to meet your end. That's the top of Canterbury Cathedral you know. It would be a much better place to jump. Certain death, I'd say. And on the way down that pretty white body of yours would probably hit a few of gargoyles sticking out. Like teeth ripping into your flesh. God is not as forgiving as the Gas Board. You'd have absolutely no chance surviving a fall from the House of God.'

'How?' asks Geroud, still unwilling to open his eyes and unable to form a full question.

'How?' repeats Titivillus. 'What a strange question. You just launch yourself. You're bound to hit some of them.'

'No,' says Geroud still unable to form the question he wants to ask. 'I mean — what?'

Titivillus yawns theatrically and takes a deep breath of the night air, seemingly oblivious to Geroud's stumbling questions. 'Do you know you can see all the way to the swimming pool from the top of the cathedral,' he says casually. 'When you're up there you feel you can almost step over the houses and land outside the pool. You know, in a moment. Just one step. Ready to take a dip. That's if you can take a dip. Without your skin bubbling up, like.'

Geroud opens his eyes. He can see he is still on top of the gasometer, looking out into the night sky. But he is also somewhere else, as if he is in two places at once. Had he been better schooled he might have said it was like living in a palimpsest, like looking out over Istanbul and seeing Istanbul, Constantinople and Byzantium, all superimposed, one over the other, over the other.[18] Except for him, the other view is from the top of Canterbury Cathedral, in the daytime, looking out over the city towards the swimming pool.

---

[18] Robert Ousterhout, 'Visualising Constantinople as Palimpsest' in Suna Çağaptay et al (eds.), *Cities as Palimpsests? Responses to Antiquity in Eastern Mediterranean Urbanism* (Oxford: Oxbow Books, 2022)

'Isn't it lovely,' mumbles Titivillus looking intently at Geroud. 'A truly lovely view. I could watch it all day and all night. Forever even. Except that strange figure running naked from the pool. What's wrong with him? He's ruining everything. But if you look to your left, you can see a beautiful little Kent village. Little more than a hamlet really. It's ever such a clear view on a day like this. But that's not right either. Can you see that pond with someone lying in it. A bit rude, I'd say. Ruining the view like that. I'd swear it's him again, the chap from the swimming pool, always ruining things. Let's look this way. That's better. A lovely country lane. Except even there there's someone taking a bath in the roadside ditch. It's him again, ruining it all. But at least that'll be the end of him. He won't survive the night out there.'

'Who are you?' asks Geroud.

'A stranger,' says Titivillus. 'Or maybe a friend. Maybe a stranger-friend. Didn't you ask for a friend?'

'I didn't ask for anything,' says Geroud.

Titivillus frowns and purses his lips. He reaches into his breast pocket again, this time retrieving not the red cigarette case, but a small piece of paper, folded in two. He opens it, and on the inside is written in blood a single word: *Karen.*

'Didn't you send me this?'

'No. I didn't send you anything.'

'Oh I think you did,' says Titivillus. 'You do remember writing on this piece of paper don't you? Writing in blood no less. That's not strictly necessary. But you do remember placing this piece of paper under that pyramid by your bedroom window?'

'Yes, but—'

'A few months ago I think,' says Titivillus. 'I'm sorry for the delay in getting back to you. I've been a bit busy, like. A lot of people to see.'

'It was last night,' mumbles Geroud.'

'What?' asks Titivillus distractedly.

'It was last night,' repeats Geroud. 'I did that last night.'

'Really?' asks Titivillus, trying to sound like he cared. 'I never can keep track of time. Always underestimating it or overestimating it. Anyway, you made the call and now we have answered, like.'

'We?' says Geroud sharply.

'I mean me,' Titivillus corrects himself, 'I have answered. You asked for help and here I am, come to help. Like George Bailey. And Clarence. Think of me as your — well, think of me as a kind of angel. A *kind of* guardian angel.'

'I don't understand,' says Geroud. 'You're an angel?'

'Well,' says Titivillus, sounding like he is going to admit a mixup at the office. 'As I said. A kind of guardian angel. Though don't imagine I'm like that Clarence. Absolutely appalling what he did to poor George Bailey. There he was, desperate to escape from a humdrum town, not unlike this one, and what does Clarence do, he condemns him to live there until the end of time, reeled out on BBC2 or the ABC Cinema every Christmas to repeat his tragedy. No matter how many times they show it, he's never going escape the prison of a Norman Rockwell life. And that's entirely Clarence's fault which doesn't sound very angelic to me. George doesn't even get to fuck pretty Violet Bicks. No matter how often you watch the film, it just doesn't happen. That on its own seems cruel. I've seen it hundreds of times and it's always the same. What do you call it round here? Copping off? He never cops off with her, like.'

'I don't understand,' says Geroud, rubbing his forehead as if trying to come to his senses. 'I don't understand!'

Titivillus begins to laugh. 'Now you really do sound like George Bailey. My apologies. I am confusing things. Look, I know we've only just met but I already like you. So if you would still like my help then here I am.' Titivillus holds up the piece of paper with Karen's name written in Geroud's blood between the index and forefinger of his left hand. Somehow it bursts into flames, vanishing into the night air. 'If you still want to jump,' continues Titivillus, 'I'll make you a promise. When you hit the ground, you'll get an instant death. No paralysis or anything like that. You'll hit the ground and that'll be it. No pain, no paralysis, just nothing. Lights out and goodnight Vienna.'

'What?' says Geroud softly, almost swooning as the daylight view from the top of Canterbury

Cathedral gives way to just being the night sky on top of the gasometer.

'You mean you don't understand my offer?'

'I do, but — I don't know — I —.'

'A minute ago you were certain,' interrupts Titivillus. 'You insisted you were going to jump.'

'A minute ago I hadn't met an angel.'

'I told you. I'm not an angel,' insists Titivillus, his voice rising in tone to sound strangely like Henry Travers. Geroud stays silent. 'But there is an alternative. Best of both worlds, like. A way to have your cake and eat it. Almost as though you'd won a prize. You do like winning prizes don't you?'

'I don't know,' answers Geroud. 'I've never won anything. Except once. *Kind of.* At school. I won a book once. But that's all.

'Really, what was the book about?' asks Titivillus.

'An owl,' answers Geroud. 'An owl who was afraid of the dark. Then he isn't.'

'It sounds like a great story!' exclaims Titivillus smiling broadly. 'I knew I was going to like you. I said you look like the bookish sort. That's why I'm going to help you. If you trust me, like.'

'How?' asks Geroud.

'Jump,' replies Titivillus. 'From here. Jump. And, as long as you trust me, you'll be fine. You know, like that owl in the book you — *kind of* — won. It had to learn to trust the darkness didn't it? And after that it started to like it. So, if you trust me you'll be fine. I'll make sure of it. You jump for me and I'll get work on that other problem for you.'

'What other problem?' asks Geroud.

'The Karen problem,' says Titivillus.

'But I'll die,' mumbles Geroud looking over the edge of the gasometer again. 'Or be paralysed. You just said I'd be paralysed.'

'Did I? I thought I promised you no paralysis. Either the instant death you wanted ten minutes ago, or no death and your dream comes true. The dream that will never come true for George Bailey and Violet Bicks. It will come true for you and this girl. But the choice is yours. In fact, I'd say you're a very lucky man. You have three choices. Climb down, go home and live miserably a *kind of* Norman Rockwell life for the rest of your seventy-four years. Or jump and I'll make sure you die quickly and painlessly. Or jump, with a little faith in me, and you'll survive and we'll have — *well, what shall we call it?* — some fun together. We'll make the peasants eat straw, like.'

There is no reason why Geroud should trust a doggy-faced little man who has climbed up the gasometer, sat next to him and said such strange things to mess with his head.

'You know it's nearly dawn,' says Titivillus, for the first time sounding impatient to bring proceedings to a close. 'You need to make up your mind up before it's light or someone will see you up here. They'll send in the psychics to talk you down.'

'Psychologists,' Geroud corrects him, snorting a small laugh as he speaks. 'They're called psychologists, not psychics.' For the first time he feels pleased with himself.

'Are they?' asks Titivillus. 'I didn't know that.' Geroud knows Titivillus is lying, but feels a small pang of gratitude for it.

'Why would you help me?' he asks.

Titivillus smiles and his dog-like features seemed to soften in what little light there is to see by. 'I told you, my dear sad, little Lonely Heart. I like you. Of course there has to be a little give and take in these things. A little something for you and a little something for me. But really you should be happy. You should be very happy indeed. It's *kind of* like you winning the lottery, me showing up like this. Or a school prize. Why shouldn't you win the school prize for once, even if it is a rather unpleasant girl called Karen?'

§11 Death at one's elbow

The fall was so quick Geroud couldn't tell how long it took to prise himself over the edge of the gasometer and arrive at the ground. Any notion his fall would seem like slow-motion — *as Scott Dachtler once told me it's like when you're in a car crash* — or that his life would flash before his eyes, was just wrong. There was a moment of being in the air, then a moment of being on the ground, the latter accompanied by a sheering pain running through his shoulder.

'Fuck!' cried Geroud. 'I can't move. Fuck!'

Titivillus was already at the bottom of the gasometer to meet Geroud when he landed. 'That's not very lady-like language,' he said.

'Fuck you!' Geroud cried out again. 'You fucker! I thought you were going to help.'

'I did help,' said Titivillus calmly. 'You've just fallen eighty-three feet and you're still alive. Some people would call that a miracle.'

'You didn't do anything?'

'You're alive,' repeated Titivillus.

'I'm not!' cried Geroud.

'Here,' said Titivillus pulling Geroud to his feet. With a sharp and unannounced yank, he pushed Geroud's shoulder blade forward, causing Geroud to let out an even louder primæval shriek. In the silence that followed Geroud began rolling his shoulder and arm, a look of disbelief on his face.

'It doesn't hurt,' he said incredulously. 'It doesn't hurt. What did you do?'

'Like I said, I'm a miracle worker. Wasn't that fun? I'm tempted to have a go myself. Shall I Geroud? Shall I?'

Without waiting for an answer, Titivillus disappeared into the nearby shadows. A moment later Geroud heard him calling from the top of the gasometer. 'Look at me, Geroud! Look at me!' As the final word fell from his lips Titivillus hurled himself into the air and like Geroud's own fall, no sooner had he launched himself than he was lying as a crumpled mess on the ground.

'Fuck!' shouted Geroud repeatedly as he ran to where Titivillus had landed. Titivillus was in a horrible state, but unlike Geroud, rather than complaining about his dislocated legs and what looked like a broken neck, he was laughing. Pulling his body this way and that, Titivillus slowly reassembled himself, methodically, as if this was nothing new to him. In no time he stood in front of Geroud as though nothing had happened.

'I knew it,' said Titivillus, still intoxicated at the thrill of his fall. 'I knew I was going to like you. I knew we'd have fun together.' He patted himself down to shake the dust from his clothes. 'Mind you, I know what you're thinking,' continued Titivillus, putting an arm around Geroud's shoulders.

'I can't believe you do,' said Geroud.

'You're thinking — what about the other problem?' Geroud tried not to flinch at being touched. 'But patience, my dear hot blooded friend. Patience, even though the sap is desperate to rise. I am working on that too.'

§12 Bigmouth strikes again

Despite Titivillus's insistence that Geroud was lucky to have him turn up, the experience of watching too many Hammer horror films at too young an age soon began to prick Geroud's conscience. In the days that followed the meeting on top of the gasometer he felt an almost instinctive need to repent. With that in mind, he had tried to enter the cathedral at Canterbury to pray for help and forgiveness, but being short of cash that day, the entry charge had put him off. Abandoning that plan he ambled down Sun Street towards the Beaney Institute Library, hoping to find some solace and advice from books in the Sorcery and Occultism section, assuming they had such a thing.

'Religion and Mythology starts in the far corner,' the librarian told him, pointing towards the end of the long room. 'From 200 through to the 300s. It is labelled.' Geroud did not feel able to ask the librarian if there was a specific book on getting out of pact with the devil, although he was sure there was one. In the movies they always found one.

Having browsed the shelves without success, Geroud left the adult lending library and stood in the entrance hallway of the Beaney. The children's library was busy with what sounded like a story being read to a group of excited infants. Geroud could hear the librarian asking them if any of them were afraid of the dark. For a moment he considered going downstairs to the record library, but upstairs, somewhere in the museum and art gallery, he could hear another voice talking loudly about vampires. The juxtaposition with the sound of the children was unsettling, but it occurred to Geroud whoever was talking about vampires might know something about dæmonic possession.

At the top of the stairs Geroud was greeted by a man seated behind a desk at the museum entrance. 'Are you here for the talk on saints and vampires?' he asked. 'It's only just started. You can creep in at the back if you're discreet.' The man pointed to a door that was still partly open. Without saying a word, Geroud walked through it and found himself in a room full of grey-haired men and women listening to another man at the front introducing the speaker.

'As well as being an authority on the writings of mediæval pilgrims,' he said, 'and the descriptions they have left us of their journeys across Europe and the Middle East, our speaker is an expert on the hagiographies of saints in mediæval manuscripts. And that is where our talk today comes in, as we discover the, perhaps surprising, affinities between the lives and afterlives of saints and vampires. And so, it is my great pleasure to welcome Dr Sarah James.'

The audience applauded as the speaker stood and walked over to the lectern. Thanking the man who had introduced her, Dr James began with a warning that much of what she was going to discuss was pretty gruesome and that it would be accompanied by slides of paintings and manuscript illuminations, some of which were quite bloody and graphic. Anyone of a nervous disposition should, she warned her audience, take the opportunity to leave. A ripple of gentle laughter passed through the clearly bloodthirsty audience, as no one took Dr James up on her advice. Dr James asked for the lights in the room to be lowered and proceeded to show images of Christian saints being tortured and dismembered with what might have been taken as a kind of glee.

'The problem for anyone trying to get rid of an erstwhile saint,' Dr James said, 'was that they appear to have been extraordinarily difficult to kill. It wasn't simply that divine intervention might save them, as in the case of the spiked wheel that was supposed to be the end of St Catharine of Alexandria, which inexplicably broke, injuring its operators instead of Catherine. Even if you did manage to hack away at the saint, the chances are they would not die.' St James Intercisus was held up as a particularly good example of this, described by Dr James as her favourite saint, whose martyrdom involved him being cut up into twenty-eight pieces, starting with his fingers being removed one by one, then his toes, feet, hands, arms and legs. Despite all this, St James Intercisus refused to die, prompting one of his torturers to eventually take out his sword and cut off the saint's head. But even in death, Dr James explained, a saint could still be trouble for the living, coming back in dreams, or even in person, to rebuke people for their un-Christian ways and in this they most resemble vampires, as a kind of undead, haunting the living.

At the end of the lecture the audience applauded and a lively debate started on the similarities between Christian saints and diabolical vampires, and whether vampires were the saints of hell. Geroud took note, wondering whether Titivillus was a fallen angel or a devilish saint, and whether there was any real difference.

It was only when most of the audience had departed that Geroud dared to approach Dr James. She was still being chaperoned by the man who had introduced her, but as Geroud drew near the man thanked her for the talk, and apologised that he had to leave as he had a finance committee meeting to attend. Seizing his chance, Geroud said, 'Dr James. Could I ask you something?'

'Of course,' replied Dr James, packing her notes into a canvas bag. 'What is it?'

'I wonder, have you ever heard of someone called Titivillus?' Dr James stopped and looked intently at Geroud. 'I mean,' continued Geroud, 'could he be one of these saints from hell you mentioned.'

Dr James seemed to gain her composure. 'Why do you ask about Titivillus? He's quite an obscure figure.'

'But you do know of him?'

'Yes, of course. In mediæval folklore he was often blamed by manuscript illuminators and scribes for causing them to make mistakes.'

'Mistakes?' repeated Geroud.

'Spelling mistakes,' explained Dr James. 'When they were copying manuscripts, if they made a mistake they would say Titivillus did it. Carvers and builders blamed him for their mistakes too. If a stone broke or they made a bad cut. I always think of him as one of the less terrifying devils.'

'Less terrifying?' asked Geroud, sounding hopeful.

'Relatively less terrifying,' Dr James corrected herself. 'They are all devils after all.'

'I see,' said Geroud. 'What if I said to you I have met him?'

Dr James stopped packing her bag again. She smiled. 'These are just stories my dear. You don't really meet with devils. Or saints for that matter.'

'But —'

'They're stories,' Dr James repeated. 'Now I really must be getting along. Whoever you met, they were probably pulling your leg. Whoever it was, it was certainly not Titivillus.'

Realising Dr James was not about to play van Helsing to his John Seward, let alone be his Father Damien, Geroud made his apologies and found himself almost running down the oak staircase to escape. He couldn't understand why, but somehow he felt he had blundered, said the wrong thing again, done something he shouldn't. Had he been a little slower getting away, and looked back, he might have noticed a figure emerge from the shadow behind Dr James. It was a man, or what seemed like a man. 'How strange,' said Dr James. 'If he had seen you, like he said, then you might have expected him to notice you standing there. Do you know him?'

'Never seen him before in my life,' said the doggy-faced man, removing a red cigarette case from his pocket. 'It's all very curious, like.'

§13 Honey, you know where to find me

The village of Barfrestone can be found in the south-eastern corner of England, almost at the most eastern extremity of the County of Kent at OS Grid Reference TR261501. The climate is temperate northern European, although local conditions in winter may veer towards more extreme weather than that found in the inland parts of the country as Kent is a promontory extending into the southern part of the North Sea. In terms of directions to Barfrestone, my advice is to follow the A2 Watling Street road from London to Dover until you reach OS Grid Reference TR236474. There leave the A2 and you will find the way is signposted. The road is generally good and paved, although somewhat narrow in places. The automobilist is advised to be aware of agricultural vehicles, which may slow progress if heading in the same direction, or force evasive action if heading towards one. Railway services operate between London Victoria and Shepherd's Well, a larger settlement not far from

Barfrestone, also known by its more ancient name of Sibertswold. From there a short walk is necessary, of approximately one-and-a-half miles, which will bring the visitor to the centre of Barfrestone.

In many ways Barfrestone is an attractive settlement, but it would not, in all probability, be enough in itself to deserve a journey or detour to see, except for the peculiarity of its parochial church. Seeing the Church of St Nicholas at Barfrestone, first time visitors will most likely be overwhelmed by the beautiful casket-like structure of the building in the pointed-arch style of the mediæval period, and more especially by its lovely twelfth-century Norman carvings. There is no doubt these are a delight. Yet for those who look a little harder there is an additional joy that points perhaps to an earlier form of Christian worship at this site — perhaps even to pre-Christian forms of worship. For although the Parish Church of St Nicholas at Barfrestone does not have a bell-tower, it does have a church bell. Set outside the building, hanging high in the branches of an ancient yew tree, sits a bronze bell, a rope hanging from it through the branches, looking almost like a swing-rope set up by the local children for their play. Thus we find, instead of shaped wood and ashlar stone forming a campanile to reverberate the chime of the call to Christian prayer, there are tree branches and spiny yew leaves through which its *adhan* must travel each Sunday morning, and on wedding-days, high days and holidays, and of course on those days when the dead are called to this place of rest.

      As many readers will already know from my previous excursions into the verdant land which I am proud to call my birth-right, yew trees have an important place in Christian mythology and are often to be found planted in church-yards across the country. In earlier times the mournful yew, as the arboreally-named Nathaniel Hawthorne described it, was often called the palm tree, at least by those with no knowledge of the actual palm, and was related in the popular imagination to the triumphant entry of Christ into Jerusalem on the day we call Palm Sunday. The yew is also said to symbolise the eternal life promised to the faithful, as no extant example of the tree has ever been known to die, at least from natural causes. The nineteenth-century architect James Wylson calculated a yew tree in the church yard at Brabourne, also in Kent, at around three-thousand years old,[19] and so it is perfectly possible the yew tree outside the Parish Church of St Nicholas at Barfrestone was planted before the present church was even built. Indeed, it does not seem too fanciful to speculate it acted as the original meeting place for the village's Christian congregation before the Norman building was erected. Were that to be the case, it would make the specimen over eight centuries old.

Alternatively, it might have been planted at the time of the building's completion, perhaps as an unofficial component in the Act of Consecration. Certainly similar ceremonial uses of long-lived trees are known from other parts of the world, such as the island of Cyprus. In that colony of ours, sycamore fig trees can frequently be found outside the most ancient of churches, including St Nicholas Cathedral, the mediæval gothic church in the centre of Famagusta,

---

[19] James Wylson, 'Timber: Its Treatment and Uses' in *The Builder*, 21 December, 1844, 628

dating from the early thirteenth century. Like the yew, sycamore fig-trees are thought never to die, and the one in Famagusta is said to be some seven-hundred years old. According to tradition it was planted, when the cathedral was built, from a cutting taken from a sycamore fig tree in Jericho in the Holy Lands. In Jericho the sycamore fig was held sacred by Christians as it was into a particular specimen of the tree that a local inn keeper, named Zaccheus, reputedly climbed to gain sight of Jesus above the huge crowds that had gathered. After the Crucifixion of Our Saviour, Zaccheus became a travelling companion to St Peter, spreading the Christian Gospel. By planting a cutting from the tree of Jericho in Famagusta, the mediæval French rulers of Cyprus seem to have been attempting to create a living link between their new church in Cyprus and the origin of Christianity in Roman Palestine.

Of course, we shall never know the truth of these claims, but if they have veracity then perhaps it is also possible that the yew tree in Barfrestone was grown from a cutting taken from a tree in another location held sacred by the Barfrestone landowners. Perhaps it came from the parent monastery of the church, or from some long-forgotten sacred shrine.

      An indication that the yew tree in Barfrestone church yard was of particular importance to the local villagers in earlier times arises from the fact the village inn is named after it. Although the Yew Tree Inn at Barfrestone was rebuilt extensively in the style known as Brewers' Tudor a few years ago, the present structure sits on the foundations of an ancient inn of far more indeterminate age. As is the fashion in our current time, the new building has been made to resemble a more ancient construction and so wooden beams dominate the saloon, together with a hearth so large it would do Mr Norman Shaw proud. Certainly it gives the impression of having been used in centuries past to roast a suckling pig or side of mutton for the pleasure of Jack Falstaff and the folk of Merrie Olde England, even if its impressive stones were cut and shaped by master masons within only the last two decades…

* * *

At some point later, after failing to locate information on how to break his pact with Titivillus, Geroud found himself in the village of Barfrestone. Some might have said he was on home turf in this neck of the woods, or some such cliché. Except Geroud never felt at home. Some might also have said that on a winter's night the snug at the Yew Tree Inn would be a comfortable shelter from the darkness of the country lanes outside. But Geroud never felt comfortable. Sitting in the snug of the Yew Tree Inn in the centre of the village, he felt particularly uncomfortable. That evening the weather was running-in straight from the North Sea, battering the promontory that is Kent. Had he been a better educated young man Geroud might have ruminated on how easily the ancient English could have mistaken the howling wind outside for Grendel's mother, full fiercely in her flight, emerging from her watery abyss to avenge her damaged son. But Geroud had never heard of Beowulf, although he did hear the howling wind.

    Geroud had entered the Yew Tree Inn alone. As he had crept through the double door he said little, other than to order, with almost apologetic deference, a pint of Fremlin's ale at the bar. The barman looked at him suspiciously suspecting this customer was well under age. But unless this was part of some police springe the barman didn't really care. He stooped to fetch a glass jar, stood upright and began to fill it from the pump.

Finding a table in the corner of the room, Geroud sat and took a sip of the Kent beer he had ordered and winced. Too hoppy for an underage drinker more used to sugared pop.

Had we the luxury of being a fly-on-the-pub-wall that night, we might think Geroud didn't notice the other man enter the room, but it was all an act. Of course he noticed. Geroud noticed everything, like hunted quarry, silent and still, terrified at every sight and sound, hoping his feigned indifference would lead the snarling hounds to pass without giving him attention. Without seeming to go near the bar, the man approached Geroud, placed a glass of red wine on the table and sat down. In the twinkling firelight the wine glinted unnaturally like liquid rubies. The man was

Titivillus. 'So here we are then,' he said cheerfully. 'What a nice little place. Do you think it's haunted?'

'That's stupid,' mumbled Geroud.

'A bit hard, Lonely Heart. Just making conversation, like. No need to be a grumpy-puss. Especially when your dream is about to come true. Ah, was that a little smile there, Lonely Heart?' Titivillus pointed at Geroud with his forefinger, teasingly wagging it towards Geroud's armpit in a mock tickling motion.

Geroud pulled away and forced his face to fall into line. 'Whatever you do, do not smile,' mumbled the voice inside.

'Oh to spoil the youth of hammer'd steel, and turn the giddy round of Fortune's wheel,' said Titivillus.

'What?' asked Geroud sharply.

'Nothing, dear Lonely Heart,' said Titivillus. 'Just a memory that came to mind, like. So this is where she lives is it?'

'So you say,' mumbled Geroud.

'That's true,' agreed Titivillus. 'That is your bone fide truth. I did say it. Because it is true. And what is also true is that in approximately four minutes and twenty-two seconds your Melusine — *or is her name Karen?* — will walk through that door ready to help her father behind the bar. Did you know the man who served you is her father?' Titivillus glanced furtively at the man who had served Geroud, his dog-like features accentuated by a mock subterfuge. 'And once she's here, it's all set up.'

Geroud did not respond.

'You know! All set up and ready to go. Houston we have lift off. Wham, bam, thank you mam. Goodnight Vienna, like.'

Still Geroud said nothing.

'All delivered, dear Lonely Heart,' said Titivillus, trying one last time. 'As promised. As stated in the deal.'

But still Geroud said nothing.

'Of course, if I'm honest, like, I don't know what you see in her. Especially after the swimming pool affair. It's a good job I stepped in. To rescue you, like.'

'To rescue me?' said Geroud sounding incredulous.

'Yes, exactly,' said Titivillus. 'She's a nasty piece of work alrighty! She might as well have pushed you off that gasometer herself. You'd be dust in a pot waiting to feed a rose bush if I hadn't've shown up.'

'It wasn't her,' mumbled Geroud.

'I beg your pardon?'

'It wasn't her,' repeated Geroud. 'In the pool, it wasn't her. It was Skinner and Scatson. Not her.'

'If you say so, my dear Lonely Heart. Although perhaps time has dulled the memory a little.'

'And who's fault's that?'

'Surely you're not suggesting it's mine.'

'A year. It's been a year.'

'Really? So long? But what's a year to someone in love. A day, a month, a year — maybe even a lifetime, just ask Dante and Petrarch. True love always waits.'

'I'm not sure I want to.'

'Not sure you want to what?'

'I don't think I want to wait. Not any more. It feels like it's too late. Like something that's passed.'

'Nonsense!' exclaimed Titivillus almost rising from his seat. 'It's all set up. This has been months in the making. You're just nervous. Everyone's nervous the first time. Just go with the flow. It's like falling off a gasometer.' Titivillus nudged Geroud with his elbow as he said the word gasometer as if sharing a private joke. 'And even though I've never really thought she's good enough for you — I mean, she's pretty and all that, but she's hardly a character — I hope you'll be very happy together. For tonight at least. *O cunning Love! With tears thou keep'st me blind, lest eyes well-seeing thy foul faults should find!* Tomorrow, of course, you have a different appointment to keep.'

Well over ten minutes after Titivillus had foretold her arrival, the door to the snug bar swung open and in walked the Melusine. 'Close the door!' shouted the barman gruffly. 'The wind'll have it off its hinges.'

'Blah, blah, blah,' the Melusine called back.

'Less of your lip girl. You're late.'

Despite the years of sharing a school classroom, and all the taunts and cruelties, the

Melusine didn't seen to notice Geroud. Opening the hatch to get behind the bar, she picked up a white bar cloth and began wiping a tray of newly-washed glasses and stacking them somewhere beneath the beer taps.

'Well, my work here is done,' said Titivillus standing as he spoke. Taking a last sip of his wine he added, 'Much as I hate goodbyes, like.'

'Where are you going?' asked Geroud grabbing hold of Titivillus's arm.

'I can't hang around here, Lonely Heart,' replied Titivillus. 'I have things to see and people to do. Besides which, ever heard of three being a crowd?'

'But what about our bargain?'

'Exactly,' said Titivillus. 'We agreed terms and I have delivered. There she is. Brought to your feet. Ripe for the plucking, if you'll forgive the pun. I have answered your cry for help. The note in the pyramid. Deal done and goods duly delivered.'

'This wasn't the deal,' said Geroud, squeezing Titivillus's arm so hard as he spoke that even the doggy little devil had to wince.

Titivillus unclasped Geroud's hand and set it gently on the table, patting it as if to encourage it to stay there. 'You worry too much, dear Lonely Heart. Relax. Everything is in order. Just go with the flow. You just have to trust me.' Titivillus sat down again. 'Of course, you are right. I knew there was something I had to tell you. You need to know how to work the spell. Its *enixus*. It's not hard. When the time seems right, just say the magic words and everything else will follow. Like I said, it's all been arranged.'

'What magic words?' asked Geroud sounding dubious.

For a moment Titivillus looked confused as though he had not thought of any magic words to pass on. 'Well, let me see — it should be something quite familiar to you. Something memorable so you don't forget it in the moment, like.' Titivillus reached for a little black notebook hiding in his breast pocket. 'Oh, yes, I know. How about, "Issy-wizzy-let's-get-busy."'

'Issy-wizzy-let's-get-busy?' repeated Geroud, sounding profoundly skeptical.

'Yes,' said Titivillus. 'Issy-wizzy-let's-get-busy. What did you expect? *O lente, lente currite, noctis equi?'* Geroud slumped back in his chair. 'Now don't forget to say the words. Choose the moment well and say the words. Faith, remember, dear Lonely Heart. Have faith. That's the real magic. *Mystérium fídei.*'

Titivillus stood again, not waiting this time to have his arm squeezed a second time, he walked straight to the door. Once there he looked back, smiled at Geroud and winked theatrically. 'And don't forget, we have our own appointment tomorrow. You and me, like. Don't be late.'

§14 Let the right one slip in

Geroud did not look up when he mumbled, 'Issy-wizzy-let's-get-busy.'

'You still here?' asked the Melusine as she appeared at his side and began to wipe the table with a damp cloth. 'You must be the last person in the place.'

'I guess so,' replied Geroud nonchalantly. The Melusine smiled.

'Funny, you remind me of someone.'

'I hope someone you like being reminded of,' said Geroud, inexplicably flirting.

Or, maybe he said, 'Someone you want to be reminded of I hope.'

Or maybe he just said, 'Someone nice, I hope.' Yes, that's it. Something succinct like that.

'He was,' replied the Melusine. 'I'd say he was the best. But he's gone now.' She sounded melancholic.

'And what made him the best?' asked Geroud.

'He was just a quiet boy. And kind. But children can be so cruel can't they?'

'Monsters,' agreed Geroud. 'Except, perhaps this boy?'

The Melusine blushed. 'No, not this boy. He wasn't a monster. Like I say, he was just a quiet boy who no one understood. At least I didn't understand him. Not really.'

'But you were friends?'

'I wish —,' the Melusine started to say. 'But, like I say, children can be so cruel.'

The table was now well-polished, but the Melusine continued to rub her cloth across it distractedly. 'It's funny, you really do look like him. What's your name?'

Something made Geroud pause. 'Titivillus. My name is Titivillus.'

The Melusine giggled. 'That's a funny name.'

'Yes, I hate it,' replied Geroud emphatically, hoping the real Titivillus was listening.

'Oh, you shouldn't hate your own name,' said the Melusine. 'I like it. Is it Greek or something? You look a bit Greek. You have that lovely olive skin.'

Geroud laughed a little too loudly. 'Do I?' he said. 'Well, maybe there's a bit of Greek in me. Who knows!'

'Do you live around here?' asked the Melusine.

'No,' said Geroud. 'Just passing through.'

'But you used to?'

'Yes, I used to. How do you know that?'

'I said you looked familiar. Are you visiting family?'

'No. I don't have any family. I mean they're gone. I'm just a tourist. Except I haven't got anywhere to stay. I meant to arrange a room in a hotel in Canterbury or somewhere, but it just slipped my mind. I wasn't really expecting to be out so late. I'm not sure how I'd even get to Canterbury at this time of night. I guess I'll have to walk.'

'You can't do that!' exclaimed the Melusine. It's miles and the weather.'

'I know, but I don't think I have a choice.'

'We have some rooms here. It used to be an inn you see. A real one, with rooms. And we still keep a couple just in case. Listen, it's still early — would you like another drink? A whiskey? Or a brandy? I'll see if you can stay in one of the guest rooms. Wait there and I'll get you a drink. Maybe I'll have one too — if you don't mind. We can drown all our sorrows together.'

'Alright,' agreed Geroud. 'But I don't know I have any sorrows to drown.'

'Everyone has sorrows,' said the Melusine, sounding wise beyond her years. 'Even if it's just that the fire's dying down and the room's getting cold.'

'You're very poetic,' said Geroud.

Or maybe he said, 'I always thought you were a poet at heart.'

'Always thought?'

'I mean, I wondered. I wondered if you are a poet. Or maybe a philosopher.'

'Here,' said the Melusine picking up a poker from the side of the fire grate and handing it to Geroud. 'You give the fire a poke and I'll get our nightcaps.'

Geroud did as he was told while the Melusine disappeared behind the bar, only to reappear with a full bottle of Glen Kella and two glasses. Her father seemed to have disappeared, almost as though he had never exist. Sitting beside Geroud, the Melusine unscrewed the top of the bottle and poured two generous measures into the glasses. 'Cheers,' said Geroud slowly, his eyes fixed on her as they clinked their glasses.

'Cheers!' replied the Melusine, her face lit brightly by the now roaring fire. 'But you haven't asked me my name.'

'No, of course, I mean,' stuttered Geroud. No he didn't stutter. He said, 'Where are my manners! May I ask your name?'

'Karen,' replied the Melusine. 'But I don't like my name either, so everyone calls me Kaz.'

'I am very pleased to meet you, *Kaz.*'

'Likewise I'm sure.'

They clinked glasses again, and continued talking until the fire had consumed even the remnants of the logs Geroud had nudged into life. It was getting late. Very late. Feeling the cold draughts of the night air more than the warmth of the dying fire, the Melusine stood, and held out her hand to Geroud. Geroud took it, and half pulled by her, half propelled by his own desire, he too stood and let the Melusine lead him across the room. They passed through a low wooden door to the right of the bar, and into a dark corridor beyond. Stumbling, Geroud held tightly onto the Melusine's hand as she led him on. The corridor was narrow, and Geroud found himself bouncing against the walls, first on one side and then the other, with persistent regularity, as he passed through it. Their walk in the darkness seemed to go on forever, as if they had entered an abyss, but eventually the Melusine stopped. Geroud stood close to her, fearing he might easily be lost and alone in the dark. The Melusine whispered a warning about a staircase ahead before moving off again, up the stairs into an ever deepening darkness. Had he been better educated maybe Geroud would have thought he was turned Eurydice to Karen's Orpheus, or Leo Vincey to Ayesha, but in his ignorance the experience had no literary meaning, only a sensual one. At the top of the stairs, they walked along another dark corridor, at the end of which the Melusine again stopped. There she opened a door to reveal a warmly-lit bedroom. A bed, with bulging turned columns set at each corner, all stained with dark varnish, dominated the room, its mattress dressed in white cotton, tightly bound at the edges, and overlaid with a red damask throw.

Like the bed, the walls might have come straight from a newly-restored room at a Landmark Trust house, each panelled in dark oak up to a height of four or five feet from the floor. Above the panelling a deep red silk paper took over with swirling floral patterns. The old-world opulence of the room continued into the ceiling which was covered in an ornate pattern of plaster strap-work that would not have looked out of place in the long gallery at Hatfield or Blickling. A whole side of the room was taken up with closed curtains, behind which must have been windows, hidden from view. In the middle of another wall was an over-large fireplace, simply carved with an ovolo surround and capped by a four-centred mantle arch. Had the fire been lit it would have instantly transported them back to the imagined Tudor or Jacobean past of the building's Edwardian architect. A better-schooled couple might even have imagined the elderly General Fairfax sitting in his wheelchair in front of that fireplace, clay pipe in hand, his mind momentarily soothed from any sense of guilt. Ah yes, Fairfax. His manly countenance striking awe and reverence into all that beheld him, while it was mixed with so much modesty and meekness, as were ever represented in the figure of an immortal man.[20]

Almost overwhelmed, Geroud turned to face Karen, the Melusine, unable now to stop tears appearing in his eyes. 'I know,' said the Melusine. 'I'm sorry.'

'You know who I am?' asked Geroud.

'Of course. Where on earth did you get that silly name Titivillus from?'

Geroud just smiled. 'It doesn't matter. Not any more.'

The Melusine took one of Geroud's hands and clasped it between both of hers. She lifted it to her lips until she could kiss the tops of Geroud's fingers, and whispered, 'No. It doesn't matter any more.'

---

[20] Paraphrased from Edward Neill, *The Fairfaxes of England and America in the Seventeenth and Eighteenth Centuries* (Albany, New York: Joel Munsell, 1868) 22

§15 Cemetery gates

The meeting with Titivillus the following day never happened. Geroud did not know why the doggy little devil never showed up, but the anxiety he felt after his visit to the Yew Tree Inn, gradually subsided over the weeks and months that followed, until he started to wonder whether he'd dreamt the whole thing up. At other times he speculated to himself that Titivillus might already have taken his eternal soul and he just hadn't noticed. Maybe you don't notice while you're alive, he thought, only once you die. None of it made sense to him, but after years passed by he almost forgot the whole thing, much as any adult in later life might forget the specific days they got drunk, or took drugs, or ran amuck as a teenager, even if they retain a vague memory of doing something like that.

It was only a coincidence, almost twenty years after he had last seen Titivillus, that momentarily sharpened the memory when Geroud found himself again in Barfrestone. This time he was not visiting the pub, but Barfrestone's little church. Like any visitor to the building, Geroud gawped at the sight of the ornate doorway, with its carved knights on horseback, and figures with bows and arrows, and strange animals that seemed to dance around its arch. Above them all was an image of Christ, seated in an oval *vesica piscis*, not that Geroud knew it was called that.

Once inside the church, he stood in the middle of the nave and looked up at the three arches dividing it from the chancel, clearly impressed at what he saw, but without any insight into what it might mean. Nor did he wonder why this tiny little church, of all the small village churches he was required to visit for his job, should be so unusual. Academic thoughts like that were alien to him. Instead he experienced his visit to St Nicholas church almost as pure æsthetic exposure — almost as if he saw the building with a child-like innocent eye.

And yet, why Geroud was in the church was not entirely innocent. Almost two decades on from his last encounter with Titivillus, Geroud was a florist, although it would be more accurate to call him a flower seller as he didn't arrange flowers or compose them into what might, in certain settings, be called works of art. Instead, he sold pre-wrapped chrysanthemums and dahlias from the back of a van, parked on a slip-road by the A2 dual carriageway, on the approach to the municipal cemetery at Womanswold. Variety did not range far for Geroud in his life as a flower seller. He had his encounters with mourners and motorists, sometimes the weather was fine and sometimes not, and every so often he would have a visit from a council official determined to view his trading licence. Even his drive each morning to collect the day's blooms was repetitive and uneventful. Arriving at the flower shop in Canterbury, the Real Florist would hand Geroud the buckets of chrysanthemums and dahlias to load onto the van. Geroud would then drive the chrysanthemums and dahlias to the outskirts of Womanswold and set up his stall. And there he would sit in wait for some unprepared mourner to come his way.

      The only real change to this routine was in the run up to the spring wedding season, when the Real Florist would hand Geroud a stack of business cards and instruct him to tour the local churches and leave a stash of cards at each of them, 'somewhere near the collection boxes,' to advertise the Real Florist's wedding services. Bouquets for brides, church flowers and buttonholes. It was an unofficial tout for business, only one step above fly-posting, but it must have worked as the Real Florist insisted on it.

    So it was, having completed his mission at St Nicholas in Barfrestone that Geroud found himself looking around the building, naïve and innocent, but with an undeniable sense of wonder. As he moved around, admiring the carvings on the inside walls of the nave, he saw a dog, or maybe it was a pig, playing pan-pipes while a mer-dog, or maybe it was a mer-pig, danced with a winged lion. He also saw the carved circles, some containing abstract shapes like stars, and others with animals and mythical beasts. There was a kind of squirrel, another lion, two winged griffins pawing at a flower, an ox and a cat with a human head. As he walked around the building the creatures seemed to get more extraordinary. The cat with a human head was followed by another mer-dog, or mer-pig, then a man with a large-head who sat watching a monkey and a donkey carrying a hare in what looked like a cooking pot hung between two poles.

Although Geroud didn't understand any of it, the carved creatures made him smile, as much a rare event now as it had been in his adolescence. The carvings affected him so much he found himself saying out loud in the empty church, 'They're lovely.' In the instant after he spoke he looked around furtively, in case someone had heard him. But the church was empty. Except — except, there was something. It was indistinct at first, but as he strained to hear more clearly Geroud realised a noise was coming from the far end of the building. It sounded like someone knocking at a door. His first thought was to ignore it. This wasn't his house, he thought. You wouldn't answer the door in someone else's house, and besides, the church door was open. He knew that, he'd only just used it. But the knocking came again, louder and more insistent this time. Geroud moved nearer to the sound, only to realise it was not coming from the main church door. It came from the west wall of the building, low down where he could see another door, much smaller this time, perhaps only three feet high, set into the wall at ground level. It might have been the old entrance to the church except it seemed too small. But it also seemed too low to be a cupboard.

Geroud knelt on one knee in front of the little door and held his hand hesitantly over the oversize wrought iron ring handle sticking out from it. The knock came again and this time a voice. 'Could you possibly open the door for me?' it asked with almost shocking civility.

'Wh— what?' said Geroud stuttering at the strangeness of the situation.

'The door,' said the voice with the confidence of a British officer in an old war film. 'I wonder, if you could see your way as to open it, like?'

'Yes,' replied Geroud, suitably deferential to the voice of authority. 'Except I don't have the key.'

'There isn't one,' said the voice. 'Just turn the handle.'

Geroud took hold of the large iron ring handle and turned it until it wouldn't go any further. He didn't pull at the door, just turning the handle enough to say he'd opened it without really opening it.

'Are you going to open the door?' asked the voice.

'Oh. Erm. It's open,' said Geroud. 'Just push.'

'It's not that simple,' said the voice. 'You need to open it for me.'

§16 William, it was really nothing

I suppose Pandora faced the same problem. The blame is always put on her, but maybe she also heard a voice from the box asking her to open it. Maybe she too had a moment of doubt. Geroud stood looking at the little door in the west end of Barfrestone church, his brow in a deep frown, unsure what to do. 'Well, are you going to open the door or not?' asked the voice again, sounding more impatient this time.

    Without answering Geroud took hold of the iron handle again, this time pulling it so the door opened. He didn't open it fully, just enough, he thought, for whatever was inside to push its own way out to freedom. Standing and moving back, he watched as whatever was inside did exactly that. He couldn't help thinking it was like a scene from some Hammer horror film, complete with swirls of smoke, or perhaps dry-ice vapour, slinking from the black space inside. Or perhaps it was more like the great reveal on *Stars in Their Eyes*. 'Tonight, Matthew, I want to be —.' But what? What could be in the little nook and what did it want to be?

For a moment, the door stood fully open with no sign of movement inside. An unnatural silence fell over the church, almost as though the white noise of the carved animals dancing to their musical instruments around the walls was stopped in silent expectation. What did appear was both extraordinary and a little disappointing. It was a foot. A human foot. It wore a very shiny black patent leather shoe with a purple sock. Attached to it was a leg. A human leg, dressed in black trousers. Then another foot appeared, and another leg. Whatever was appearing seemed to be human, but it was being born backend first. When it was fully free from the doorway the apparition remained on its knees, its back to Geroud, shuffling its body as if trying to settle itself on firm earth again. It was dressed in a jacket that matched its trousers, all impeccably black, laundered and pressed, despite emerging from what was clearly a very dusty cupboard. The figure moved gingerly into an upright position, as though it had not stood on its legs for a very long time. Still with its back to Geroud, it stretched, pushing its arms upwards and to the sides, and rolling its shoulders, as if to give a theatrical impression of stretching, rather than exercising any real need. Only when this performance was ended did the figure turn around, slowly with equally deliberate theatricality.

'Titivillus!' exclaimed Geroud.

§17 I thought you were dead

'Hello Lonely Heart!' said Titivillus, a large grin on his dog-like face.

'What do you mean hello?' asked Geroud, still unable to understand what he had seen.

'It's a simple enough greeting, like,' replied Titivillus, still pushing his arms left and right and rolling his shoulder blades.

'Where have you been? What are you doing in there?'

'Reading,' replied Titivillus casually, as though it was perfectly normal for a fully-grown man to squeeze himself through the three-foot door to a dark cupboard at the west end of a mediæval church. He walked stiffly past Geroud to the nearby font. There he took some of the sacred water to wash his hands before settling himself onto one of the nearby pews. 'It was a really odd book as it happens. You were in it. And me. And this church. Oh, and that gasometer where we first met. Spooky!'

'But you were in a cupboard?' said Geroud.

'Is that a statement or a question?' asked Titivillus raising his eyebrows. Geroud didn't answer. 'Well,' continued Titivillus sounding as if he was about to explain himself as opaquely as possible. 'If I am honest — *absolutely honest I mean* — I didn't really mean to be in there.' He stretched his legs as he spoke, then bent them at the knee, back and forth, first one then the other making the kneecaps crack like knuckles. 'If I'm honest like — *really honest, I mean* — and of course I am always *really* honest with you, I had a bit of an accident. Or perhaps I should say I was tricked. Last night, after I left you, I had planned to set up another little surprise. A present, like. For you. I thought, know, I'm going to do my dear sweet Lonely Heart a special favour. An extra special favour. Without him even asking, like.'

'Last night?' asked Geroud.

'Yes,' continued Titivillus. 'In that pub. The Oak Tree — isn't that what it's called?'

'Yew Tree,' said Geroud. 'It was the Yew Tree. But it wasn't last night. It was twenty years ago.'

'Twenty years?' said Titivillus calmly. 'Are you sure.' Titivillus looked intently at Geroud's face as if examining a piece of evidence. 'I find that hard to believe. Mind you, you do look different. Oh well! It must have been that book. I always lose track of time when reading a really good book. Did you miss me?'

'Miss you?' said Geroud. 'I thought you were dead. Or that I imagined you.'

Titivillus laughed. 'I see your sense of humour has improved. But of course I'm immortal. I cannot die. And it wouldn't be fair. The world needs me.'

'If you say so,' replied Geroud. 'Although I've managed perfectly well without you.'

'Now, now, dear Lonely Heart. I like to think we need each other. Think of all the fun times. Like when we fell of that gasometer —'

'Don't change the subject,' interrupted Geroud. 'You abandoned me.'

'I say, my dear Lonely Heart,' said Titivillus sounding genuinely hurt. 'You know I've always had a soft spot for you. I wouldn't ever abandon you. Ever. Cross my heart. Not that I can hope to die. Twenty minutes or twenty years, what difference does it make when you're the cherry on my cake?'

'What favour?' Geroud asked, feeling uncomfortable.

'Cherry.'

'What?'

'The flavour. Cherry. You're always the *cherry* on my cake.'

'I said favour, not flavour. You said you were doing me a favour. What favour?'

'Ah yes, I'm glad you asked me that. Otherwise you might not know how good a friend I am. It was a big favour. A really big favour, like.'

'What?' asked Geroud.

'Well,' said Titivillus, 'When we were in that pub, I thought, I know I'll do Lonely Heart a really big favour.'

'You've said that. What did you do?'

Titivillus laughed nervously. 'You'll love this. I thought I'd teach that hideous boy a lesson. You know the one who looks like a fat pig.'

'Looked. I don't know what he looks like now. He'd be old by now. Like me.'

'Old? Hardly my dear boy. You don't look a day over forty.'

'I'm thirty-six.'

'Spot on then. As for that boy, he probably looks like an even fatter pig by now.'

'We're not meant to say things like that any more,' said Geroud sounding unconvinced at his own words. 'Times have changed. It's fattist. You're just some throwback. Like Austin Powers.'

'Who?' asked Titivillus, sounding as though he couldn't care less who Austin Powers might be. 'Still, I cannot believe humanity has stopped calling each other names. Personally I've always thought any weapon is valid when used against an enemy, especially if your enemy has the upper hand. It is always legitimate to resort to counter stigmatisation.'[21]

---

[21] See Nobert Elias, *The Established and the Outsiders* (London: Sage Publications, 1965; 1994) xxi. See also Norbert Elias, *The Court Society* (Oxford: Blackwells, 1969; 1983), for examples of the way in which labelling and counter-labelling was used to bolster and attack the aristocracy in 18th-century France.

'Yeah, well, you've been away a long time. But what did you do?'

'Fear!' replied Titivillus trying to sound ominous. 'I decided to put the fear of God into him. The fat pig. To scare the little shit witless, like. After I left you, I went into the village and I found his house. And —' Titivillus trailed off, as though realising his story was not going to have the triumphant ending he wanted. 'Well I found him and I taught him, like. You know — a lesson.' Geroud looked at Titivillus blankly. 'Except it didn't quite work out. I wasn't going to do anything too bad of course. Just frighten him to death. I was in my best devil wear. All the bells and whistles. You know, satanic apparition on a dark night, with a second head coming out of my backside screaming for mercy, and a penis shaped like a pitch fork ready to prod him. It was all very old school.'

'And was he frightened?'

'Oh yes!' exclaimed Titivillus grinning. 'He was pissing himself. Literally. Three times as I recall. Fat pigs have big bladders. Anyway, we ran around the whole village. It was great fun.'

'So how did you end up in there?' asked Geroud pointing to cupboard door.

Titivillus looked sheepish. 'You mean in the Devil's Nook?' he said, trying to sound confident again.

'Is that what they call it?'

'I don't know, but they should. It sounds catchy. Or maybe Hob's nook to get in a bit of olde English village dialect. You know to add a sense of authenticity.'

'Can you go on?'

'Oh yes. Well, I can only presume he decided to find God. The fat pig I mean. He stopped running around the village and headed for the church. I'm surprised it was even open. All these lunatics running around at night, you'd think they'd lock it up as a precaution. Very remiss. Anything could happen —'

'The point. Get to the point.'

'Yes, of course. Anyway, he ran into the church and I followed him.'

'I see,' said Geroud. 'And you lost your powers?'

'What?' replied Titivillus, sounding confused. 'Why would that happen?'

'Because — *you know?* — it's a church.'

'Exactly,' said Titivillus. 'It's a church, so my powers should have been at their height. Their zenith, like. This is one of those places where your mundane little world meets all the other worlds. A liminal zone. Hypostatic space. A matrixial space no less! Fluid and magical. Especially *this* church with its carvings. All very apotropaic.'

'Even if you're a devil?' said Geroud sounding disappointed.

'Oh, I see,' said Titivillus, sighing deeply. 'After all these years and you still think in such binary terms — I'm a boy and you're a girl, this is good and that is bad. Nothing is so straightforward I'm afraid. As someone once said, *Why must we assume that life, which has evolved into such a diversity of creatures, should be expressed in a single category of understanding?*[22]

Geroud looked at Titivillus blankly.

---

[22] Herbert Read, *The Philosophy of Modern Art* (London: Faber, 1952) 97

Titivillus continued: 'Well, my point is that reality is more complex and more exciting than just yin-yang-ing everything. My world and yours meet in a place like this whether you're a devil or a saint. We touch. Intimately. Mind you, I suppose that's the point of yin-yang. Anyway, I chased him in here, and I let out a plume of foul smelling vapour from the mouth in my backside, and then —'

'And then?' asked Geroud.

'And then—. If I am honest — *and I am always honest with you* — if I am honest I'd have to say I lost concentration. Just for a moment, like. All that vapour. I guess. It goes to your head. In the confusion the fat pig opened the door to that cupboard, pushed me inside and well, hey presto, here we are. End of. Like.'

This time it was Geroud's turn to let out a loud laugh. It was perhaps a little too loud, a little forced, as though it came from someone who didn't often laugh. Calming himself, Geroud asked, 'Why didn't you just push the door open?'

'He locked me in,' said Titivillus.

'I don't think so,' said Geroud. 'It wasn't locked when I found you. You told me so yourself.'

'Ah,' replied Titivillus trying to look conspiratorial. 'That's probably a plot device. To be honest I don't know why I couldn't open it and you could. Maybe you have some mystical powers after all. Or maybe I didn't even try. I did get lost in that strange book I found inside, but let's leave these speculative questions open for future generations to argue. You need to just accept I couldn't open the door from the inside.'

'Even if any of that made sense, you could have forced it open. It's not that solid.'

'And damage an old building like this!' replied Titivillus, sounding genuinely shocked.

'Well, it proves I was right to doubt your divine powers after the disaster at the pub,' said Geroud.

'What disaster?' asked Titivillus. 'I've just been reading about it in that book I found. It all went to plan. You copped off with her. That Melusine girl. Look, it's here in black and white. Just as I promised. And in a four poster bed in an oak-panelled room too. Very romantic.' Titivillus opened the book in his hand and pointed to page 141.

'That's what you promised,' agreed Geroud, sounding as angry as he could after twenty years of calming down. 'Sign an insignificant piece of paper and you'll get the one thing you want more than anything else in the world. A night with her.'

'Exactly, a night with that dull little girl. All delivered as promised!'

'Yes, a night with her was promised. Except, all I got was a miserable night alone in the pub and a long walk home in the rain.'

'On your own?' asked Titivillus.

'Of course on my own, who else with?'

'But what happened to the Melusine?'

'I'll tell you what happened. You didn't stop to think that someone else might turn up, order a drink at the bar, and when it took a little longer to arrive than he expected he'd shout "Come on girl! Issy-wizzy-let's-get-busy!"'

'Issy-wizzy-let's-get-busy. He said those words?'

'Yes.'

'Issy-wizzy-let's-get-busy?'

'Yes.'

'He said them? Not you?'

'Yes, he said them, not me.'

'Well, who'd have guessed it,' said Titivillus. He stood and started pacing around. 'It really is almost like the plot in a book. You'd think — *I mean* — I mean you really would think, that of all the things you could say in the world — *I mean* — what are the chances of some random stranger, randomly saying those exact words. At that moment in time, in that exact place? I mean, like, it would be — '

'Impossible?' asked Geroud.

'Exactly,' agreed Titivillus. 'Well, nigh impossible, like.'

'That's what I thought, so I assumed you'd set the whole thing up as a joke. A cruel joke.'

'I wouldn't do that, dear Lonely Heart. I must admit it would be a good joke, but I wouldn't. Not to you. How was I to know some stranger would arrive and say that exact spell?'

'Except it wasn't a stranger.'

Titivillus looked confused. 'But you said some man walked in and ordered a drink.'

'Not some man. A man. A man called Scatson. Remember him? Skinner's friend.'

'Oh yes,' said Titivillus as it dawned on him how calamitous the cock-up had been. 'The slightly more charming thug. A thin pig so to speak.'

They sat in silence for a moment, before Titivillus began laughing. 'Oh Fate,' he tried to say repeatedly. 'Oh Fate, you make fools of us all.'

'It's really not funny,' insisted Geroud.

'No, no, of course not,' agreed Titivillus unconvincingly. 'Well maybe a little. And it does show you can't trust anything you read these days. In that book it says you and that Melusine shared a bottle of very good whiskey when all the other customers had gone home.'

'Nothing like that happened. You can trust me on that. Unlike you or that book, I was there.'

'So she didn't tell you to poke the fire?'

Geroud frowned as he looked at Titivillus, pursing his lips to avoid swearing in the church.

'And she didn't lead you upstairs and along a dark corridor to a panelled bedroom?'

'No.'

'And she didn't take one of your hands and clasp it between hers?'

'No.'

'And she didn't lift your hand to her lips to kiss the top of your fingers?'

'Are you trying to rub it in? If that was the plan, she did it to him, not me.'

'And you didn't —'

'No, we didn't.'

'Then I guess you're right. That slightly more charming thug must have got the benefit. But it's your own fault. You really should have been quicker off the mark. With the *issy-wizzy-let's-get-busy* business I mean. That's always been your problem, if I might say so. Sometimes I think you like to miss your chances. There's comfort in being a victim all the time.'

For a moment the silence of the church tried to take hold of them again, but it was held back by Titivillus, gently sniggering as he worked out the difference between what had really happened at the Yew Tree Inn twenty years earlier and what he had read in the book in the cupboard. Geroud stared at him sternly. 'You really do have to see the funny side, dear Lonely Heart,' said Titivillus.

'You mean the funny side how the devil makes you sign a contract and then fails to deliver?' asked Geroud.

'Well, that is quite funny,' said Titivillus. 'I get locked in a church cupboard and you lose your soul for nothing. We do make a right pair when you think of it. Like Laurel and Hardy. I knew we'd be good friends. We're two of a kind you and me.'

Despite the litany of cock-ups, or maybe because of them, Geroud couldn't help smiling. There really was something ridiculous about it all. It was not the first time since he had met Titivillus that he felt he'd been saddled with a second-class demon, but maybe that was because he was a second-class sinner. He hadn't asked for unbridled power, unimaginable wealth, or revenge, death and destruction on a global scale. He hadn't asked to be president of the United States, or a media mogul. His teenage self had just asked to cop off, *as Titivillus had so delicately put it,* with a girl at school because she had a pretty face and he was lonely. It had always been a pathetic request so why wouldn't the outcome be equally pathetic. He could have asked for anything, but he had in truth asked for nothing. Mind you, dear reader, at that age I might have asked for something similar and I don't think it would have seemed like nothing to me. Not at that age, like. It would have seemed necessary, like a profound and desperate need.[23]

---

[23] The late Augustine Shutte had some interesting things to say on this kind of thing. See Augustine Shutte, 'The Human Predicament and the Transcendent' in *New Blackfriars,* vol. 68, no. 801, January 1987, 25-35

§18 My love life

After Titivillus had emerged, backside first, from the nook in Barfrestone church, Geroud might have been forgiven for thinking his pact with the doggy little devil was null and void. Something along the lines of an agreement made and a contract breached. Although Geroud had never felt any great loss in signing away his soul, there was still a lightness in the tone of his voice as he mentioned this to Titivillus, which might have been interpreted as a sign of relief.

Titivillus frowned. 'Why would you think that?' he asked.

'It's obvious,' said Geroud. 'You didn't deliver. Isn't there something in the Sale of Goods Act about things like that? Failure to deliver.'

'I think, dear Lonely Heart, you'll find I did deliver,' said Titivillus. 'You didn't collect. If you order a pint of beer at a bar and don't drink it do you think you can ask for a refund?'

'You can at Marks and Spencer. Maybe not beer, but shirts. And knickers.'

'Language,' replied Titivillus. 'This is the House of God.'

Geroud was silenced by Titivillus's sudden bout of piety. Eventually he said, 'But you can't mean you're still going to claim my soul?'

Titivillus nodded.

'But I didn't get anything for it.'

Titivillus shrugged.

'Is that all I'm worth?' asked Geroud, sounding hurt.

Titivillus frowned. There appeared to be a genuine pang of conscience in his voice as he said, 'It's not such big a deal. And look at how things have turned out! After twenty years, I'm reunited with my *bestest, bestest* boy. It's like the old team back together. Like Laurel and Hardy, Flanagan and Allan —'

'Chalk and cheese,' interrupted Geroud.

Titivillus laughed. 'I knew you'd develop a sense of humour. You know, I've always thought that if I ever did decide to believe in God I would become a Calvinist. I'd be as good as any dour Scot and I'd use predestination to explain why we met. Why you were always mine.'

'You sound like some creepy stalker,' said Geroud.

'It's exactly like that,' replied Titivillus his voice becoming animated at the idea of a new metaphor to play with. 'Isn't it creepy that you were a dysfunctional little boy who couldn't even make a single friend in a school filled with hundreds of other dysfunctional little boys? And isn't it creepy that you fell for such an unpleasant girl, even though she couldn't stand the sight of you? And that you happened to find a book on witchcraft that taught you to make a magic pyramid? And that when you decided to jump off that gasometer, I just happened to be passing by? And today! Today you happen to be in this church, so we meet again! Isn't it all a bit too creepy? A bit preordained? It's almost as though we're characters in a book or something. *Deus ex machina,* like.'

'If you read anyone's life back to them it would probably sound like that,' said Georud. 'There isn't a pattern in the carpet, it just seems that way.'

'There isn't a pattern in the carpet, it just seems that way.' repeated Titivillus. 'You've become a philosopher over the years. Perhaps a poet too.'

'No, I just sell flowers.'

'A flower seller. Is that a cryptic metaphor for something? I presume you're really something to do with this church. Are you the vicar? Or the bishop. Maybe you're an Inspector of Parishes. I hope you're an Inspector of Parishes. We can some fun with that. Or are you here for the architecture? That's it! You're an art historian, here to survey this lovely building. Is that it?'

'No,' replied Geroud starting to sound annoyed. 'Why are you asking? You know what I am.'

'Only God knows who we really are my son,' said Titivillus with mock solemnity.

Geroud's anger subsided. He let out a short snorting laugh. 'This is ridiculous, I'm not a vicar or a historian. I'm a flower seller. Cheap flowers from the back of a van in a lay-by.'

'Ah, mon Dieu!' exclaimed Titivillus, looking as though he wanted to dance at the news. 'I love flowers

and you're a florist!' He stood up and walked briskly, almost running, towards the large display of lilies at the side of the high altar, sticking his face into the blooms, one after the other, until his dog-like nose was covered in orange pollen. Turning again to face Geroud, he said: 'You know, if I have been born a dull and ordinary little mortal like you, I would have been a florist. What a noble profession. All that beauty! Who needs fame and fortune. All I want is flowers!'

'Fame and fortune might be nice too,' mumbled Geroud.

'Pah!' exclaimed Titivillus. 'Pah! Pah! Fame and fortune is for tossers.'

'Tossers who don't have to worry about paying the gas bill and get to drive fast cars, and go skiing in St. Moritz.'

'Yes, those tossers,' agreed Titivillus. 'But St Moritz — you'd hate it. It's full of tossers who can afford to be there and don't have to worry about paying the gas bill. Not your sort of people at all. You know, even the mountains hate them. That's why they knock a few of them off each year. When they get the chance, like.

An avalanche here, an unexpected dive off-piste there. Pop-pop-pop! You don't want to be like them. Trust me, you are better off as a florist.'

'Flower seller.'

'Tomato! Tomato! You know it's like we live in a bubble of space, you and me. And in this bubble of space miracles happen. And I'm glad of it. It means we're back together again. In real life that doesn't happen. In real life people don't meet up with old friends after twenty years and it's like they only met yesterday. It only happens in a miraculous bubble of space like this one.'

'So you think we're friends?' asked Geroud.

'No, you are right,' agreed Titivillus. 'We have always been more than friends. And that makes me feel like celebrating now we're back together — how do you like to celebrate?'

'I don't,' mumbled Geroud.

'You don't?' said Titivillus, sounding genuinely confused. 'You must celebrate sometimes. With your friends? Family? Girlfriend? Boyfriend?' Geroud shuffled uncomfortably and for a moment he thought he heard the building mumble. Maybe it was the creatures carved on the walls, whispering about him.

Titivillus sat on one of the pews nearest the altar and it appeared as though he was in a kind of secret communion with someone, or something. Although he said nothing, a stream of tiny smiles played across his mouth and cheeks and Geroud wondered for a moment if he was praying. But to what?

After a while Titivillus stood and walked in almost total silence through the arch separating the nave from the chancel. There he began to look closely at the wonky geometric carving of that ran just above head height around the north and south walls of the chancel. In another age he would have passed for an antiquarian on a motoring tour, with Arthur Mee on hand waxing lyrically on Barfreston's ancient beauty:

> Through the high chancel arch, dominating the whole interior, is the great wheel window above three Norman lancets. It is tracery in the full flush of its early splendour. Each of the eight spokes of the wheel is a sturdy little sculptured

> column, and the whole effect of the window is to make us feel that we are in the presence of the beginning of that Gothic glory, the Rose Window, which was soon to follow.[24]

In the chancel were set two heavy wooden chairs, one on either side of the altar table. Titivillus walked over to one of them, grabbed it by the top of its tall back and pulled it slightly further away from the altar. The chair legs scraped loudly on the flagstone floor causing Geroud to wince. Titivillus sat down. Geroud was not surprised to see him being so cavalier with the furniture by the altar and it was just a chair, after all, presumably placed there so someone could sit on it. More shocking was the way Titivillus proceeded to place first one leg, then the other, on the altar table. His legs now resting comfortably on the holy shrine, the doggy little devil, who had only moments ago upbraided Geroud for saying the word *knickers* in a church, pulled from the breast pocked the same bright red cigarette

---

[24] Arthur Mee, *The King's England: Kent* (London: Hodder and Stoughton, 1936; 1969) 25-6

case Geroud remembered seeing on top of the gasometer two decades earlier. A kind of giddiness came over Geroud as he watched Titivillus's theatrical actions. He knew it was a performance just for him. He couldn't help smiling, imperceptibly to anyone who might have been watching, but he felt it in his own face. It was as if he was watching a TV show, so unreal it was not really disrespectful at all. Even the cigarette case seemed to be in on the act, appearing almost magnified in Geroud's sight, as though an unseen TV director had ordered a close-up. Geroud could see clearly that the cigarette case had a golden double-headed bird, some kind of eagle, set into it. When Titivillus opened it Geroud saw a row of cigarettes, each wrapped in black paper crowned with gold-coloured filters. Without looking up Titivillus said, 'It was given to me by the Tsar you know.' Geroud blinked repeatedly and shook his head slightly as if trying to break out of a reverie. 'The cigarette case,' continued Titivillus. 'The Russian Tsar that is. Nicholas the —oh, which one was it? The one they shot.'

'I don't know,' said Geroud.

'The Second. Yes, that's it, Nicholas-the-Second,' continued Titivillus. 'He gave it to me as a thank-you.'

'For what?' asked Geroud.

'For making him a saint.'

'You made Nicholas II a saint? That doesn't sound likely.'

'I know what you mean!' agreed Titivillus. 'He was hardly holy material. A nasty piece of work, with shit for brains. Not in the remotest sense holy, but ideal material for sainthood. And now he spends his days in hell, boiled in oil day after day for all eternity, but happy as Larry just because he's a saint up here. St Nicholas the Passion-Bearer they call him. That's the Church for you. Putin's up next. He's a KGB thug. St Putin the Peacemaker is what the Russian Orthodox Church will call him. He's got a few other sins to get out of his system first, but honestly, you couldn't make it up.'

'Do you often do the Lord's work?' asked Geroud sarcastically.

Titivillus laughed, but ignored the question. 'And these are Sobranie Black Russians,' he said taking one of the black and gold cigarettes from the case. 'You have to have Russian cigarettes in a Russian cigarette case, don't you think? Leave the John Player Specials for the cool kids at the far end of the school field. Of course the irony is that the cool kids were really so uncool they wouldn't have ever known these are the cool cigarettes. Stupid people never see their own stupidity. You know what I mean, dear Lonely Heart?' Geroud knew exactly what he meant.

> When dad came back from his trips to Cyprus he'd always bring us a present. Most of the time he'd buy it at the airport, a giant tube of Smarties or a huge Toblerone. In those days you only got things like that at airports. I don't think real shops even sold Toblerone. Sometimes he'd bring a handful of seven-inch singles, each of them so exotic, from the mysterious Greek script written on the label to the green and brown vinyl that we'd never seen on any English record. And then the tunes, a kind of high-

powered folk music, turbo-charged with amps and synthesisers — Greek bangra. But one time he brought my mother a box of cigarettes, 200 duty free, but not her usual brand. Not Player's No. 6. They were called Sobranies. The packets were an unusual shape, like little cigar boxes. But it was the cigarettes themselves that was most exciting. Instead of white paper, they were brightly coloured, each a different shade, red, purple, yellow, pink and green, and all with gleaming gold tips. It was all very James Bond.

With so many packets in that big box how would me mam miss just one? So I took it. Just one. One packet that is.

That day, for the first and only time in my life, the walk to school seemed exhilarating. I had an unusual show-and-tell, a secret to share with the likes of Skinner, and Scatson, and the Melusine, and the smokers at the end of the field. Something to make me belong. Except it didn't work out like that. It never did. It never does. Life's a pigsty full of pigs. Some friend of the Melusine saw them first and made a grab. Had they stayed in her greedy hands my efforts might still have opened the door to a better life. A new role for me as chief supplier of exotic fancy goods. But Skinner arrived. He snarled and called me names. The others laughed. They began walking to the end of the field to try the new candy-coloured cigarettes and I started walking with them. Skinner stopped. I sensed I should do the same.

I often wonder what would have happened if I have just kept walking, ignoring Skinner. Maybe I should have run over to the excited group of girls in front of me, each choosing their favourite colour as they walked. But that never happened. Skinner stopped, so I

**stopped. He asked me where the fuck I
thought I was going, but I was too frightened
to answer. He called me a fucking bent
bastard and started walking away. I decided
not to follow. Something told me I'd got off
lightly that time.**

    'I don't think —' Geroud started to say, but Titivillus interrupted him.
    'You don't think they're still on the JPS? Maybe not. Too old school. Can you even buy JPS any more? Why knows! So maybe Marlboro Lights. Whatever — they're still not cool enough to be on Sobranies. And if they are on Sobranies it's just because of an accident. Opportunist theft or vulgar expropriation. Besides which, if we're really lucky they'll all die of lung cancer anyway.' Geroud remembered thinking the same on the day he'd lost his box of multicoloured Sobranies. But hearing Titivillus say it out loud shocked him.
    'I was going to say I don't think you should smoke in here,' said Geroud.

'Why not?' replied Titivillus indignantly. 'You don't think I'm one of the cool cats.'

'Cool cats?' said Geroud sarcastically.

'Yes, cool cats,' repeated Titivillus. 'But what would you know about it?'

Titivillus began patting his the top of his jacket as Geroud remembered he had done on the top of the gasometer. And as he had before, Titivillus located the box of Lucifer matches and took them out. He placed one of the black cigarettes in his mouth and lit it so the end fizzled audibly in the near silent church. He then took a long drag causing the cigarette to burn unnaturally fast. It disappeared in a matter of seconds as though caught in its own bubble of time-lapse space. As it burnt out Titivillus threw the smouldering butt onto the stone floor by the altar, apparently unconcerned at the fire risk, and exhaled what looked to Geroud like an entire cigarette's-worth of smoke into the air. The chancel filled with a dense fug. It spilled into the nave of the church and reached Geroud. Geroud might have expected to cough at the sulphurous fumes, but instead the smoke smelled sweet, almost like incense. Titivillus leaned back contentedly in the chair.

'You shouldn't smoke at all,' said Geroud.

'True,' agreed Titivillus sounding like he couldn't care less. 'But I'm hoping for an early death.' Geroud couldn't tell if he was joking. 'But listen, enough of this chit-chat. We've been thinking, like.'

'We?'

'I've been thinking. What if we start again? On a different track, like? You've lost your soul and didn't quite get what you wanted for it. How about if we make — *I mean, I make* — a *kind of* good-will gesture?'

'You'll give me my soul back?' asked Geroud.

'Not quite. That's not quite in my power. But I can do something for you. As a friend, like. As a friendly good-will gesture. So you don't feel cheated, like.'

§19 First of the gang to die

'Hiya Gez, what you got there?'

'Oh nothing really. Me dad's just got back from Cyprus. He bought me mam some of these, so I nabbed a pack.'

'What are they?'

'Don't know really. Smokes, but funny'uns. Different colours.'

'Cool! Hey look guys. Gez has some weird smokes.'

'Wow, Gez, what are they? How d'they taste?'

'Let's find out. Come on Gez — the usual place.'

'Where?'

'Yeah, like you don't know. There! Under the trees. But you've not been there have you?'

'No. I wouldn't be welcome.'

'Oh fuck off. You would. 'Specially with smokes like this.'

'What about Skinner?'

'Oh fuck him, he knows where we are. Let's have the smokes before the greedy pig gets here. He'll have 'em all.'

'Great! What colour d'you want?'

'Dunno. Let's try 'em all.'

§20 How can anybody possibly know how I feel?

'Yes,' said Titivillus distractedly.'

'What?' asked Geroud.

'What what?'

'You said yes in that meaningful way. It's really annoying.'

'Oh, it's nothing,' said Titivillus as if rousing himself from a daydream. 'I was just thinking, like. Wouldn't it be nice if you could replace a real memory with a dream? So you could remember the dream instead of what really happened, like.'

'It depends if the dream's a nightmare I suppose.'

Titivillus frowned. 'Is your glass always half empty?'

'It's all empty.'

Titivillus smiled. He was still resting his feet on the altar in Barfrestone church, sat on a great oak arm chair. 'As I was saying, a kind of good-will gesture. One in which we turn all this nonsense to our advantage.

Not that I'm admitting liability, like. It's your fault that night didn't work out, I think we're agreed on that.'

'I don't — '

'It's alright don't apologise, we can sort it out. What if we rethink the whole thing. I mean, you know your original wish was a bit pathetic. Selling your soul just to shag that hideous knob-grinder. What were you thinking?'

Geroud frowned at Titivillus's description of the Melusine. 'It seemed —' He wanted to say it seemed important at the time. The solution to his loneliness. His pain. But now Titivillus was right, in his description, if not in his language, it did seem stupid.

'Not just stupid,' said Titivillus loudly as if reading Geroud's thoughts. 'Pathetic. But still, teenage infatuation. It seems so real. At the time. But teenage thoughts are really all pathetic despite what anyone says. Teenagers are stupid creatures.'

'Yes. I thought it was real. At the time. But it's hard to remember.'

'So why not try to forget?' asked Titivillus. 'Or rather, why not replace the reality with a dream?'

'Do you mean you're going to make me think I did sleep with her? Isn't that called something. False memory or something?'

Titivillus laughed. 'I'm not sure even I could manage that. I'd have to wipe out all your other memories of the last twenty years too. Even a planted memory of you shagging the girl of your teenage dreams couldn't wipe out all those years.'

'Like you say. Teenage infatuation. And I'm not a teenager any more. I've outgrown all that.'

'It sounds like you've never read *Death in Venice*. Infatuation and desire are not all in the hands of the young you know. I'll vouch for that. You can be as old as the heavens and still fall in love.'

'I do read,' said Geroud, trying to change the subject. For some reason he felt uncomfortable at the way Titivillus seemed to be opening up to him. 'I sit day after day outside the cemetery selling flowers and when I'm not selling flowers I read. But I haven't read any books on Venice. You always said I was the bookish sort —'

'Did I? When?'

'On top of that gasometer. You said you thought I looked like the sensitive bookish sort. Well I wasn't then. Maybe I'm not now. But I do read.'

'Really?' exclaimed Titivillus, leaping from his chair. 'Then that's what we'll work with. With the goodwill gesture. Something more obviously Faust-like.'

'What's forced-like?' asked Geroud.

'You haven't read the story of Faust? A few have been written.'

'No. I don't think so.'

'Faust, my dear Lonely Heart, sold his soul for knowledge and power. Wealth as well. He was a bit more ambitious than you, or rather John Dee was.'

'John Dee?'

'Yes. Dee was the man they based Faust on. The writers I mean. He was a magician in the court of Elizabeth I. He sold his soul for knowledge, wealth and power. You can ask him about it yourself soon enough.'

'What do you have in mind?' asked Geroud nervously.

'Not the wealth and power bit. That's a bit clichéd. Although I do like the idea of a comic interlude or two.' Geroud looked at him blankly. 'You know peasants eating straw. That kind of thing. Anyway, not wealth and power, but world renown. Intellectual kudos. Academic respect. *Fame! I want to live forever!* Doesn't that sound exciting?'

'To be honest I'm not sure I can be bothered. Not now. What's the point? If I'm going to hell let's just get on with it.'

'Empty glass again! You need to recognise when your glass is filling up. And when that glass is really an oak tree.'

'What?'

'Ah ha!' exclaimed Titivillus. 'That's what we'll make you. An authority on art. An art historian. A great art historian!'

'An art historian?'

'Yes, a sexy art historian. Everyone loves an art historian! Especially an art historian who hums-and-ahs over a mediæval truss or can muster a far-away look when faced with a newly-built branch of ASDA. It's a look that says, I know you're an ugly brute of a building, *un péché volontaire,* but I'm a sexy art historian so I know the DNA running through your concrete veins goes back to Gropius and Behrens, and Morris and Webb. I can see the goodness in your soul! We'll make you an expert on architecture, an architectural historian!'

'Can't you just make me president of the United States?'

'Of course I can,' said Titivillus. 'I could give you all that with the click of my fingers. I can even give you the power to make peasants eat straw if you like. But where's the fun in that? I want you to make — *well, to feel like you've made* — a difference. It's not the magic that's the hard bit. Of course there will have to be a bit of magic. I can always do the magic. This has to be something else.'

'Alright, why not make me an expert on literature then?' asked Geroud. 'At least I've read some books.'

'Oh I don't think so. No I don't think so. That wouldn't work at all. I wouldn't want to make you an expert in English literature. No one likes English teachers. You don't get people looking back on their school days and saying how much they liked their English teacher. No, no, no. Everyone looks back and says they loved their art history teacher. Especially their sexy art history teacher.'

'Are you sure?' asked Geroud. 'I don't think I even had an art history teacher?'

'Of course you did. This is a civilised country. You must have done.'

'You really are deluded.'

'And you are an innocent when it comes to the ways of the world, dear Lonely Heart. Which is why you need me. And even if there are not as many art historians as there should be, it doesn't matter. Nine times out of ten someone asks to be made President of the United States, or a famous English teacher. They're a bunch of clichés. There's no point being a cliché.'

'What is the point then?'

'You, dear Lonely Heart. The point is you. Something about you. Something that comes from you and makes a difference.'

Geroud was frowning again. 'A difference to what?'

'Does it matter?' asked Titivillus. 'A difference, that's all. Something to make it feel like it's all been worthwhile. That life has been worthwhile.'

§21 Nowhere fast

The journey to London was annoying. Geroud couldn't understand why he felt annoyed, he just did. Like waking up with an aching neck or arm — *presumably because you've slept in a strange position* — he'd woken up feeling annoyed. His annoy ached.

    Of course it could have been Titivillus who was annoying. He seemed distant that morning, to the point of being disdainful. He wouldn't explain why they were going to London together, he just told Geroud to trust him in that annoying way and that Geroud didn't need to know anything yet. That was especially annoying. Or maybe it was the weather that annoyed him. Low cloud hung over Kent, and by the time their railway train reached the outskirts of London, passing through the last of the true countryside around St Mary Cray, it was raining heavily. Then again, it could have been the woman sat in the seat opposite Geroud and Titivillus. She was really annoying.

    Somewhere outside Sittingbourne, Titivillus had stood up in the swaying carriage and announced he was going to find the buffet car. Geroud told him Kent trains did not have buffet cars, at which the woman opposite give him a strange look as though she was judging him. Titivillus ignored Geroud and walked down the train carriage in search of a coffee that Geroud knew he could simply magic up if he wanted to. Geroud gave a wan smile to the woman and shrugged his shoulders as if to say, *he won't listen*. She looked away and began rummaging in her handbag, as if trying to find an excuse not to engage. The woman's hand soon emerged holding a nail file, a sharp metal one. It felt like a subtle threat, but soon it was being used on her nails, creating a rasping noise that really annoyed Geroud. He winced as the visible flecks of nail flew into the air towards him. That wasn't just annoying, it was disgusting. He wondered how the woman would feel if he started picking his nose in front of her. He wanted to tell her to stop, that it was unfair and unhygienic, but he stayed silent, bottling up his resentment. Instead he just looked at her and saw her scowl. That annoyed him even more.

Despite all this, the woman looked vaguely familiar, although Geroud could not place where he had seen her. She must have been his age. Old enough to know how to behave in public. She stopped filing her nails, put the dagger-like file back in her bag and stood up. She looked around, ostentatiously casting her eyes above Geroud's head to avoid his gaze, before walking down the aisle, presumably to find an empty seat in the next carriage, away from the strange man staring at her.

Titivillus returned, followed by a man in a stiffly pressed white suit, holding a silver tray set with two cups of coffee in white china cups, and a plate with two French croissants. Titivillus sat down and the man in the white suit placed the tray on the table in front of him. 'Is there anything else I can do for you sir?' he asked.

'No, that will be all,' replied Titivillus. 'Except, what time will we be arriving into Victoria?'

'We are due in at eleven-fifty-two, sir. Although, I believe we might even be a few minutes early today. The track conditions being so good.' Geroud looked at the rain falling outside and wondered how that made the track conditions good. Titivillus thanked the exile from the Orient Express for his service, tipping him with what looked like a large silver coin.

The train arrived in Victoria at eleven-forty-four. Outside the ticket barrier Geroud saw the woman from the carriage. This time she was with a man, and both looked at him, mumbling conspiratorially. Geroud kept his head down as he passed, but thought he could hear the man saying, *do you think he suspects something?*

In front of the station Titivillus walked straight to the front of a long queue of people waiting for a taxi to arrive. As he did so, a black cab pulled up, the driver put out his arm to open the door and Titivillus climbed in, beckoning Geroud to do the same. No one in the queue seemed to notice or care that they were pushing in.

Near Old Compton Street the traffic ground to a halt, leading Titivillus to declare they would walk the rest of the way. Titivillus walked fast, almost as though he was keen to get out of the shower, except, even in the heavy rain, he did not seem to get wet. It wasn't that the rain didn't land on him, more that each drop colliding with his body seemed to regret its error in landing there and, after a very English apology, made its excuses to depart as quickly as it could. Not even the hair on Titivillus's head was willing to take on the falling water. Like Marcello Mastroianni fresh from make-up, Titivillus managed to look perfect.

On Geroud the rain settled like visiting relatives unable to take a hint to leave. It didn't just soak into his coat, it pried its way inside until all his clothes were wet, his skin was wet, everything was wet. Most of all, London was wet — people, places and things. Everything in fact, except Titivillus. Looking at Titivillus Geroud couldn't help noticing how different he seemed to the silly little devil who had crawled out of the Devil's Nook at Barfrestone church only a few weeks earlier. He wondered if he was the same man at all. Or should that be the same creature?

Despite the rain, Old Compton Street was busy. It would take a global pandemic to empty this small corner of London. Like the rain itself, other pedestrians seemed to swerve to avoid Titivillus, not out of fear, but a sense of how inappropriate it would be to collide with him. He seemed to exude an aura that told people to step aside. Geroud on the other hand found himself swerving one way to sidestep a passer-by, then another to dodge the splash from a puddle, as though his aura invited everyone or everything to walk right over him. And so they did.

    When Titivillus finally stopped it was sudden enough for Geroud to crash into his back. Titivillus seemed barely to notice the collision as Geroud ricocheted onto the wet pavement. Neither did Titivillus do anything to help Geroud to his feet, leaving it to a passing stranger to offer his hand. Instead, Titivillus seemed more intent to sniff the air with his dog-like nose, as though trailing a quarry.

§22 Driving your girlfriend home

'Do you think he suspects something?'

The woman didn't answer.

'He doesn't look like a private dick?'

'What do they look like?' asked the woman, looking at Geroud as he scurried past, across the station concourse.

'Not like him,' replied the man. 'He'd be shit scared of his own shadow.'

The woman laughed. 'True. But he does look familiar.'

'Yes,' agreed the man. 'But if Skinner has sent some mug to follow you, shouldn't he be following us? That creep's run off.'

'The mean bastard's probably got someone on the cheap.'

'Or it's a double bluff and we're being watched right now by someone else.' They cast their eyes around the station, wondering who could be the real spy on them. Dozens fitted the bill.

'Can we go?' said the woman. 'If he is having me followed, he'll know all he needs to by now.'

'In that case,' said the man, putting his arms around the woman and kissing her on the lips. 'In that case, it doesn't matter any more. Let's start making plans. I mean proper plans.'

The woman smiled. 'Yes,' she said. 'Let's start making plans.'

§23 Oscillate Wildely

Behind a large desk, piled high with stacks of tatty paper, on top of which a troop of overflowing ash trays balanced like trapeze artists swaying on a pole, sat a slender woman, a mug of coffee in one hand, a cocktail-length cigarette holder in the other, looking simultaneously unaffected and elegant.

At the end of the cigarette holder, a garishly pink and gold Sobranie cigarette smouldered lazily, as though something other than tobacco was burning in its lugubrious tip. The woman showed no sign of wanting to puff on the cigarette and it is possible she had long since followed government advice to quit smoking, but had neglected to quit lighting up. As her cigarette burned the woman would flick its ageing grey head, almost imperceptibly, with little more than a twitch of her forefinger, into one of the rocking ashtrays, never looking for her mark and never missing it. Professor Fortnum never missed her mark.

In the corners of the room more precarious towers echoed those on the desk, this time formed of books, the volumes placed on their sides, one on top of the other, some with spines and titles facing outwards, others not, and none in any apparent order. One pile had collapsed, but had fallen close to the wall, and posing no immediate hazard, had been left to rest in its preferred location, like a well-known drunk left supine in the street. Other books were open, face up or face down, often pressed against each other in what looked like a biblioplicit mating ritual, possibly in the hope of producing little novellas of their own.

The overall effect of this scene was contradictory, exuding simultaneously both seediness and sophistication, like coming across a collared vicar in the "five items or less" queue at ASDA.

Professor Rachel Fortnum had no need of the psychic abilities of Alison Dubois to know when a visit from Tittivillus was due. A unique — some might say special — feeling would gradually creep up on her as the hour approached, like a bout of colic. That feeling was rising now as she sat amongst the piles of books and papers, drinking strong black coffee and lighting unsmoked cigarettes. So it was no surprise that

Professor Fortnum also felt the urge to stand and look out of the grime covered window onto the dirty-wet London street below. Looking down onto the still cobbled surface of Chenies Mews, she could see Titivillus. He was dressed in a black-ribbed polo-neck sweater and dark crisply-pressed trousers, topped by a long and closely tailored olive green leather trench coat, unbuttoned but tied tightly around his thin waist with a broad belt matching the coat. With him was a sorry-looking figure she didn't know, following the doggy little devil's purposeful strides with short trotting footsteps, like a small child following an impatient parent to an unknown destination. It was a sight that made her smile. It reminded her of herself a few years earlier. Or was it longer? Time was so indeterminate when it came to Titivillus.

Although it might have been difficult to discern from the semi-squalor of her office, Titivillus had brought Professor Fortnum the power, fame and fortune she desired, allowing her to rise through the academic ranks, from one-star part-time tutor, to lecturer, to senior lecturer, to reader, to associate professor, until she had been given the rank of five-star professor, all at breakneck speed. And now she was a Dean. For the previous two years it was as though the start of each new term had brought to her door a new letter of appointment and not once had any of her colleagues queried her rise as being anything unusual, unexpected or exceptionally quick. At least no one who'd survived her appointment to Dean. She smiled again. And then again at the realisation that if Titivillus was visiting he must want something. And if he wanted something he would be willing to give something in return. Whatever it was she knew a letter inviting her to become the university's new Vice-Chancellor would soon be in the post. She licked her lips at the thought of an addendum to her original contract with that lovely little devil who was now crossing the cobbled street below, and was now standing outside her building, and was now opening the front door below, and was now asking the security guard for directions to her office, and was now climbing the narrow stairs, and was now walking the corridor of her floor, and was now knocking at the door her assistant's office. And now he was entering her chambers. Professor Fortnum smiled even more broadly at the thought of him in the adjacent room, waiting and wanting something from her. She placed the cigarette holder into her mouth and took in a deep draught of tobacco smoke. So, she had not given up smoking at all.

§24 Some girls are bigger than others

Titivillus stood in front of an empty desk, apparently vacated by Professor Fortnum's assistant, although there was every reason to suspect it had never been occupied. Perhaps the whole room had never really been occupied. Everything appearing incongruously new and unused, from the desk itself, to the typewriter and the intercom system, to the swivel chair and the somewhat spartan furniture that occupied the rest of the room. The filing cabinet in the corner even had its protective wrapping still attached. There were no personal touches either, like the photograph of a spouse or child or an anæmic pot plant.

      Behind Titivillus stood Geroud. He couldn't help staring at Titivillus in mild amusement at the way the little devil seemed to be sniffing the air and squinting his eyes, like a hunting dog when it first senses its prey. From the start Geroud had felt there there was a general doggyness about Titivillus. It was not a big friendly doggyness, or a sweet lapdog doggyness, it was a more elegant doggyness, like a cirneco or beauceron, or even the dog-headed Egyptian god Anubis — austere, angular and slightly unnerving. Geroud might have gone on with this line of thought had it not been for the only other presence in the room, a young woman who was sat bolt upright on an uncomfortable-looking black Viennese café chair by the door. She was so unobtrusive Geroud had missed her when they first arrived, and he might have assumed the same of Titivillus, except when the doggy little devil barked loudly, 'Is Professor Fortnum available?' At first Geroud was unsure whom Titivillus was addressing, even wondering for a moment if an invisible sprite was sitting behind the desk. It was only when Titivillus turned to face the seated young woman that it became obvious he was talking to her. 'Professor Fortnum,' he said again with pointed formality. 'Is she by any chance available to see us?' The woman frowned, all the while looking Titivillus directly in the eye. Breaking the stare, she turned her head slightly to address Geroud.

'I don't know. I'm waiting to see her myself. I don't work here.'

Titivillus ignored the woman's explanation. 'Would you mind letting Professor Fortnum know we are here? I'm sure she's expecting us.' The woman remained seated, barely concealing her contempt at the doggy little devil telling her what to do.

'As I said,' said the woman slowly, again addressing her reply to Geroud, and speaking as though trying to explain a simple concept to an idiot, 'I —do—not—work—here. I am waiting to see Professor Fortnum myself. I was told to wait here.'

'You might not work here yet, young lady,' said Titivillus returning the woman's condescension in spades. 'But I presume you are here in search of work. You are dressed very formally, and you do not seem to have the nervous energy of a prospective young scholar, so I presume your desired work must be administrative in nature. In other words I presume you have applied for the recently-advertised post as Professor Fortnum's secretary.'

'Personal Assistant,' said the woman.

'Personal Assistant,' repeated Titivillus, a slight smile playing on his lips. 'With that in mind, what better way to prove your worth to Professor Fortnum than stepping into the role of her — Personal Assistant — without being asked? Take over the role. Make yourself indispensable. As my father used to say, make a job for yourself.'

'You had a father?' mumbled Geroud, but Titivillus ignored him.

'It's called initiative,' continued Titivillus patronisingly. 'And a Personal Assistant needs always to show initiative. In other words, he needs to assist the person.'

'She,' said the woman. 'You said he. I'm not a he, I'm a she. I'm not a man.'

'Then stop acting like one. Show the initiative of your sex. As a woman the world is stacked against you. The whole patriarchal system is against you. Power is against you. You have to work twice as hard just to stand still. In the time it has taken for us to have this conversation, your brother, were he here,' — Titivillus paused a moment as if trying to catch the woman out by knowing all about her — 'your brother, were he here, would probably have risen to Senior

Vice-Presidential-Provost by now, not because he is any better than you — he may even be worse — but because the world is handed to him on a proverbial plate, without him having to lift a finger to deserve it. It's called privilege. Male privilege. It is all stacked in his favour for no other reason than he is was born a man. As a woman you have to show more — spunk.'

'Spunk?' queried the woman.

'Spunk,' repeated Titivillus. 'And so, will you let Professor Fortnum know we are here?'

Had the woman really been her brother, Geroud thought, she might have punched Titivillus in the face for making a speech like that. Instead, after a deep breath, the woman stood, walked to the door leading to Professor Fortnum's office and raised her hand to knock.

'Not like that!' called Titivillus. He pointed to the desk. 'Use the intercom. Like a professional. It's all about being professional.'

The woman glowered at Titivillus with absolute contempt, but seemed to accept his instruction. She stepped away from the door and moved behind the desk. Without stooping, and barely breaking her hard stare directly at Titivillus, she pressed a button on the grey and brown GEC746 intercom. As she did, through the door to the adjacent room a buzzer could be heard, and over the intercom came a woman's voice, rendered alien and metallic through the tiny speaker. 'Yes, what is it?' asked the voice.

'Professor Fortnum,' said the woman. 'There are two,' — she paused momentarily, looking first at Titivillus and then at Geroud — 'gentlemen to see you. They claim you are expecting them, but they are not in the diary.' There was no reply from Professor Fortnum, but everyone knew the message had been heard. In the silence the woman sat on the swivel chair and seemed to accept her new role as Personal Assistant to Professor Fortnum, even if no job offer or contract had ever existed. Geroud gazed at Titivillus with a look of amazement on his face. 'How did —' he started to say.

'What you have to understand, dear Lonely Heart, is that Professor Fortnum is a hard-headed creature, at least when it comes to negotiating contracts and sealing deals. I can vouch for that from experience. But she is also a lover of art — she is an artist herself one might say — her mind is on the higher things of life, and even beyond life, and so when it comes to dealing with appointing a new secretary —'

'Personal Assistant!' interrupted the newly installed Personal Assistant.

'My apologies. When it comes to appointing a new Personal Assistant she is far too busy to waste her time on actually organising such mundane matters. That is why Professor Fortnum is a woman after my own heart — were I in possession of such a thing. So the truth is, our young friend here already had the job as Professor Fortnum's Personal Assistant as soon as she walked through the door this morning. By just turning up she was in effect appointed. No doubt when she arrived Professor Fortnum told her to her to sit down, or something of that nature, but what she really meant to say was sit down and start work. Anyway, in six seconds time Professor Fortnum will walk through that door and it will be as if this young lady had been here forever.'

'But isn't that all a bit ridiculous?' said Geroud drolly. 'Almost as if someone's making it all up. How did she know about the diary?'

'Why don't you ask her?' suggested Titivillus, but the newly appointed Personal Assistant seemed far too busy to be interrupted, with piles of paper inexplicably appearing on the desk in front of her, through which she was now working in a methodical fashion. 'There is no God and no machine if that's what you mean,' continued Titivillus. 'No *deus ex machina*. That really would be ridiculous.'

'So it's just a coincidence this woman is here today? I only ask because, if this was a story, this would look rather like an attempt by the author to add some mildly amusing colour to it. And perhaps tell us a little more about Professor Fortnum.'

Titivillus laughed. 'You really have changed. But as someone very important once said, it is true there is a tendency for mediæval folk tales to develop clear objective narratives, and in doing so they inevitably become encumbered with odd inconsequential, but startlingly vivid and concrete, details.[25] But we are not in a mediæval folk tale are we, so that idea would be a somewhat ridiculous, like.'

'Still it is weird,' insisted Geroud.

'Ridiculous, as I said,' replied Titivillus. 'But it's ridiculous the way the sun seems to rise in the east and set in the west each day. If this were a novel, then at this moment in time this young woman might be a newly introduced character, maybe your love interest, or mine—'. The woman looked up, peering over her spectacles with an undisguised look of disgust on her face.

'Or she might just be a bit of inconsequential detail. We cannot be sure. It doesn't matter, what matters is — .'

Just as Titivillus was about to explain what mattered, the door to the inner chamber burst open, and Professor Fortnum stepped into the room. A newly lit bright purple Sobranie cigarette was perched on the end of her long cigarette holder, its gold filter glistening in the light. 'Did I hear someone talking about love?' she called out theatrically as she entered.

---

[25] Herbert Read, *English Prose Style* (London: Bell, 1928; 1980) 127

'Is it worth talking about anything else?' exclaimed Titivillus, equally theatrically. 'Professor Fortnum! As I live and breathe, can it really be you?' Titivillus swept himself forward and embraced Professor Fortnum warmly, planting a kiss in the air on either side of her face.

'Can it be me? Can it really be me?' repeated Professor Fortnum. 'These days I often doubt it really can be me. If it is really me, would I have to do so much work for myself? So often I am alone, I wonder if it really can be me, or at least the me you promised all those years ago. You see my secretary here? Ten years we've been together, and yet still she doesn't know where anything is. Almost like a newly-born kitten.'

'Actually —' the newly-born kitten began to say but Professor Fortnum leaned close to Titivillus and whispered loudly, 'You see, I have to do everything. Everything! All I get from this girl is backchat. Backchat! Yes! All! All! All I get is backchat. Why, I would even have to clean my own office if it wasn't for —' Professor

Fortnum paused, more for dramatic effect, Geroud thought, than necessity. 'My condition.'

'But this cannot be so,' said Titivillus. 'I know for a fact you have had a succession of little helpers. I make sure of that. This little girl behind the desk —'

'Yes!' interrupted Professor Fortnum. 'She is no more than a little girl. A baby, newly arrived and in need of mothering. But how shall I find time to mother and nurture her? I never can. Why do you send me children! I have to mother to them all, and yet I must also mother myself. You are so lucky to have this strong young man with you.' She moved towards Geroud as she spoke, placing her forefinger on his cheek and drawing it slowly down towards his chin. 'He has a strong jaw-line as only the young may have. Yet, I can see he has already known something of the world. And there is no doubt he will one day end up making love to my dear innocent little secretary.'

'I doubt that,' said the dear innocent little secretary in a deadpan voice.

'Yes!' continued Professor Fortnum, ignoring the denial. 'Yes, he will. It is inevitable. He is already thinking of how to seduce her. He is a man of the world, charming no doubt, but one who preys on the innocent. Yes, I can see he has known the bitter disappointment of life and it has warped his sense of right and wrong. Warped I say! Whereas this darling daughter of mine, she has known nothing of the world. She is easy meat for him. No doubt they have already been meeting — behind my back — in my office after dark — for weeks!'

'Actually,' said the darling, trying to interrupt, 'I have only just —'

'You are so right, my dear, so right,' interrupted Titivillus, taking Professor Fortnum by the arm. 'The young are such easy prey for each other. They think they know it all. They say *this is right* and *that is wrong*. Why do they never say, *I just don't know?* Whatever happened to deference? Deference to the old and the wise, and most of all deference to the artistic? They are so certain of everything. They do not understand our only aim in life is to protect them from themselves and each other.'

'Yes!' agreed Professor Fortnum. 'They think they are all philologists. Philologists, every one of them! And German philologists at that!'

'You are so right my dear,' agreed Titivillus. 'Everyone is so clever nowadays. Everyone is a German philologist.'

'You mean everyone thinks they are a German philologist,' Professor Fortnum corrected him. 'But in truth they mask such profound ignorance with such profound certainty.' She drawled the words profound with great profundity.

'And where will such certainty end?' asked Titivillus.

'Why! In disappointment of course. If one is so certain one is right, what else will happen when we finally see we are wrong?'

'Despite that, you must look after your sweet innocent little child,' said Titivillus. 'You see my young friend here is passionately in love with her. They were childhood sweethearts, ever since they held hands on a dark night on a barren sea wall at Graveney and looked out over the black abyss. It was then they realised we must love today because tomorrow we are nothing.'

'That's not —' Geroud started to say.

'Ah the young,' continued Professor Fortnum. 'I do not deny they must have their romance. Not unlike you and I at one time, my little Titi.' The personal assistant sniggered, but Geroud just stared at the couple in front of him and thought there was something beautiful in the scene. It was false, theatrical and in many ways ridiculous, but like an operatic love scene, it was strangely beautiful. For his part, Titivillus just gazed into Professor Fortnum's eyes, as if she really was an old flame. And perhaps she was. 'Do you remember that time?' asked Professor Fortnum.

'It is still that time,' replied Titivillus. 'It will always be that time!' Sweeping Professor Fortnum, almost improbably, up in his arms, Titivillus carried her into her inner chamber and closed the door with his foot behind them, leaving Geroud and the newly installed personal assistant alone in the outer office.

§25 I just want to see the boy happy

It was after five when Titivillus finished his meeting with Professor Fortnum. The Personal Assistant had cleared the desk of the work she had found to do and shown so little interest in Geroud, who stayed sat in front of her throughout, that she spoke to him only once more that day, and even then only as she was about to leave. Gathering her coat and handbag she told Geroud to remind Professor Fortnum that there was an Academic Promotion Committee meeting in the morning and the list she had asked for was typed up in a folder on the professor's desk. Only later did Geroud wonder how an instruction to type up anything had reached the Personal Assistant and how the said typing had been placed on the Professor's desk without the Personal Assistant speaking to anyone while he was there or ever leaving her own chair.

At some time after five the door to the inner office opened and Titivillus emerged, looking as fresh as he had at the start the day. 'Right,' he said as he stood in front of Geroud. He was smirking. 'Right,' he repeated. 'Let's go.' Titivillus walked to the door. He held it open and, with a theatrical sweep of the arm, encouraged Geroud to take the lead in leaving the building. Geroud obliged and took the stairs to the ground floor, Titivillus following closely behind. When they reached the street Geroud stopped and turned to Titivillus. The smirk on the doggy little devil's face was bigger than ever to the point where he could no longer stop it turning into hysterical laughter.

'You're not going to believe it,' Titivillus tried to say repeatedly, each time laughter interrupting his speech. 'Not— no—'.

'What?' asked Geroud. 'Tell me what?'

'Aah, wowsers! What a woman! She'd do anything for me you know. And I'd do anything for her. Almost anything anyway. Some of her suggestions go past even my limits. You know, if I didn't care so much for you, dear Lonely Heart, I think I might spend the rest of my days with her. But fear not, I thought about you all of the time. And I have come up Top-Donald-

Trumps on this one. You! Who'd have thought it? You're not going to believe it.'

'Believe what?' asked Geroud.

'You! Who'd have thought you'd rise so far so fast? Apparently there is some kind of committee meeting tomorrow to decide on promotions in the university.'

'Yes, the Academic Promotion Committee.'

'You know about it already!' exclaimed Titivillus. 'You really are a genius.'

'Not quite,' explained Geroud. 'That PA asked me to remind the professor about it, but I forgot.'

'Never mind, never mind,' said Titivillus. 'She knows all about it. The girl left a folder on the professor's desk, like. But the point is she's the key figure. The professor I mean. Everyone else on the committee, they're all *yes men.* I know that as a fact as I put them there. But what's important is who's top of the list for promotion. You know. In the folder, like.' Titivillus nudged Geroud with his elbow. 'You know?'

'I have no idea,' said Geroud.

'Y. O. U.' said Titivillus, this time poking Geroud's chest with his forefinger as he spoke. 'You.'

'Me?' asked Geroud.

'You!' said Titivillus triumphantly. 'You're going to be a professor. The meeting's at 11am, it ends at 1pm and so, by my reckoning, by 2pm you will have your *litteras confirmationis*. You do know what I mean? By two-o'clock tomorrow afternoon you will be able to call yourself Professor Geroud. Are you pleased?'

'That's stupid,' replied Geroud sounding more peeved than pleased. 'It doesn't make any sense. I'm a florist. No, I'm not even a florist. I sell flowers by the side of the road. I don't know anything.'

'Pah!' scoffed Titivillus. 'You don't need to know anything to be a professor.'

'I haven't even been to university.'

'Pah! Pah!' scoffed Titivillus again. 'That has nothing to do with it. Professorships are not like getting a school leaving certificate. You don't sit an exam to get them. It's all based on who you know and who you suck up to. If you want to become a professor get on your knees, put your tongue out far as you can, and stick it up the arse of the nearest passing provost or vice-chancellor. Except in this case I did that job for you.'

Geroud felt slightly sick at the image. 'I don't even work at a university,' he said.

'Didn't. Past tense, dear Lonely Heart. You didn't work at a university, but you do now. Apparently they have a little art school somewhere. I think she said Kensington, I can't remember the details. Anyway, they'll let you know all that. Apparently they need a professor there'.

'But what am I going to be a professor of?' asked Geroud. 'I don't know anything.'

'You're not listening, dear Lonely Heart. I told you, you don't need to know anything. Especially as you're going to be the university's new Professor of Art, like.'

'Art!' exclaimed Geroud. 'I don't know anything about art.'

'What's there to know my dear chap? It's hardly epidemiology. Just go to a few art exhibitions and quote Walter Benjamin at people. Learn to say things like: "This painting is the embodiment of Walter Benjamin's wreckage strewn at the feet of the Angel of History." Even better, look slightly distracted and then say, "I always find her work brings to mind Benjamin's Angel of History." It's easy! Just remember to always call him Valter Ben-yamin. That always sounds clever. You try.'

'Falter Ben-varmin,' said Geroud.

'Near enough,' said Titivillus. 'And who knows, all that flower arranging might even come in handy. You can get the students to paint some flowers or something. Call it neo-nature-morté. Very avant-garde.'

'And when they ask me about — I don't know — Picasso or something, what am I meant to say?' asked Geroud.

'I knew it, you're a natural!' exclaimed Titivillus. 'You already know about Picasso. Thank God I didn't insist on you becoming Professor of Epidemiology. That was my first choice.'

'I'll be a fraud. Of course, I've heard of Picasso but I don't know anything about him.'

'That's wonderful, Lonely Heart,' replied Titivillus excitedly. 'You're sounding more professorial every time you speak. Only say, "The more I look at

Picasso the more I realise I know nothing about Picasso!" You just need to learn to call your own ignorance ambiguity. The ambiguity of art, like. It's all very Empson. And don't worry about giving lectures —'

'Lectures!' exclaimed Geroud.

'Of course,' said Titivillus. 'You're going to be a university professor. You have to give lecturers. Not many. Being a professor I mean. But one or two.'

'On art?'

'On art history to be more exact.'

'So on a subject I know nothing about?'

'You obviously do know about it. You've just told me that one of the most interesting ways of looking at Picasso is from a perspective of knowing nothing about Picasso.'

'I didn't say that,' said Geroud. 'I said I don't know what it means.'

'Exactly, that is what that means. You don't know what it means and neither will anyone else. The most authoritative voice in art is very clearly the voice that says it knows nothing. Just try to sound more confident in asserting your ignorance. It will make you sound very clever.'

'And what happens when a student asks me a question?' asked Geroud. 'Do I just say I know nothing?'

'Oh, goodness me,' replied Titivillus sounding almost disgusted. 'You can be so naïve, dear Lonely Heart. What sort of professor would allow a student ask them a question? What you need to understand is that professors only talk to other professors. It's the first law of academia. When it comes to students your only role is to ask the questions. You ask them the questions and let them give you the answers.'

'This is ridiculous!'

'Not at all. Okay, if a student is foolish enough to ask something like *What did Picasso mean when he said, "The hidden harmony is better than the obvious,"* just give them the professorial answer.'

'Which is?'

'You just say, *That is certainly something you should be asking yourself young man.* Or young woman as the case may be. Then simply walk away.

Keep that one in permanent reserve. All professors use it.'

Geroud started hitting his hand against his forehead in despair. Even Titivillus was astute enough to realise the good news was not going down as well as he had hoped. He tried to sound reassuring. 'Like I say, don't worry. I'll be around. I'll write your lectures. I'll ask Gombrich or Hauser to help. You've a good memory. Or, if you like I can send you some help. A little sprite to take your place, like.'

'Ridiculous! Ridiculous! Ridiculous!' exclaimed Geroud. 'How is any of this supposed to make up for you abandoning me for twenty years? Or maybe this is some kind of hellish joke where you make things even worse.'

'I wouldn't do that to you, Lonely Heart,' replied Titivillus sounding genuinely hurt. 'Really, I wouldn't do that to you. I want to make everything up to you by making you famous.'

'I'll be famous for being an idiot!' exclaimed Geroud.

'Never! You're going to change the course of art history. I am going to see that. With your inaugural lecture.'

'My what?' asked Geroud.

'Your inaugural lecture,' continued Titivillus. 'It's nothing to worry about. It's like an announcement. A public statement on what you stand for, like. All professors do them. It's the second law of academia. Having reached such dizzying academic heights, professors show their humility by giving an inaugural lecture to a packed lecture hall full of other professors.'

Titivillus ignored the look of horror on Geroud's face. 'You're going to come up with a rather natty little theory based on your extensive research into the stone carvings at that church in Barfrestone.'

'You mean the quick look I had at them?' asked Geroud sarcastically.

'Do you know, that's exactly what I love about you,' said Titivillus. 'You come at things from a unique angle. A quick look and you have a whole new theory of art. Who else would be capable of that? It's what I call real-life experience, like. You can't train someone to do that. You're either born with it or you are not. It's very clear to me this really is your vocation in life, dear Lonely Heart. You're not going to be one of those ordinary professors who knows things.'

'No, I don't know anything.'

'Exactly, you have real-life experience. You're so — *what's the word* — authentic. It's almost as if you are real. And I found you. Like Cimabue finding Giotto in the sheepfold. When you go into the senior common room at the university, you'll be able to boast about it. You can enjoy a bit of inverted snobbery, like. In fact, that should be your line. If some knob of a professor tries to pull rank just say something off-hand about the facile thoughts of the privileged classes. That always shuts them up. Nothing terrifies academics more than coming face to face with real-life. Especially in the arts. It calls their bluff. They all think they're the real thing, but you really are the real thing. Fuck me, it's going to be so brutal.'

'For who?' grumbled Geroud. 'You keep forgetting — I DON'T KNOW ANYTHING!'

'And I keep telling you you don't need to know anything. You just have to understand, my dear, dear Lonely Heart. Being an academic is all an act. It's about overcoming your own doubts. Your own lack of self worth. Academics even have a name for it. They call it *imposter syndrome*. It's very on trend to have imposter syndrome. There's hardly an academic in the land who won't tell you they have imposter syndrome these days. It means you have to overcome the feeling that you are an imposter, whilst always droning on about feeling like an imposter. You'll be one of the greats.'

'But *I am* an imposter!'

'That's the ticket, although perhaps say you are racked with the fear of being an imposter because of your humble background and your lack of opportunities. And yet you fought against all the disadvantages of your life and now you have reached this exalted position. The problem is, while you can rationalise the fact you have made it, you can still never quite shake off the deeply ingrained feeling that have no real right to be here. Trust me, they'll love that line. *He's so original,* they'll say. *So great, but so, so humble.*'

§26 Frankly, Mr Shankly

Some six months and three days after the meeting at Rachel Fortnum's office, the newly ennobled Professor Geroud stood alone outside the art school. He let out a soft sigh most people would not have noticed, not deep enough to suggest a profound discontent with anything that had happened or was about to happen, more a resigned sigh at promises not kept and promises unkeepable. It was the sigh of unfulfilment.

Geroud had never fully signed up to Titivillus's attempt to make amends with a final moment of glory before his body would be discarded and his soul dragged to unknown torments in hell. It felt like being given a complimentary voucher to eat at a restaurant that had just given you food poisoning. Titivillus seemed to think that, as Geroud faced in the agony of the abyss awaiting him, he would somehow be comforted by the knowledge that in the land of the living some lauded academic with a bevy of students would sing his praises as the defining name in the science of art history. Even if that outcome was in any way likely or possible, he still felt it was a paltry recompense. And besides, for the past six months Geroud had hardly enjoyed been Professor Geroud. It was true, having money was nice, and the work he was expected to do was not that much of a burden, even if his colleagues complained about it at every turn. At worst it was a bit mundane, but better than sitting in a lay-by selling chrysanthemums. Apart from allowing the creature sent to by Titivillus to use his body to deliver a carefully crafted lecture on art every so often, written by some of the greatest art historians of all time — *all now resident in hell* — Titivillus's prediction that professors rarely taught had proven correct. Teaching was the work of doctors, senior lecturers, associate lecturers and sessional tutors in descending order of pay and status, and ascending order of workload.

Of course, Geroud was required to attend a weekly faculty meeting, but these proved even less of a problem. He soon discovered it was best to say nothing, or when forced to speak to agree in principle with the head of the school, while recognising the merits of a colleague's arguments, a tactic that won him friends in high places. If he was forced to air his own opinion, Geroud would follow Titivillus's advice and say he wanted to see how things panned out, understand the lay of the land, grasp the environment before committing himself to anything too definite. Very quickly this led to Geroud being seen as possessing a kind of Solomonic wisdom. The phrase *fools rush in* was soon associated with his name, followed by the rider *but Professor Geroud waits to see what's best.* The only problem with this approach, if it was a problem, was that it left Geroud feeling isolated amongst the staff. He cut a lonely figure, seated alone each lunchtime, eating a sandwich bought from the cafeteria in the art school's pretty little courtyard garden, beside a happy fig tree. Almost everyone would say hello as they passed by, but few would stop to chat. He was liked insofar as he was not disliked, but he was also unaligned to any faction which made him an unlikely soul with whom to share lunchtime gossip. 'If I fell in the Thames and drowned today,' Geroud sometimes thought, 'they would all come to my funeral tomorrow, and all forget about me by the middle of next week. So much for being famous!'

Perhaps Professor Geroud was expecting too much. Many professors live out lives very like this one, eminent without being extraordinary, and for many people his current life would have seemed an achievement in itself. It was an extraordinary step-up from being an unremarked flower-seller in a lay-by on the A2 to being an unremarked professor in a university art department. Back then no one would have even have come to his funeral. Perhaps no one would even have marked his passing with any of the cheap flowers he sold. Now, at least, they would say, 'He was not your typical professor-type you know. No airs and graces. Damn it! He was just a thoroughly decent chap.' And then they would pause. And then they would reflect. And then they would forget. A step up, no doubt, but hardly a figure to live on in memory until the end of time. Goodbye Mr Chips.

The sighs over, Geroud entered the art school and made his way to his office on the third floor of the Georgian brick terrace building. As always, on his desk was the latest script sent by Titivillus. As he sat down Geroud wondered if Titivillus himself might turn up today. He wondered the same thing every day as he had barely seen Titivillus since he started the new job. He sighed again. Success really wasn't all it was cracked up to be.

Picking up the script, Geroud saw his name printed in the top left-left hand corner, written in the same size of type as the rest of the paper, designed to look like a working document: businesslike, matter-of-fact, and not something intended to blazon the ego or the prestige of its alleged author. 'No airs and graces. Damn it! A thoroughly decent chap.' He put the script down again and looked around the office. He recognised it was slowly starting to resemble the old office of Professor Fortnum. Not that she inhabited that any more. Six months earlier, she had inexplicably risen to become the university's new Vice-Chancellor, following the unexpected death of the previous incumbent in a freak accident involving a long-dormant volcano on the island of Milos. Bizarrely the former VC had been its only victim, at which point the volcano had miraculously plugged itself up, and returned to sleep.

Piles of books, seemingly half-read, some open, some closed, some pressed against each other and some tottering in piles, were beginning to grow, as though academia was subject to some immutable process of ossification, the piles of books, read and unread student papers and stacks of dull-looking journals forming like stalagmites in an academic grotto in every academic's office.

Geroud wished Titivillus would visit today.

§28 Seasick yet still docked

In my experience, outsiders always write the best essays. It cannot be because they suffer from a lack of confidence — there seems no logical reason why that should make you a good writer. But it is their lack of arrogance. Those who are comfortable in the world of academia have an arrogance that comes from believing success is rooted in mastering the education system, accepting its tedious mysteries and applying them with soulless rigidity. The outsider lacks both confidence and arrogance, and so the rigidity of the academic mind is also lacking in them. If you get them to overcome their lack of confidence, persuade them that it is all a trick — *a confidence trick no less* — and that they have as much right to write on Picasso or the Mona Lisa as any dull art history student at Cambridge or St Andrews, they will often produce something profoundly original and interesting. I have no pride in myself, but I do have a deep sense of pride in the students I have taught who have felt able to follow my advice on this. Some of them have written astonishing essays that even resemble works of art, although, when I think of it, in over thirty years of teaching art history, I don't think I have ever had a student write on Picasso or the Mona Lisa. Does anyone write on those things any more I wonder.

But I digress. I like to think Geroud would have reached a similar conclusions to mine had he taught long enough at the university art school. Had he done so he might have been apt to follow Herbert Read, writing in *The Criterion* in 1925, at the moment when his own personal struggle between conformity and rebellion was starting to take hold, in quoting Andre Gide:

> It is important to remember that the struggle between classicism and romanticism also exists inside each mind. And it is from this very struggle that the work is born; the classic work of art relates the triumph of order and measure over an inner romanticism. And the wilder the riot to be tamed the more beautiful your work will

be. If the thing is orderly in its inception, the work will be cold and without interest.[26]

But of course Geroud was really a flower-seller, so he never needed to read Gide, or Read for that matter. Apart from what little he picked up listening to the beautiful creature inside him deliver the scripts sent by Titivillus, he remained unsullied by the arid order of the classical mind.

* * *

Geroud looked out of his office window. There was little movement in the garden outside, although someone seemed to be chiselling stone closer than usual to the wall beneath his window, possibly right under the window. In the carving studio itself there seemed to be a meeting taking place. He assumed it was a Staff-Student Liaison Committee meeting and wondered why

---

[26] Herbert Read, 'Reason and Romanticism' in Herbert Read, *Essays in Literary Criticism* (London: Faber, 1926) 92

he hadn't been invited. Too easily forgotten, he thought. Why else would Titivillus abandon him yet again?

'Cup of tea,' said Geroud out loud suddenly, as though another part of his brain was trying to stop its own depressive thoughts. A cup of tea would do that. A cup of tea would be a positive thing, comforting for mind, body and soul. There might even be someone to talk to in the little cafe downstairs, even if only to say *hello,* or, *I'm sorry are you in the queue?* Or, *I thought you were dead*.

Geroud left the office and descended the creaking narrow staircase to emerge into the sunlit garden. Whoever had been carving under his window was gone, but had left, chiselled in large letters on the wall the words: מְנֵא מְנֵא תְּקֵל וּפַרְסִין . I'm surprised they were allowed to do that, he thought.

In the cafe no one else was waiting, but Geroud was still able to exchange a few pleasantries with the tattooed young man serving behind the counter. He ordered a tea, stirred the tea-bag in the paper cup, added milk and removed the tea-bag, in that order, as always and as always without any sense that anything unusual was happening around him. Except when he came to pay. 'We no longer accept money here,' said Kelly, the young man serving.

'How do I pay?' asked Geroud

'By service to the community,' said Kelly. 'I serve you, you serve the community. If you serve the community then you pay me.'

Geroud laughed nervously, unsure if Kelly was joking. As he turned to walk away he expected to be called back with *Not really, of course you have to pay.* But no call came.

In the garden, another new sign had appeared under the newly carved Hebrew. This one was more improvised, handwritten on a wooden board and attached to the wall.

Interim Guild for the Implementation of Visual Acuity (Readian Affiliation)

Underneath this was added, the word *Welcome,* in what looked like an after-thought.

'Are you coming?' asked a voice. Geroud turned around quickly, spilling his tea. It was Titivillus.

'Titivillus,' exclaimed Geroud, trying to wipe his scalded hand. 'What are you doing here? And where have you been?'

'What are you talking about, Lonely Heart,' replied Titivillus nonchalantly. 'I told you last week about today.'

'I haven't seen you in months,' said Geroud, trying to sound stern.

'I find that hard to believe,' replied Titivillus. 'I am sure — *certain in fact* — that only last week we sat in this very garden and I handed you today's lecture.'

'What lecture? I don't know what you're talking about.'

'Tut, tut!' said Titivillus calmly, as if trying to chastise a child without riling it to anger. 'Porky pies, my dear Lonely Heart. Porky pies. Is all this because you haven't done your homework?'

'No, it's because I don't know what you're talking about,' insisted Geroud. 'I'm telling you we haven't seen each other in months.'

Titivillus sat on a low wall by a large acanthus plant so he resembled some diabolical doggy figure peering out from a mediæval church capital. He looked up at Geroud, cocked his head slightly to one side, as if trying to gauge Geroud's honesty and reached into his top jacket pocket. Geroud expected the cigarette case normally housed there to appear, but instead Titivillus pulled out a paperback book. To judge by the grim grey cover it must have been a dull read, but Titivillus began flicking through it as though consulting the Bible. 'Ah,' he said softly pointing to a particular page in the book. 'That explains it. It's the cheap binding. Glue you see. It should have been sewn. Otherwise pages, and even whole chapters, fall out and disappear, like. That's what's happened. Chapter 27 is missing. Or maybe it was never printed at all. You know bad editing. This writer is always being accused of bad editing. Or could it be that the author is a crook and never got round to writing it. I guess we'll never know. But, it does explain why you don't remember our meeting. In chapter 27 I told you about this very important lecture you are going to give to the newly formed *Interim Guild for the Implementation of Visual Acuity (Readian Affiliation).*'

'You mean that?' said Geroud pointing to the sign behind him. 'What is it?'

'The new name for the art school. Catchy isn't it. While you were doing whatever it is you do in your office all day, the students down here staged a revolution and broke away from the university. Now the art school is an independent anarchist commune. Readian affiliation. *Your benign influence methinks!* And now those same students want you to give them a lecture to help consolidate their new found freedom. It's all to help pave the way for your inaugural professorial lecture next week in Barfrestone.'

'Next week?' asked Geroud

'Oh dear, that's in chapter 27 as well. Anyway, we — *or rather you* — have organised a carving festival in Barfrestone, where the students will demonstrate some of their lovely carving skills and learn about the equally lovely church down there. That's where you'll give your inaugural lecture as a professor. Except it's two lectures. Over two days. Clementina got a bit carried away and wrote rather more than she was asked to, then Hauser wanted a go, and then Gombrich said he wanted to add his bit, and in the end you had a dozen or more of them all chipping in. Like watching carp feed in a pond. So, you will be giving these two lectures at Barfrestone next week, like. It's very smart of you really.'

'Is it? Why?'

'It's in the middle of nowhere so hopefully none of your university colleagues will be bothered to turn up, which means you won't have to face scrutiny from all those other professors. I expect your audience will be the local vicar and all these students you claim to have been teaching for months. Lots of friendly familiar faces. Nothing too demanding, like. Certainly nothing to worry about.'

Somewhere out of sight, deep inside the carving studios there was a murmur from the students and a raised voice asked for a show of hands. Apart from that, and the new signage on the wall, there was nothing to suggest a revolution had happened. No one appeared to have lost their head or been strung up from a lamp-post, at least not for the moment. It must have been a very polite revolution, Geroud thought.

'Chop-chop,' said Titivillus, interrupting Geroud's thoughts. 'There are some eager students in there desperate to hear what you have to say. But it's such a lovely day, let's do the lecture out here. I'll round them up, you go get that script on your desk and then we'll do the you-know-what.'

§29 Mute witness

'A few years ago I wrote a rather intemperate review of John Carey's book *What Good Are the Arts?* I did so with good reason, it is a profoundly ignorant book. So, while I have modified my views on many of the artists and art critics I have reviewed in the past, to the point where I frequently find myself blushing with a deep sense of shame at what I once said, in the case of Carey I stand by every word. His was a book that should not have been written, let alone published.[27]

'Despite this I will say that in one small respect Carey was almost right. While Carey stupidly argued that those who enjoy art are socially-divisive individuals who value human life less than the existence of artworks, he was almost right in seeing art as a kind of death cult. He was just too blinded by his dislike of art to understand what that idea really meant.

'To call art a death cult does not mean art-lovers are homicidal psychopaths, rather it is to

---

[27] Michael Paraskos, Review of John Carey's *What Good Are the Arts?* in *The Art Book,* vol.13, no.1, 2003, 47-8

recognise that art transports its makers and its viewers into a realm of existence that has affinities with death, something recognised by ancient shamanistic cultures in their use of ritualistic carved objects, and by the Greeks and Romans in their conceptualisation of the living nature of sculpture, and by the mediæval Byzantine painters in their understanding of the nature of painting as a window onto another world. As the followers of the musician Orpheus knew when they practised what we know as the Orphic Mysteries, one of the functions of art was to help facilitate transaction between the living and the dead.[28]

'Put this way, rather than seeing art as a death cult for the living, perhaps we should see art as a life cult for the dead, or as a space in which the dead, and perhaps even the inanimate, can have a life-like voice. This seems to me to be an important point in any attempt to understand art, which I would like to explore in my talk to you today. Art as somehow on the

---

[28] See Yulia Ustinova 'To Live in Joy and Die with Hope: Experiential Aspects of Ancient Greek Mystery Rites' in *The Bulletin of the Institute of Classical Studies*, vol. 56, no. 2, 2013, 105f

boundary of life and death, at times like the living, and at times like the dead.

'As I have already indicated, in the ancient worlds, a belief that art animated, or gave life to, the seemingly inanimate was relatively commonplace, but this survived into the modern period. It was certainly there in Shakespeare, who played with the idea in *A Winter's Tale,* with the ambiguous position of Hermione existing as a living sculpture. In the later seventeenth century a similar idea was present in Molière's Dom Juan, and a century later in Mozart's opera Don Giovanni. In the early nineteenth century Alexander Pushkin explored the idea in his poem 'The Bronze Horseman: A Petersburg Tale' and at the end of that century it informed Oscar Wilde's *The Happy Prince.* In the twentieth century it could be found in novels like Gustav Meyrink's *Der Golem,* published in 1914, and in the cinema it was seen John Baines's classic horror film *Dead of Night,* made in 1945. I could go on giving examples, but I will restrict myself to just two more, both from that great film franchise, *Ghostbusters,* in which the giant 'Stay Puft' marshmallow man, and the Statue of Liberty, come to life.

'Needless to say, there is a long artistic tradition of animating the inanimate. And for the academic art historian, there is a bountiful seam to mine of examples of this genre, all of which can be fitted into a mainstream academic book or paper. But to do that is to miss an essential quality of that tradition. For many of those who engaged originally with the idea that art can animate the inanimate, there was a reality to the phenomenon that is not adequately captured by academic convention. To capture it one must enter a different mode of thought, one closer to the creative act itself, rather than offering a commentary on it, and perhaps accept that a different kind of cultural theory is necessary to understand the reality of animating the inanimate. For me the model for this different kind of cultural theory is Herbert Read's 1934 novel *The Green Child,* and it is that which I would like to explore with you today.

'Just before he wrote *The Green Child* Read had a direct encounter with the idea of animating the inanimate when he wrote an article in praise of Jean Cocteau's surrealist-inspired film *The Poet's Blood*, made in 1930.[29] In that film, we again see animate sculptures. But what Read made clear in his article was that the justification for such a flight of fancy was that the filmic space was not the same as real space. Like all artistic, or poetic, spaces it was, he said, *emancipated from space and time*. This is significant. Read forces us to rethink the question as to how inanimate objects can speak by turning it into a new question: where can inanimate objects speak? In effect, it becomes a spatial question, which provokes the equally spatial answer: inanimate objects speak in a world of art that is emancipated from space and time.

'The problem with this question, and its answer, is that mainstream critical theory does not allow for time and space to be emancipated in this way. Even non-mainstream critical, cultural and political frameworks, such as anarchism, can have problems with it. But I have argued elsewhere that this is not an inevitable

---

[29] Reproduced in Herbert Read, *A Coat of Many Colours* (London, Faber, 1947) 229

position for anarchist cultural studies to take.[30] The implied radicalism of anarchist theory allows it to diverge from mainstream cultural theory by accepting a place for the human imagination that is a transcendent space. I hasten to add that not all anarchist theorists will accept this, but there is no denying it has historically been a feature of aspects of anarchist cultural theory. Indeed, it is, arguably, one of the ways in which radical anarchist cultural theory differs from Marxist cultural theory. Unlike Marxism, anarchism can choose to reject the idea that we are inescapably trapped within pre-existing social, economic and cultural structures, condemned merely to rearrange the deckchairs to make their use more equitable, like victims of a Schopenhauerian nightmare. Instead we can imagine ourselves into another reality.

'In historical anarchist thought this idea has been articulated in terms of envisioning in art the future paradise to which an anarchist revolution would inevitably lead. This is seen in the works of the late

---

[30] See Michael Paraskos, 'Anarsist Bir Rembrandt Nasil Olurdu?', *Sanat Dünyamiz*, vol. 131, Kasım-Aralık 2012

impressionist artists, Henri-Edmond Cross and Paul Signac. In correspondence with Signac, Cross wrote:

> Until now, pictures dealing with the theme of anarchy always depicted revolt, either directly or indirectly, through scenes of poignant misery. But let us imagine instead the dreamed-of age of happiness and well-being and let us show the actions of men, their play and their work in this era of general harmony.[31]

'Both artists' brightly coloured paintings of the Côte d'Azur, such as Cross's *By the Mediterranean* and Signac's *Au temps de l'harmonie* should be seen in the light of this correspondence. Although it is not impossible to imagine these paintings as reflections of leisure time in the existing reality of our world, the extraordinary vibrancy of their colours hints at something very different, something otherworldly. In effect, they are images of an alternative reality

---

[31] Undated letter, quoted in A. Dymond, 'A Politicised Pastoral', in V. Jirat-Wasiutynski (ed.), *Modern Art and the Idea of the Mediterranean* (Toronto, University of Toronto Press, 2007) 125

constructed through the artifice of art. Consequently, Cross and Signac are much closer in their paintings to the writings of Charles Fourier, with his vision of a world of vegetarian animals, and seas that taste of lemonade, and closer too to earlier Christian eschatology, in all of which existing reality literally disappears, and a new reality comes into being. Indeed, it is no accident that Cross and Signac's anarchist utopias are so reminiscent of earlier visions of the Garden of Eden.

'The idea of the artist as a kind of magician, conjuring up images of a utopian post-revolutionary space, comes to life in Signac's extraordinary 1890 portrait of the anarchist journalist and art critic, Félix Fénéon. Fénéon is set in the midst of a swirling mass of abstract colour, and appears to be pulling a flower from his top hat, as readily as Louis Comte would pull a rabbit from his. The phrase that comes to mind when thinking of this painting as anarchist art is that it represents a form of transcendental anarchism, a phenomenon sadly sometimes derided by anarchist activists, but frequently adopted by anarchist artists. This becomes even clearer in relation to Fénéon's own writings on Signac, particularly his 1890 biography. There Fénéon presented the material basis of Signac's neo-impressionist technique as a means to transcend existing material reality and achieve a 'new way of seeing'. Signac sacrificed 'the fleeting to the permanent, and in its celebrations and its magic, confers on Nature, which at last grew weary of its precarious reality, an authentic Reality.'[32]

'That Read also fell into the camp of transcendental anarchists is apparent in the introduction to his 1954 book *Anarchy and Order.* Read wrote: 'Society exists to transcend itself, and the progressive force of its evolution is the poetic imagination'. He suggested that transcendence leads not simply to a dream that the banks and factories might have nicer managers, or other mundane visions of utopia, but to what Read described as 'new fields of consciousness'.[33] Significantly, Read himself connected all this to *The Green Child,* published some

---

[32] Quoted in R. Roslak, *Neo-Impressionism and Anarchism in Fin-de-Siècle France: Painting, Politics and Landscape* (London, Routledge, 2007) 2

[33] Herbert Read, *Anarchy and Order,* (London: Faber, 1954; 1971) 23

twenty years earlier in 1935. In the same paragraph he stated that this was what he was trying to show 'symbolically' in *The Green Child*.

'The Green Child is organised into three sections, each set in a distinct location: rural Yorkshire; then, a fictional south American country called Roncador; and finally, a subterranean utopia. The lead character in the novel, Oliver, who visits each of these locations, is a fictionalised version of Read himself. In the first location, rural Yorkshire, we see evidence of progressive nineteenth-century liberal capitalism in action, with Oliver employed as a local schoolteacher. The fallacy of this model of progress soon leads him to abandon Yorkshire, and he finds himself in a fictional south American country. Almost accidentally, Oliver becomes the country's leader, and he soon adopts the role of a benign Tzar. But Oliver becomes disillusioned with the society he has created, and leaves again. This time he ends up in a subterranean world populated by green-skinned people. In this world there are no leaders, free love is practised, and intellectual desires

are satisfied through debates on the nature of the universe.

'It is not difficult to map this tripartite schema onto Read's rejection of the ideal society as simply the equitable distribution of wealth. Rather there is a psychological, and some might say spiritual, need to experience new fields of consciousness. However, to understand the origin of *The Green Child* it is helpful to go back into the 1920s.

'Newly demobbed from the army, and having only recently served in some of the most horrific battles of the First World War, Read was at this time something of a lost soul, in search of a purpose in life. Working as a civil servant, there was no obvious outlet for Read's creative ambitions as a writer. As he later wrote:

> My mind was full of projects – projects for novels, plays and long poems which needed seclusion and ample leisure for their execution. As month after month went by with nothing

accomplished, I worked myself into a desperate state of dissatisfaction and revolt.[34]

A kind of salvation for Read came in the form of T.S. Eliot. During the war Read had encouraged Frank Rutter, the editor of the journal *Art and Letters,* to publish some of Eliot's early poetry, and this act of faith was reciprocated after the war when with Eliot invited Read to join the editorial board of his new journal *The Criterion.* But Eliot's classicist conception of modernism was a difficult fit with Read's already well-developed sense of modernism as a romantic movement. As Andrew Causey stated, Eliot's preference was for:

> a stern culture, anti-popular and concerned – outwardly at least – more with standards than experiment. With watchwords like order, authority, tradition and the impersonal, it saw

---

[34] Herbert Read, *Annals of Innocence and Experience* (London: Faber, 1940) 164-65

itself as reacting to the chaos in cultural and spiritual values.[35]

As a result, Read spent much of the 1920s hiding his romanticist tendencies, penning somewhat unconvincing pæans to classicist writers, such as Julien Benda, Georges Sorel and Irving Babbitt.[36]

'Given the sheer aggression of some of the other figures on *The Criterion* editorial board,[37] I believe that Read's involvement with *The Criterion* led to an extreme repression of his genuine beliefs on modernism. Consequently, when Read moved away from Eliot and *The Criterion* circle in the early 1930s, he went through an equally extreme opposite reaction to classicist modernism, like a pendulum swinging from

---

[35] Andrew Causey 'Herbert Read and the North European Tradition', in Benedict Read and David Thistlewood (eds), *Herbert Read: A British Vision of World Art* (London: Lund Humphries, 1993) 38f

[36] See Michael Paraskos, *Herbert Read: Art and Idealism* (London: Orage Press, 2014) 45f.

[37] The American poet John Gould Fletcher accused Read of being a 'romantic spy' at *Criterion* meetings. See Jason Harding, *The Criterion: Cultural Politics and Periodical Networks in Inter-War Britain* (Oxford: Oxford University Press, 2002) 16 and 40.

one amplitude to the other. Certainly by 1932 he had embraced what he called romanticist ideas, including Jungian psychology, anarchist politics and Surrealist art. *The Green Child* is accordingly a novel predicated in part on a rejection of Eliot's preference for a classicist revival.

'However, I want to suggest that *The Green Child* is also founded on the rejection of another manifestation of classical order, namely normative or mainstream academia. We know Read had some antipathy towards academia from an early age. As a student at Leeds University, just before the First World War, he bemoaned the lack of intellectual and practical ambition in his fellow students:

> I have found that most people whose minds have responded to a formal university education are like monoliths. They are bodies at rest. They have acquired during their university years a

choice armoury of information, and they assume that it will serve them for the rest of their lives.[38]

Read picked up this tack again in his introduction to the catalogue to the International Surrealist Exhibition, held in London in 1936:

> Our culture is altogether on the guidebook model; Shakespeare has four stars, Milton three, Donne and Blake one. We do not stop to ask on what system, and by whom, the stars were awarded. If we did, we should discover some dusty college of pedants, their noses buried in a profit and loss account of biographical data, critical overdrafts and vested interests. If we dared to travel without a guide, to trust our eyes and ears and our contemporary sensibility, the result would be catastrophic. Schoolmasters and professors would wander about helplessly like myopic men deprived of their glasses; textbooks

---

[38] Herbert Read, *Annals of Innocence and Experience* (London: Faber, 1940) 88

would be irrelevant and teaching an
imposition.[39]

It seems to me that the moment when Read wrote this was extremely significant. It was a moment when the study of art history was increasingly being integrated into academia as one of the classical humanities. In Britain this was largely due to the work of the Courtauld Institute of Art, founded in 1932.[40] Consequently, it is possible to see *The Green Child* as an attempt to influence the development of academic art history in a non-classicist way and I would suggest that this means we can see *The Green Child* not simply as a work of fiction, but as an art theory text. A creative art history text, which is perhaps the first overt work of what has been called Art-Art History.

---

[39] Herbert Read (ed.), *Surrealism* (London: Faber, 1936; 1971) 44-45
[40] See Richard Woodfield, *Art History as Cultural History: Warburg's Projects* (London: Routledge, 2001) 264. I disagree profoundly with Woodfield's overarching statement that prior to the establishment of the Courtauld Institute, English art history was a matter solely of connoisseurship or criticism, but it's a matter of opinion I suppose.

'That claim might seem far-fetched, but it is certainly the case that *The Green Child* is full of art. If we begin with the world of the green-skinned people itself, it is made of 'luminous obsidian'. Obsidian is a hard glass-like volcanic rock that was used by Mesoamerican sculptors, who were a well-known influence on Henry Moore. This suggests the subterranean world is, in some sense, a Mesoamerican sculpture. Alternatively, perhaps the subterranean world is set inside a Barbara Hepworth or Henry Moore sculpture itself, inside of one the holes they so famously cut into their works in the 1930s. This seems particularly plausible given Read's Moore-ish descriptions of one of the subterranean caverns:

> [T]he wall arched upwards shallowly concave until they reached the high apex, which was round and deep, glistening and bluish, like the freshly exposed socket of a bone.

'Hepworth's sculptures are also evident elsewhere in the subterranean world. Towards the end of the book, we learn that the primary goal of the green people is to achieve a guru-like status, in which they spend their time in secluded silence, contemplating crystalline objects. As described by Read, these objects bear a striking resemblance to Hepworth's sculptures of the mid-1930s. They comprise 'seven planes without symmetry, but with axes meeting in a single point'.[41]

That Read had almost no connection with the Courtauld after its foundation, despite its position as the leading centre for art history in Britain and (to some extent) the wider English-speaking world, and his position as one of the leading authorities on art from the 1930s to the 1960s, surely speaks volumes. Read's attempts to influence the development of academic art history were undertaken as an outsider to the Courtauld establishment, and he inevitably failed. Yet, in *The Green Child* we see a glimpse — or at least a starting point — as to what that alternative might have looked like, as Read sets out an alternative reality, a space so unlike our reality it is one in which sculptures, like the

---

[41] Herbert Read, *The Green Child* (London: William Heineman, 1935; 1989 reprint) 192

dead in the Orphic mysteries, can speak for themselves. Consequently it falls at the point at which it meets the rational conception of reality posited by normative academia. The truth is that talking sculptures can never be incorporated into classical academic investigations into art history because they only exist in spaces where they can talk, namely the artistic spaces of art, books, poetry, theatre and films. Outside of those spaces the notion of talking sculptures appears absurd.

'We know also that Read was not averse to the idea of giving voice to art objects in other settings too. In addition to writing the 1936 surrealist exhibition catalogue introduction, Read participated in the opening events, with a spoken prose piece called *The Surrealist Object*. In this he stated:

> This is the surrealist object speaking to the British public. It has become necessary for the objects to explain themselves to the people. For

> convenience, I speak on behalf of other
> objects.[42]

In this act Read forced his audience to face an inanimate object that speaks for itself. The object is thus empowered and possesses agency, at least in a Surrealist space, something that is also true of the Green-skinned, sculpture-like, characters in *The Green Child* who are empowered and possess agency in the novel's alternative space. From this it should be clear that I believe Read wanted us to see the green-skinned people as carvings by Henry Moore, something very much apparent in their description. According to Read, they were:

> excessively slender, their heads egg-shaped;
> they had no perceptible eyebrows, their eyes
> were tiny, but bright like a ferret's.[43]

---

[42] A recording of Herbert Read reading this exists. H. Read, 'The Surrealist Object', reproduced on LTM Recordings, *Surrealism Reviewed,* CD recording, LTMCD 2343.

[43] Herbert Read, *The Green Child* (London, William Heineman, 1935; 1989) 166

It is not difficult to find sculptural works by Moore from the 1930s that fit this description. Because of this, I do not think it unreasonable to view the green people as animate sculptures, and in the alternative reality of the book's space, they are able to speak for themselves. Notably, whilst in the book's evocation of our world the green child of the title is silent, once she is returned to the subterranean alternative reality in which she belongs, she regains her name and speaks. Her first words, spoken in her native language, are 'I am Siloën'. In saying this Siloën asserts her right to speak with the commensurate right to agency and self-determination, thereby breaking what Ellen Friendman and Miriam Fuchs have called the patriarchal sequence of narrative 'in order to give presence and voice to what was denied and repressed'.[44]

'I would argue that, with all the examples given here, there is a sense we are being invited into an

---

[44] Ellen Friendman and Miriam Fuchs, *Breaking the Sequence: Women's Experimental Fiction* (Princeton: Princeton University Press, 2014) 15

alternative reality, not as an act of escapist fantasy, but to be philosophically engaged, politically active and psychologically transformed. That is why I believe Read was using *The Green Child* as a kind of manifesto for a different, creative kind of art history.

'Of course, if we were to follow him in this we would have to place art and art education in a wholly different sphere to the presumed objectivity of the historian or scientist, turning the pursuit of art history and theory into an art itself, rather than just another version of the humanities. That might seem a bizarre suggestion, but it is worth remembering that art history began life not in the universities but in the art schools as an aspect of a creative practitioner's education. Moreover, we should remember that Read saw the academicisation of art history happening before his eyes at the Courtauld and elsewhere, a change that gained for the subject the gloss of scientific impartiality, and consequent credibility, but perhaps lost from it something more important, the potential to be a transcendent creative act in itself.'

§30 All you need is me

Some indeterminate time after giving the rather ridiculous lecture on the possibility that inanimate sculptures might speak to us, Professor Geroud stood on the bottom step of a Lehane Motors coach and looked back into the vehicle to check all had disembarked. He turned and called to the students outside with a nervous gentle voice that they should all make their way to the field on the opposite side of the road. The students picked up their rucksacks and obeyed, and were soon trailing after Geroud through the car park of the Yew Tree Inn in Barfrestone, across the road and into the field as directed. Once there, Geroud waited for the students to gather around him again. 'Okay, find a spot to pitch your tent. There are the public toilets at the far end of the pub garden, but if you prefer, the male students, can use the bathroom upstairs in the main pub building, in room 101. Female students the one in room 102.'

This time the students didn't move. Geroud looked at a young man standing near by: 'Richard,' he mumbled. 'What are they waiting for?'

'Nothing,' replied Richard. 'It's just inertia. A body at rest will remain at rest unless it is acted upon by a force.'

'Will it?' asked Geroud.

'Oh yes. Newton's First Law of Motion.'

Richard walked forward into the field, determined to act with force on the inert students. At some point, and for some inscrutable reason, he stopped, looked around him, and selected a patch of the rough grass-covered ground to call his own. He unhitched the rucksack from his back and began to lay out its contents on the ground in front of him. All this was done with enough natural theatricality for the other students to take note and follow suit. In less than half an hour, a small tent village had appeared and, with the New Barfrestone commune duly established, the students were quick to find their way to the public bar of the Yew Tree Inn, for much-needed refreshment. Geroud watched them drift away in small groups, chatting and laughing, and felt a kind of bereavement, as if they were leaving him forever.

'You can come with us,' said Richard as he passed. 'We do quite like you, you know.'

In the twenty years since he had thrown himself off a gasometer for a bet, Geroud couldn't remember anyone saying they liked his company. Longer, in fact. It felt like a metaphorical hug, an act of psychological touch so palpable that it seemed as though some muscle deep inside him, clenched for so long he couldn't remember a time when it wasn't set in clamped spasm, at last managed to relax.

§31 There is a light and it never goes out

The journalist was dissatisfied. It wasn't that national-treasure-television-sculpture-celeb, Richard Barnes, didn't answer her questions, more that his answers seemed evasive. No, I don't mean evasive, I mean they were unsatisfactory, like the mystery of a cryptic crossword clue for someone perfectly able to do a quickword in less time than it takes a Northern Line train to get from Balham and to Kennington. The things he said sounded as though they had meaning for someone, but for any one else it was hard to see the point of his Orphic mystery.

She decided on a different tack. She asked him about the new series of his hit television show *The Great British Carve Off*. She said the premise seems to start with the fact that carving sculpture is a dying art — you know, why spend weeks struggling with a block of stone or wood when a 3D printer could knock-up an equivalent overnight, *sans* fuss, *sans* bother and *sans* any real skill? The art was no longer in the hands of an elite. It was democratised. Except that TV's sculpture-celeb, Richie Barnes was on hand to tell the great British public something different. He would say that a carving by a laser-guided cutting machine, or an equivalent knocked-up by a 3D printer, was not the same thing at all. Looking straight to camera, long hair and piercing eyes, like some Biblical prophet, he declared there is magic in taking hammer to chisel to wood or stone. And in that magic lay the possibility of true greatness, the kind of greatness no machine could ever reach. In the opening titles he could be seen taking a large sledgehammer to a Ultimaker S3 3D printer, midway through it printing a statue of a golden calf, sending its shattered guts across the screen. It was all very televisual.

The show had been an unexpected hit, moving in three seasons from BBC4 to BBC2, then onto prime time BBC1. In its wake there was a revival in carving, with high street studios springing up in empty old shops offering carving classes for birthday parties and hen nights out.

Barnes himself was in demand too. As well as appearing on his own show, he had gained a near permanent spot on a slew of TV and radio quizzes, chat shows and pod casts. Book deals followed — *Learn to Carve in a Fortnight*, *Carving for Christmas* and his latest sensation *Carving on Ice.* Or was that *Carving in Ice?* Whatever the case, he was a success. Far from being a dead art, carving was now alive and well, and it had made him famous. Rich and famous. What right had he to be cryptic, thought the journalist. Unless he was really trying to hide the truth. The truth that carving really wasn't that special.

Asking Barnes about the new show released the script drilled into him by a publicist. But Barnes seemed tired of repeating the same old stock phrases. Of course it was about fun, but there's a serious side to carving. It puts us in touch with a really ancient tradition, going back to Babylon and Egypt and the carvers of the cathedrals, but also it had a spiritual side. It was a healing thing. Something about the tactile self, something about being a complete human, not just sitting at a desk or a computer, but actually doing things. *Blah, blah, blah.*

The journalist scented blood. 'Do you really believe any of that?' she asked provocatively. Barnes looked at her suspiciously. He knew she was trying to catch him out. It was so blatant he couldn't help smiling. For a moment he wondered whether to help her with a minor scoop.

'When you touch a piece of rock,' Barnes started to say. 'I mean.' He stopped again. So she had fazed him with her bluntness. 'What do you want me to say?' he asked. 'What is it you want? Do you want me to say it's all bollocks and that you cannot resurrect an entire industry on the back of a TV show? Or maybe that TV is not a creative medium, it's a parasite medium, run by parasite people? Is that what you want? But if he did that then surely it wouldn't be any more true than saying this is the start of a new age of carving? For that to happen you'd need to have truly creative people pick up a hammer and chisel and to start carving, not a celebrity newsreader or a ex-footballer.'

Barnes stopped. He wondered if he had given the journalist the headline she wanted. 'Isn't that a bit elitist,' she asked.

'For fucks sake!' exclaimed Barnes. 'What's elitism got to do with it? People only say that to shut you up. And it's a shitty way of shutting you up. If you're going to use that old line then you'd better declare yourself. You should tell us where you went to school and university before using the E word.'

'I just mean,' replied the journalist, taken aback by the aggression in Barnes's voice, 'most people don't have the opportunity to pick up a hammer and chisel, or a paint brush or anything like that. So they do what they can. The next best thing. A mobile phone to take a picture, or a little film, or a 3D printer to carve a sculpture. And then someone like you comes along and you say that because they don't do those things in the way you say they should, they're missing out on some kind of spiritual experience. That's what I mean by elitist. Isn't the truth that you don't really want a revival of carving? That you don't really want us to do any of these things, because it means you can feel superior and mock us for not doing them?' Barnes frowned deeply. It seemed a hard line of questioning from the *TV Times.*

'Perhaps we should move on,' said the journalist, realising she might have gone too far. 'You're working on a memorial to the art historian Michael Paraskos.' A sense of relief came over Barnes's body as though he'd been released from a trap, although he didn't know if he'd really escaped. Only the next morning's headlines would reveal that. But talking about something else still felt like a release.

'Yes,' he replied. 'He was one of my tutors. He was a great tutor.'

'And what kind of monument will it be?' asked the journalist.

'It's a group work,' explained Barnes. 'All great carving is the work of a group. Michael taught us that. He said look at the mediæval cathedrals. Every surface is carved, but it is the work of the group. The guild. He said we need to recapture that collective spirit. After he died all his past students went on a torch-lit parade through the centre of London. Thousands of us were there to say thank you, walking through the streets, from Kennington to Trafalgar Square, a single collective guild. And afterwards, some of us wanted to create a permanent memorial. In Venice. Where he died.'

'Is that going to happen?' asked the journalist.

'We think so,' replied Barnes. 'There's space in the church of San Zorzi Mazor.'

'And you are carving the actual statue of him?' asked the journalist.

'Yes,' replied Barnes. 'But it's not just a statue. It's designed to be a living thing, with real clothes on the stone body. So it will not just be a representation of him, it will be him. The idea is for his friends to gather once a year on his birthday to strip him down, wash the stone body and then dress him in new clothes. Like a mediæval saint. There'll be a kind of ritual. Once a year. Carving shouldn't end when the chisel is put down. It should become part of life. A living ritual.'

'And that's what those socks are for I see you knitting?' asked the journalist.

'Carving,' Barnes corrected her. 'I'm carving him socks in wool using knitting needles.'

'I see,' said the journalist sounding doubtful. 'And the sculpture of Paraskos, is it accurate or more abstract?'

'See for yourself.' Barnes stood up and walked to the end of the workshop where a large object sat hidden beneath a dirty grey dust-sheet. Pulling the sheet aside revealed the top half of a standing figure carved in a marble-like stone. 'Actually it's travertine stone,' said Barnes, as if answering an unspoken question. 'As most people know, travertine is not a true marble. But it's a very English stone. A bit like Michael. Of course he was very foreign really — loved flashing his European passport around when the rest of us were waiting in the immigration queue at Marco Polo Airport. But you wouldn't find anyone more English than him. You know, he spoke BBC English with just a dash of Yorkshire. And he wore cardigans a lot. Very English.' Barnes pulled the rest of the dust-sheet away to reveal the full sculpture. 'As to whether it's accurate — well I suppose you could say it's an accurate representation, but it doesn't really look like him. The stone itself demands a say on the final outcome so you can't just force a likeness onto it.'

'What about the — ' For the first time the journalist blushed at her own question. 'I mean, why does he have such a large — '

'Cock and balls?' interrupted Barnes laughing. 'He'd have wanted it that way. About a year ago — or was it two? — when we all got together in the Prince of Wales pub to agree the design — those of us involved in the carving I mean — we said give him a big cock and massive balls to match. It was unanimous. I think we also said we'd need somewhere to hang the towel when we wash him. It's form following function. Also we wanted to do a homage to that Gormley sculpture in South Kensington. You know, the one with big cock. He worked near there you see.'

'Yes, I see,' said the journalist. 'But how did he die?'

§32 Let me kiss you

'It was such a heroic death. How could it be anything else? It was worthy of Byron at Messolonghi.[45]

'My old tutor was a fitness fanatic. Not in the sense of developing a sportsman-like physique — although his body was a sight to behold — but as something more elevated, something more like the Greek ideal of creating harmony between body and soul. It was as though he was born with the beautiful goddess Sophrosyne whispering softly in his ear.

'It wasn't that he was without pride. Some might say he was excessively proud. But his physique deserved some pride. If he stood at the water's edge on that Venetian island, outside the classical perfection of Palladio's San Zorzi Mazor, and looked in wonder at his own reflection, who could have blamed him if for a moment he was seized by the vision in the water, and stood motionless, his face fixed like stone, his perfect body a statue carved in marble? On those days many boys and girls must have desired him, but his pride

---

[45] Is he being ironic?

kept him distant. Many looked, but no one dare to touch, except of course Sophrosyne still whispering in his ear.

'And so he would swim. To swim around the island of San Zorzi Mazor, the distance is approximately one mile. It was a daily routine, and shortly after dawn each day he would set off from the staith in front of Palladio's church. Setting a brisk pace in the water he would round the island in a highly respectable thirty minutes. This daily ritual done, he would return to the staith and rise from the water, his body wet and gleaming in the Venetian sunshine, like *Adonis Anadyomenos,* to stand before the church. Except that day. The day we all remember. On that day he didn't return.'

'What happened to him?'

'They think he was hit by a vaporetto. An ignominious end. They found his body a few hours later. Apparently it wasn't a pretty sight.'

§33 You have killed me

'It wasn't a heroic death. How could it be? It was quiet and unnoticed. Like the man himself. Murder some say, but there was no proof. Maybe he jumped. He said he often thought to jump.

'We had eaten in the Ghetto — the Venice Ghetto I mean — at Gam Gam. There were lots of us there. Sixteen or more, but no one saw a thing. At the restaurant, we were surprised they had room for us. At such sort notice. But that's the floods. Most people didn't go out. Tourists — sensible tourists — holed up in their upper floor hotel rooms until the tide had passed. But we were not sensible tourists. We washed up in a ground floor bar and a ground floor restaurant and we drank and ate without much thought for the ground floor flood.

'Leaving the restaurant we noticed the water had overflowed the canal path of the Fondamenta Cannaregio, but we waded though to the Ponte delle Guglie, laughing as we splashed our way forward. And then we walked whatever still dry land we could find to the Ferrovia stop at Santa Lucia railway station. With no water bus in sight we walked to the Piazzale Roma, our feet again wading through shin-high water, and from there we took a bus to Tronchetto and a batèlo heading to our base at San Zorzi Mazor. It was a stormy crossing, with waves more like the open sea than those of a sheltered lagoon. All along the banks of the Canal della Guidecca the paths were flooded, as high as a man's waist, and yet the street lamps burned as though their footings were set in nothing more than mildly damp ground. A few people could be seen wading where the footpaths should have been, each looking perilously close to becoming lost souls.

'I suppose we were vaguely aware that he went to the open deck at the back of the water bus, and stood alone out there surveying the water all around us. Perhaps he wondered where a boat could land if there was no land. And if it could not land, could it stay adrift on the open sea forever, like some batèlo Marie Celeste? Some said they thought they saw a woman join him out there, but it was all very vague. Inside the cabin we chatted excitedly and nervously as we crossed the Canal de ła Zueca and reached our waterlogged stop. There we bustled to get off the boat, until we realised we could not see him any more. Not so vague any more. Is he still outside? Is he at the back? Is he at the front?'

'What happened to him?'

'No one knows. We do know he went overboard. They found his body the following morning. No clues. Nothing definitive anyway. Maybe a sudden wave hit the boat and knocked him over. If there was someone else out on deck that night they could not be found. So maybe he jumped. Like I said, he often thought to jump.'

§34 Found found found

'I don't know if you could call it a heroic death. At least not in the conventional sense

'He walked ahead as we left the drowned vaporetto stop at San Zorzi Mazor. I guess he felt the need to take the lead. You know, do his tutoring duty, despite often saying that after five he was off the clock.

'The way from the staith to our accommodation in the old monastery was completely flooded. Even the pontoons raised above the water were floating in the waves. He stepped onto the first of them only to find it sink below the waterline as it took his weight. The dirty water covered his foot as high as his knee. He called out to us to tread carefully, and to try and stay in the middle of the floating boards. We followed his instruction gingerly, each of us in turn crying out, half in laughter, half in fear as our feet were overwhelmed. He went ahead until he reached the steps of Palladio's beautiful church where there was some semblance of dry land. Not so wet anyway. But from there the pontoon bridge, set on the narrow path that skirted the island, which was the only way to reach the accommodation, had washed away. Looking to the corner of the church, where the Canal de ła Zueca gives way to the Łaguna, the water was deeper and seemed rougher. It had overwhelmed the narrow path giving the impression you would have to wade through open sea.

'In our group we had a little girl, six years old, too young to wade through that. I suppose that was meant to be his moment of heroism. He told her to climb on his back, and like St Christopher bearing the infant Christ, he waded through the deeper water.

'At first it all seemed fine. It seemed like the little girl might even have made it on her own and he needn't have worried. But you couldn't see what lay beneath. How deep the water was. Or if the path itself had washed away. Perhaps there was some debris hidden beneath, or a loose stone, or maybe it was just the push of a wave. Whatever it was, he lost his footing. Of course his instinct was to save the child. He managed to push her from his back onto the flooded path, where she sat in the water, wet but safe. But as he turned to save himself it was as though the long flowing hair of Cymopoleia wrapped itself around his legs. He struggled, seemed to right himself for a moment, before toppling again, into the water.'

'What happened to him?'

'In the end nobody knows. We all rushed forward, but the sea wouldn't let him go. He disappeared beneath the waves. I suppose he is still down there. Somewhere in the mud at the bottom of the lagoon, holding up the weight of that lovely old church, like a human pile. You see, they never found his body.'

§35 Please, please, please let me get what I want

Professor Geroud's students, sufficiently refreshed in the public bar of the Yew Tree Inn, were surprisingly quick at finding their way to the nearby church and they soon seated themselves in its nave, among the local inhabitants in what was possibly the largest congregation the building had seen since the repeal of the Act of Uniformity. Certainly the building felt pleased at the turn out, exuding a warmth that was welcoming to the visitors. Titivillus was also pleased, almost as though he was really an extension of the building, one of its carved grotesques freed from imprisonment in the stone of the walls.

Like his students, Professor Geroud had ensured he had also imbibed enough refreshment, in his case to dull the doubt he had about the wisdom of standing in front of such a large crowd, to talk on a topic he knew nothing about. Even so, he felt sick. Imposter sick and now mildly inebriated imposter sick.

An impatient cough from the audience flew past him like a warning shot. He had to start. Standing in front of the altar Geroud sensed the creature about to enter his body emerge from a shadow somewhere. As usual, it stood behind him for a moment. Glancing over his shoulder Geroud could see it was dressed in its familiar smart light grey suit, its dark hair held in place with gel or Brylcreem, like a tribute act to a young Tony Hadley. In Geroud's eyes the creature was so corporeal he was amazed not one person in the crowd before him saw it, let alone witness it disappear inside him. Every time he wondered why no one screamed.

As usual, the beautiful creature took Geroud's hands into his, closing them so they each formed a double fist. It then moved close until it pressed against Geroud back. Geroud heard it mumble something in a language he could not understand, and then it was inside him and in control. He was possessed. Except, to say it possessed him is not quite right. Of course Geroud knew it was not really him speaking. The words that flowed so fluently from his mouth were not his, and yet it still felt like him. It was not so much possession as a kind of union, so that for the moments when the creature controlled his body it felt to Geroud that he was a different Geroud. That different Geroud still had all his thoughts and feelings, and all his memories, but he was, by all accounts, confident and charming and knowledgeable. At no point did Geroud feel he was not in control of himself, and had anyone ever questioned him on the matter, he might have said that he knew he could push the creature out at any moment, if he wanted to. He just never wanted to. In fact, when the creature left him, Geroud even felt a kind of loss, as if bereft of a part of himself he liked. Titivillus had told him this is what artists call poetic fury. Like being taken over by a muse. Or a *kind of* muse.

Whatever the case, the creature empowered Geroud. With its help he began to describe what his audience could see easily enough for themselves by glancing over his talking head. Sometimes, according to Titivillus, you have to point out the things that are obvious before anyone can see them. Vaguely gesturing at the walls of the ancient building as he spoke, to any casual observer Geroud might have appeared the consummate academic, perhaps even professorial. But Geroud knew it was all a fraud and he suspected his audience knew it too.

* * *

'Thank you ladies and gentlemen. Students. I suppose one of the joys of visiting St Nicholas parish church here in the east Kent village of Barfrestone, is the first sight you get of the building, set high on a bank above a narrow country lane that passes through the village. Even when you have already seen pictures of the church online or in guidebooks, it still comes as something of a shock to see such a beautiful and unlikely building looming over you, looking more like something from south-west France or even the eastern Mediterranean than a typical Kent village church.

'I first experienced this in the late 1980s when I was a student of art history at the University of Leeds. I was studying mediæval architecture at the time, and wanting to impress my tutor, Dr Stephen Chaplin, I asked him if there were any good churches in Kent I could visit during the holidays. It was a stupid question that said more about my ignorance than it did my keenness for mediæval buildings. Kent is full of good mediæval churches to visit. It is full of astonishing churches. But Stephen was kind enough not to mock me, and said the one he would recommend was at Barfrestone. He said it would make a good comparison with the twelfth-century parish church at Adel near Leeds. He was right, the two churches are ideal subjects for an undergraduate compare-and-contrast essay, if such things still exist. But my trip to Barfrestone became more than just an exercise in ticking off yet another romanesque church from my list of places to visit. It became something like a pilgrimage as I alighted the train at Shepherdswell railway station, a couple of miles from here, and walked down the narrow country lane, towards this church. Perhaps it was all the unknowns that made that first visit seem extraordinary. In the days before mobile phones and the internet, I didn't have a map and so I was unsure if I was even walking in the right direction. I think I assumed if the church was recommended by my tutor it must be signposted. Of course it wasn't. Then there was the possibility the church would be locked, something less likely to be true then, but still a possibility. And there was, of course, the even greater likelihood St Nicholas would not live up to its billing. Again, before the internet it was very difficult to access pictures of small parish churches like this, so I had no idea what the church would look like, other than the written description in my copy of Pevsner's *Buildings of England*. I was stepping into the unknown, and to make matters worse, despite it being the Easter holidays, the weather was still firmly set to winter. Midway along the country lane that might or might not have been leading me to Barfrestone, I was caught in a icy rain storm that soaked my clothes and left me feeling absolutely dejected.

'Maybe no one will believe me now, and maybe it's just a false memory, but from what I recall, as I turned down into the depression in which the village of Barfrestone sits, and looked up at the church I saw it bathed in a shaft of golden sunlight streaming down, straight from heaven. Like a mediæval pilgrim arriving at the goal of some long and arduous trip, my spirits lifted and the church really did look like some ornate mediæval reliquary, as if crafted from gleaming gold. At least that's how I remember it, and today, whenever I visit the church, and I round that same corner, usually now seated in a car rather than on foot, I still see the church as a golden casket, regardless of the actual weather. Such is the power of memory, or possibly the power of imagination on our memories.

'Of course, I do realise a two mile trek down a country lane in a little bit of rain is not really comparable to the experience of a mediæval pilgrim walking through rain and shine from Paris to Santiago de Compostela, or from London to Jerusalem, facing untold dangers. I also know that the goal of my journey does not really compare to finally seeing something like the Church of the Holy Sepulchre after such a journey. But I am entitled to my memories and they are strangely strong memories when it comes to this building. For some reason it seems to have seared itself into my memory, or perhaps I should say into my psyche, in ways I cannot fully understand or explain. It has become part of me, a touch of the divine in the heart of an atheist. It is part of what makes me think of myself as a secular Christian.

'In the early twentieth century, the influential art theorist Herbert Read suggested that one of the purposes of art was to provide humanity with what he called reconciling images. He suggested we live in a world that is in many ways hostile, arbitrary and frightening, and as a mechanism to survive in a world like that humankind had evolved a kind of second reality in which we perceive ourselves to live. We might call this a mental reality. Although this is based in large part on what the real world is actually like, it also shields us from the most disturbing aspects of that real world. The reconciling image is a mechanism to maintain the link between our mental image of the world, and the actuality of the world, and in that sense it is both a comforter that ameliorates our experience of reality, and a reality check that keeps our mental reality in a working relationship with the real world.

'Forgive me for mentioning this at some length. I only do so because it seems important to what I want to talk about here, to what I want to tell you. It is important to me because in my mind, when I think of myself back then as a dysfunctionally shy twenty-year-old who was finding life very difficult, and who, if I am honest, was suffering from quite serious mental health issues, this building, with its carvings, was a reconciling image for me. When I rounded that corner into the village and saw the church bathed in sunlight, for a moment I felt whole again. Or maybe whole for the first time. A physical material object — a work of art no less — so beautiful and complete, despite its time-worn state, seemed to be capable of healing. Was capable of healing. Did heal.

'I am well aware that this does not quite make sense in terms of Herbert Read's theory, as a work of art the best part of a thousand years old should not be capable of acting as a reconciling image so long after its creation. I have no explanation for that, only a subjective judgement that it did. Maybe some works of art are capable of transcending time in this way, I cannot say. All I know is what I remember happening that day, and that the afterglow of it has never really left me. I was not cured of my melancholy — *indeed it was to get much worse before it got better* — but for a brief moment I felt cleansed. And I wonder whether that was what this place was like for its original creators. Or at least intended to be like.

'Of course, it should go without saying that the church we see today is not the church that would have been seen by those who created it in the twelfth century. They would probably ask why we haven't restored it to its former glory. If they did we might have to explain events like the Reformation, the Puritan Republic, changes in religious taste and how we like our old buildings to look old. If we did, I don't think they would understand a word of what we tell them. And I suppose we would have to tell them about the disastrous attempt at a restoration in the 1840s, by the Victorian architect Richard Charles Hussey. I say disastrous, simply because of what was lost under Hussey's watch, including a series of rare mediæval wall paintings, which I suspect would have modified dramatically our understanding of this church. That loss was by accident. Deliberate losses include the removal of a pointed arch gothic windows from the chancel in order to make the building appear more coherently romanesque.[46] But maybe I should not be so scornful. Hussey claimed he had to do what he did to Barfrestone in order to save what remains today. Ancient buildings do fall down if they are not repaired and restored. But like Thomas Hardy, I cannot help thinking they lose some of their integrity when they are.[47]

'And so I suppose I should not like Hussey — and yet, somehow I do. I like the way he speculated, as best he could in the circumstances, about the things he found when he began work on St Nicholas Barfrestone. In the absence of written evidence, we are only left with the physical materials of a building like this from which we have to speculate. Just as it is estimated that as little as 7% of medieval literature has survived to the

---

[46] E Hessing, *Barfreystone Church* (Canterbury: Kentish Gazette, nd.) 12

[47] See Benjamin Zenas Cannon, *Disappearing Walls: Architecture and Literature in Victorian Britain,* unpublished PhD, (University of California, Berkeley, Spring 2014)

present day,[48] a similar or even lower amount of medieval material culture survives,[49] all of which is why restorers must tread carefully when they replace wood and stone work. They are removing the only evidence we have.

'Visiting the village of Barfrestone today one of the most striking things is how small the place is. If it didn't have its remarkable parish church, we would probably call a hamlet rather than a village, a semi-detached extension to nearby Shepherdswell or Eythorne, as much as a place in its own right. In saying that I am probably being unfair to the community at Barfrestone, and I have no intention of being rude. I simply make the point that Barfrestone is small. Very small. And, as far as we can tell, it has always been small. There is no evidence of a much larger village in the past, or that it was the country seat of some great lord of the manor, or the site of any monastic

---

[48] Mike Kestemont et al, 'Forgotten books: The application of unseen species models to the survival of culture' in *Science* no. 375, 18 February 2022, 765f

[49] See James Tapper, 'Praise Be! Medieval archbishop revealed as lost English saint' in *The Observer* newspaper, 4 February 2024, 22

settlement. And yet, this tiny village has one of the most extraordinary and beautiful examples of a twelfth-century romanesque parish church architecture anywhere in England. Of course people speculate as to why.

'The church itself sits on a raised shelf-like bank high above one of the two lanes that form the village. It is surrounded by the grass and graves of the church yard, high trees, and along the edge of the road a napped-flint stone wall capped with red terracotta bricks. The church is multicoloured, or polychromatic, with a grey flint galetted stone lower section, almost resembling rubble in the way it is put together, typical of this part of the country. More unusual is above the flint level, where the wall is in warm-white Caen limestone, a high status material imported from Normandy. On top of this is the bright red roof made from terracotta tiles. Despite its diminutive size, the effect of the church is both uplifting and grand, giving the appearance of a two-storey building, with a ground level and clerestory, when it has in fact only a single floor.

'These are the things we might notice straight away, long before we have started to look closely at the carvings on the outside of the building. Already these elements indicate this is an unexpectedly elevated mediæval structure for a tiny village. The Caen limestone alone is a material more readily associated with the major showpiece buildings erected in England after the Norman invasion and occupation in 1066, used in places such as Westminster Abbey, the Tower of London and Canterbury Cathedral, rather than in minor parish churches. And that realisation might lead us on to the ornate carvings, not only around the door, but across the whole building, inside and out, all of which again suggest the church had a relatively high-status.

'Except that might be a speculation too far. The truth is that so little survives of the parish churches of the Norman period in England it can be difficult to be certain if Barfrestone's ornateness was particularly unusual. The earliest parts of the building are late eleventh century, so initial work on it began not long after the Norman invasion. However, most historians seem to agree that the decorative carving dates from about a century later, begun some time in the 1180s. This is a date first suggested by the building's most extensive biographer, Edward Hessing, in his undated guidebook to the church, published by the Kentish Gazette newspaper probably during the 1960s. In a bid to explain the more unusual aspects of the church Hessing placed Barfrestone in the context of the church of St Mary in the village of Patrixbourne, located some eight miles away, with its impressive Romanesque carvings around the south door and a wheel window, just as we see at Barfrestone.[50] Patrixbourne too is partially made of Caen limestone and is seen generally as contemporary with Barfrestone, which might suggest such buildings were relatively common. To add to this supposition, other churches nearby also show evidence of high-status twelfth-century building work, including Holy Innocents, Adisham, Saints Peter and Paul, Aylesford and St Clement, Sandwich. However, with the exception of St Mary Patrixbourne, of these only St

---

[50] E Hessing, *Barfreystone Church* (Canterbury: Kentish Gazette, nd.) 8

Clement Sandwich comes close to Barfrestone in terms of the exceptional quality of the stonework, in its case in the crossing tower, again partially made from Caen limestone. But the problem in using Sandwich as a point of comparison is that mediæval Sandwich was a much more significant settlement than Barfrestone, and in it we might expect to find some high-status building work. As is so often the situation with early mediæval parish churches, the material evidence appears to throw up more questions than answers. In this instance we are left with the possibility that either large numbers of highly decorated English parish churches were built in the Norman period, but they were so modified in the gothic period that all evidence of them has been lost, or Barfrestone and its nearby cousin Patrixbourne are anomalies.

'We might hope that in the absence of almost any documentary evidence for most early English parish churches, archæology can provide answers to some of questions we might have. Even if an early mediæval church was rebuilt in the later mediæval period, archæologists might have found fragments of romanesque carvings from the earlier building, either in church grounds or embedded in the later structure as hardcore. Unfortunately very little archæological work has been done on English parish churches and so there is both a lack of archæological work relating to specific buildings, and a lack of wider material from which to generalise. My personal belief is that early parish churches were not generally ornate in terms of carving, although less costly painted decoration was likely to have been ubiquitous. Consequently, I think Barfrestone was always an unusual example, and it is, paradoxically, also one of the few parish churches where something approaching an archæological investigation has happened.

'Some time after his restoration work, Hussey appears to have been highly sensitive to his legacy as a church conservator, which led him to write in the 1880s an unusually detailed record of the work he carried out at Barfrestone. Notably he published this in the archæology journal *Archæologia Cantiana* in 1886, and his text does have an archæological tone to it, giving it an air of scientific objectivity. Hussey always claimed his restoration was necessary to save the building at Barfrestone from collapse — *and I see no evidence to doubt that claim* — but he clearly felt the need to justify what he had done in print. That justification also included an analysis of some unusual aspects in the structure of the building and speculation on its origins. Particularly notable was his claim that:

> In the upper part of the Northern portion of the West Wall of the nave, a piece of string moulding, corresponding with that on the outside of the building, was found, much worn by exposure to the weather. It has been worked on the back edge of a corbel carved with a rose, and suitable for the external cornice; the rose was quite clean, as if new, and, from its style, perhaps, rather older than the string moulding. In the same place was also found another small head, and a corbel-head like those in the cornice, and another small he head of apparently later date. In all the walls, fragments of squared stones and ashlar, which had been

> used in some former building were found; as were also two or three fragments of patterns inlaid in stone, of character resembling that marked above.

Hussey was convinced this was evidence that the stones had originally been used in another building, and necessarily modified for re-use at Barfrestone.

> It is apparent from what has been brought to light in these repairs… that certainly a large part, and probably the whole, of the wrought stone used in the church was not primarily prepared for it; and had been built into some other erection.[51]

'But Hussey was not a trained archæologist, and when he was investigating the state of the building prior to his 1840 work he was not specifically looking at it with a view to writing an archæological report.

---

[51] R.C. Hussey, 'Barfreston Church in A.D. 1840' in *Archæologia Cantiana*, vol. 15: 1886, 151

Consequently we do need to treat his *ex post facto* report with some caution. Despite this, there is something admirable in Hussey's 1886 description which reads as being strikingly modern. In the absence of documentary evidence he looked at the building and found the phenomena of hidden carved and dressed stones (ashlar) and recut structural elements, and these led him to make a speculative suggestion as to why they were used in the building. They showed no sign of weathering, he wrote, suggesting to him that whatever building they originally came from could not have been standing for long.

Almost following Jules Prown's art historical model a century before it was written,[52] Hussey went on the hunt for documentary evidence that could back up his speculations, and alighted on a short-lived structure, commissioned in 1186 by the Archbishop of Canterbury, Baldwin, at Hackington, just north of Canterbury. The documentary evidence was not enough to provide proof, but the very existence of the

---

[52] Jules David Prown, 'Mind in Matter: An Introduction to Material Culture Theory and Method' in *Winterthur Portfolio*, Vol. 17, No. 1 (Spring, 1982)

building at Hackington led Hussey to think it could have provided the spolia for constructing Barfrestone church. Baldwin had wanted to establish a new college of secular priests at Hackington, with an accompanying 'cathedral' church, in an attempt to dilute the influence on his manor of the monastic community of Christchurch Canterbury. Christchurch is what we today call Canterbury Cathedral, and it was already rich and powerful institution, and growing more so in the aftermath of the death and canonisation of Thomas Becket, which had made it a major pilgrimage site. Whatever form Archbishop Baldwin's building was intended to take, it is reasonable to assume it would have comprised a high-status structure, with expensive carvings made of high quality materials, such as Caen limestone, which is exactly what we see at Barfrestone. Unfortunately for Baldwin, the monks at Christchurch petitioned both the king and Pope and the project was eventually abandoned in 1189, or rather it was transferred to Lambeth, where it would eventually become Lambeth Palace. That aside, the assumption Hussey made was that the building project at

Hackington was begun, and rather than waste the completed masonry and stone carvings after its adandonment, they were redirected to Barfrestone.

'I admit I quite like Hussey's suggestion. I can imagine sitting with him, perhaps in the public bar at Birmingham's Grand Hotel one evening, enjoying a glass of port, and hearing his theory as to where the stones of Barfrestone must have come from. I can imagine too, in my alcoholic haze, agreeing with him that his theory must be right. Absolutely right Richard, no doubt about it! It rings true. The problem is, as I might realise as I emerged from my babalas the following morning, there is no real evidence for this theory whatsoever. It is highly speculative. As Charles Coulson noted in 2014, Hussey's theory has given rise:

> to speculation about re-use in c.1175-80 of materials from Hackington college by Canterbury, a hypothesis advanced by Hussey and reinforced by the very astute and scholarly Rector (Edward) Hessing (1964-71), but on

> specific as well as general grounds quite
> untenable.[53]

Even Hessing thought the Hackington connection an 'unnecessary complication'. It is a theory we probably need to put away and only bring out in future as an historical curiosity. It is untenable, not because it is definitively untrue, but because it is an arbitrary connection made between a building at Hackington that might not even have existed, and one at Barfrestone that does exist. That in turn leads me to suggest it is more reasonable to look for an immanent explanation for the existence of such a high status church at Barfrestone, focusing on the church and its location, to think about what it might have meant in the late twelfth century. I admit this will, in some respects, be as speculative as Hussey invoking Hackington, but that is the nature of so much investigation into mediæval parish churches, where we have a material history in the form of the building in front of us, but very little

---

[53] Charles Coulson, 'The Barfrestone Conundrum: 'Much Restored' but 'Virtually Unaltered' in *Archæologia Cantiana,* 134 (2014):153-186

documentary evidence. In the absence of documentary evidence we often end up with no more than possibilities. If we are lucky those possibilities will turn into likelihoods, but that may be as far as we go. In that context I think Hussey did quite well with his speculation, and I hope I can get at least as far in terms of plausibility.

'In taking this approach, one of the first things I would note is not the building itself, but its location. Barfrestone is almost literally mid-way between the port of Dover and the city of Canterbury, and is not much of a detour from the road linking Canterbury to the mediæval port of Sandwich. In the middle ages both Dover and Sandwich were major embarkation points between England and continental Europe, and both towns show plenty of evidence that this made them thriving settlements.[54] In the case of Dover there is the surviving Maison Dieu, founded in 1227 by Hubert de Burgh, with the specific aim of housing pilgrims arriving

---

[54] See Helen Clarke et al, *Completest Medieval Town in England* (Oxford: Oxbow Books 2010) 30

from the continent, en route to the shrine of St Thomas Becket at Canterbury.

'Dover's Maison Dieu also had claims to be a pilgrimage destination in its own right, with the nearby chapel dedicated to St Edmund. This modest little building was in fact founded by a man who would also become a saint, Richard, Bishop of Chichester.[55] In mentioning this, what I am drawing your attention to is that pilgrimage in the middle ages was not a matter of reaching a single destination. It was a question of taking a journey through a religious landscape, in which a pilgrim would stop off at a variety of different holy sites, not all of them fitting in with the traditional image of a cathedral or monastic cult site.[56]

'Barfrestone's location, effectively midway between Dover and Canterbury, would seem to make it an ideal setting for either another 'maison dieu'[57] or

---

[55] A rather old, but entertaining account of the Maison Dieu is given by John Lyon, *The History of the Town and Port of Dover and Dover Castle* (London: Longman, 1813) 39f

[56] See Ross T. McIntire, *In the Footsteps of the Holy: Sacred Landscapes and the Cult of Saints in the Anglo-Norman World, 1066-1220* (PhD: University of York, 2019) 40 and *passim*

[57] Such as that to be found at Faversham in Kent.

another secondary pilgrimage site. The only problem with this is that there is no evidence that the church or surrounding buildings operated in either capacity. Besides which, it is unlikely pilgrims would have needed a rest-place, like a maison dieu, in this location. The distance from Canterbury to Dover is less than 20 miles, well within the 30 mile distance posited by Marjorie Nice Boyer as typical for daily foot travel in the period.[58] And yet this does not negate the possibility that Barfrestone's was a stopping off point for at least some pilgrims travelling between Canterbury and Dover, perhaps not as a place of overnight rest, but as a place of thanksgiving with specific connotations linked, in part, specifically to the carved decorative detailing of the church.

'In some ways that decorative detailing is fairly typical of the age in terms of its form and variety. Hessing links the more fantastical creatures shown to the manuscript bestiary known as *The Book of Creatures* by the Norman poet Philip de Thaun, written

---

[58] Marjorie N. Boyer, 'A Day's Journey in Mediæval France' in *Speculum, vol.* 26, no. 4 (1951) 599

between 1121 and 1139.[59] Although possible, this seems an unnecessarily specific source to cite, but whatever the origin of the imagery, around the exterior of the arch above the main south-west entrance we see the voussoirs, capitals and tympanum all carved with high quality images. This is a three-stepped romanesque arch, with the outer layer showing a mixture of figurative images, including allegorical figures representing the signs of the zodiac and agricultural and artisan workers at their labours, each set in shallow roundels. The next ring appears more playful, with animals playing musical instruments, a creature possibly representing a satyr, again playing a musical instrument, a figure on horseback and what look like hunting dogs. The inner arch comprises abstract and foliate forms.

'As I have suggested, much of this seems typical of the age, but a few details do stand out, not least the number of animals represented and their frequent ability to play musical instruments. Mary

---

[59] Hessing connects this imagery to E Hessing, *Barfreystone Church* (Canterbury: Kentish Gazette, nd.) 13

Remnant has suggested that we should not see the animals playing musical instruments in the carvings as fantastical at all, noting that the legs of the creatures appear to be too human in form. As a consequence she suggests we look at them as semi-realist representations of human minstrels dressed up as animals at some kind of celebration.[60] Although George Nebolsine's suggestion that Barfrestone's portal is close in style to doorways at Charente in France seems arbitrary, it does illustrate that Barfrestone's image of Christ in Majesty appearing in an aureole, and surrounded by angels, may be familiar from other romanesque buildings, but it is still remarkable.

An extensive description of the carvings written by Arthur Collins in 1933 is still one of the best speculative enquiries into what the images surrounding Christ might be and what they might symbolise. Particularly noteworthy is the question of the keystone, on which appears what looks to be the sculpted image of a bishop. Although this could be St Nicholas, Bishop

---

[60] Mary Remnant *English Bowed Instruments* (Oxford: Clarendon Press, 1986) 59

of Myra, to whom the church is dedicated, it has been interpreted as St Thomas Becket, the murdered Archbishop of Canterbury. The dating of the carvings to the late twelfth century makes this plausible, given St Thomas's murder at Canterbury Cathedral in 1170, and his rapid canonisation in 1173, but as Collins points out, if it is Becket his representation wearing this form of mitre is uncomfortably early in date.[61] This raises the possibility it is either not Becket (in which case who or what is it?) or it is a later addition.

'That said, the cult of Becket following canonisation spread remarkably quickly, and his shrine at Canterbury very soon became a major cult site, attracting visitors from all over western Europe. Because of this, the appearance of a carving of Becket at Barfrestone is not inconceivable. If it is Becket then we might have a strong indication that the church at Barfrestone is indeed connected to the pilgrimage route to and from Canterbury, but if that is the case, what is the connection?

---

[61] Arthur Collins, 'The Sculpted Ornament of the South Doorway of Barfreston Church', in *Archæologia Cantiana,* vol. 45: 1933.8f

'Possibly the other carvings provide a clue. At the side of the romanesque portal, on one of the capitals are two knights on horseback possibly jousting, but equally possibly engaged in actual battle. Given the repeated appearance of military figures on the doorway, such as the roundel on the extreme left hand side of the door, containing a recognisable Norman soldier, dressed in a hauberk, and sporting a Norman-style conical helmet, complete with a long shield and sword, it is tempting to speculate whether another contemporary event was exercising the minds of the carvers making these images at Barfrestone. That event was, of course, the Crusades. The possible date for the carvings in the 1180s puts them within tantalisingly close proximity to the calling of the Third Crusade to the Holy Lands in 1189, but even without that, the Second Crusade, fought from 1145–1149, would still have been fresh in people's minds. If this is a legitimate connection it might suggest Barfrestone is a building not simply focussed on the Canterbury pilgrimage site of St Thomas Becket, but more specifically on the Crusades as an act of pilgrimage.

Although today we might not so readily associate religious pilgrimage with the idea of military Crusades, that was not the case in the mediæval period when western crusaders habitually described their battles as pilgrimages. This could suggest that the church at Barfrestone was indeed a pilgrimage church, but with a particular orientation towards crusader-pilgrimage and that this is signified through its cycle of sculptural decoration. I am wary of taking my speculation further than the evidence allows, but is it not possible that the militaristic imagery of the carvings at Barfrestone is a concrete representation of the liturgical developments in this period that saw the standard blessings given to pilgrims at the start of their journeys develop into specific military blessings given to pilgrims as they set out to join the Christian armies fighting in Western Asia?[62] This could mean we need to understand Barfrestone as a kind of thanksgiving church, aimed at a specific group of people, perhaps the crusading

---

[62] For an extensive exploration of the development of the pilgrimage blessing into the crusading blessing see M. Cecilia Gaposchkin, 'From Pilgrimage to Crusade: The Liturgy of Departure, 1095-1300' in *Speculum,* vol. 88, no. 1 (January 2013), 44f

knights and soldiers depicted so extensively on the main portal. It is possible there was a social class element in all of this, so that for less elevated individuals, simply on pilgrimage rather than crusade, a blessing to turn them into Christian pilgrims, as it were, could have taken place at the port of Dover, maybe at St Edmund's Chapel adjacent to the Maison Dieu. It could even have taken place at their home parish church. This is highly speculative, but for the knightly class, bound together by a distinct aristocratic social status, and as crusaders having a significantly different experience of pilgrimage, a dedicated space such as this chapel-like church at Barfrestone might have been desirable. If so, the military imagery on the church might then have more meaning than being mere decoration.

'More evidence suggestive of this comes from other carved elements on the building. Lionel Wall has pointed out something interesting that, I must admit, passed me by, namely the relatively high degree of anatomical accuracy and detailing of some of the carvings, including one of the mounted knights and his horse. We have already noted a similar comment from Mary Remnant in relation to the human-like anatomy of the carved animals playing musical instruments, but Wall writes that while we might quibble about the proportions of the mounted knight on the right hand capital of the main door, 'compared with… contemporary illustrations of the period this is a fine depiction. Our knight has a lance from which a banner hangs. We can see a saddle and some vestiges of reins and bridle.' To my mind this could suggest a close and specific knowledge of how the animals and, crucially, the knights and their paraphernalia appeared in real life. This, as Wall also notes, is also to be seen in the nearby carved lion, which succeeds in simultaneously evoking a rampant heraldic lion whilst also being anatomically believable. As Wall states, 'The marvellous thing about this lion carving is that the sculptor - unusually - seems to know vaguely what a lion looks like!'[63]

---

[63] Lion Wall, 'Great English Churches', online resource <www.greatenglishchurches.co.uk/html/barfreston.html> accessed 1 August 2023

'I think there is some validity in Wall's assessment and to my mind the combination of something that is both quasi-heraldic and anatomically conceivable may be connected to the potential origin of this image. Consequently, is it possible that the carver of this lion had been to the Holy Lands and that there he had seen not only early (possibly Islamic) heraldic lions, but also a real lion?

'Yet, a curiosity for me is not just the carved lion, but the row of smaller, again almost heraldic, beasts carved into the abacus above the line. These three chimeric beasts in small roundels again seem to my eye to come from a lexicon of images with eastern Mediterranean origin, almost evidence of what Eva Hoffman and Scott Redford have identified as the encounters with antiquity that characterised the experience of western Christian crusaders and non-combatant pilgrims to the eastern Mediterranean during the western mediæval period. Carved and other visual forms from the ancient civilisations of the region appear, they argue, to find a new life in the emergent Western crusader culture of the early mediæval period, as well as in Byzantine and Islamic culture at this time.[64]

'Of course I accept quite readily that there is no way to prove this as a point of origin for the imagery we see at Barfrestone, except for a typological, comparison of the images with Mediterranean equivalents. But the possibility this could be a crusader-pilgrim church, complete with subject-specific imagery, evoking not only martial qualities, but broader imagery that can be read as having Levantine origins, offers a fascinating departure point for further speculation in this area.'

---

[64] Eva Hoffman and Scott Redford, 'Transculturation in the Eastern Mediterranean' in Finbarr Barry Flood and Gülru Necipoğlu (eds.), *A Companion to Islamic Art and Architecture* (London: Wiley, 2017) 409f

§36 Vicar in a tutu

'Quite extraordinary Professor,' said the vicar, shaking Geroud vigorously by the hand. 'In all my years at this church I have never thought of the building in terms of — what did you call it? — a crusader thanksgiving church. And it is true. Compared to heraldic beasts our lions do look more realistic, as if the carver did see a real lion'

'Relatively,' interjected Geroud, or rather the creature inside him did, still directing his words.

'Oh yes. Yes, quite right,' agreed the vicar. 'Relatively realistic. But you think our carver could have been to Palestine? And seen a lion there?'

'Maybe, but it's only speculation,' admitted Geroud. 'We can never know something like that for certain. I would just point out that so many of the images and forms on the building do seem to be derived from things someone might have seen if they had been to Jerusalem, whether as a crusader or a standard pilgrim. It's Scott Redford's theory really. And Eva Hoffman. They call it transculturation. The way a culture can absorb aspects of other cultures so it becomes a kind of hybrid culture.'

'Multiculturalism,' suggested the vicar.

'Similar, except that suggests multiple cultures co-existing. Here the returning carver, if we assume he had been to the east, seems to have absorbed the forms he saw, whether it was a living lion or an ancient Greek statue from the ruins of, say, Ephesus. It was transferred into him and became part of him. Part of his own internalised culture. The same with the rather wonky Greek key motif. The same with mince pies and Christmas pudding. We know they came into England from the Middle East in the middle ages, but they seem very English now. We have absorbed them and we celebrate with them. So why not think of a carved lion, a Greek meander or a grotesque Melusine in the same way. They come from the east and maybe the departing or returning crusaders wanted them here in this church to create a *kind of* symbolic link to the Levant. Rather like taking a cutting from a particular tree to plant in your garden to create a metaphorical or even a metaphysical link to the place it came from.'

'Remarkable!' exclaimed the vicar. 'You make it sound so simple. And you are so right. I have an olive tree growing in a pot I grew from a cutting I took on a pilgrimage of my own some years ago. To Jerusalem as it happens. It means so much to me. You know, I must introduce you to a friend of mine. Richard Hull. Mediævalist at Cambridge. Coming tomorrow for your second talk. Good man to know. Also makes a mean gin sling.' At that moment Geroud felt himself convulse as the creature inside him left his body. 'Are you alright?' asked the vicar. 'You look rather pale. Gin slings are entirely optional you know.'

'What?' mumbled Geroud. 'No, it's not that. I just need to sit down.'

'Of course, of course. Hard work lecturing. I know! Three times Sunday. Weddings, baptisms, funerals. Survive this week, you might think about a life in the priesthood.'

'If I survive this week,' repeated Geroud distractedly.

The vicar laughed and walked away leaving Geroud alone with Titivillus. 'A really wonderful talk,' said Titivillus. 'If I might say so myself. You'll be the talk of the village.'

'What did he mean by *if I survive this week?*'

'Who?'

'That vicar. He said, *if I survive this week.*'

'Just a turn of phrase, like.'

'So he wasn't another of your creatures. Reminding me of the contract?'

'The vicar!' exclaimed Titivillus laughing. 'My dear Lonely Heart, the rather sweet reverend of this parish is one of the most upright of men you could meet. A nice man too. He doesn't have anything to do with me.'

'That's true,' agreed Geroud. 'He just ignored you completely.'

'Yes, I supposed he did,' replied Titivillus, smiling. 'People often do.'

'Yes, they do, don't they. Why is that?'

'No time to think about that now, my dear Lonely Heart. Tomorrow is another day. In fact tomorrow is another important day. Your second lecture in the morning, this time with a bus full of your colleagues from the university.'

'I thought you said they wouldn't come all this way to see me.'

'It's Vice-Chancellor Fortnum's doing, not mine. A three line whip, like. But don't worry. A good night's sleep and you'll be at the top of your game. And I know just the thing for that. So shall we join the students in the pub?'

'In a minute,' replied Georud. 'I just want to clear my head.'

'Of course,' said Titivillus. 'But don't dwell on things. You delivered a great talk. Honestly.'

'Maybe I did,' said Geroud. 'But it wasn't really my talk was it. You wrote it. And your creature read it. I was just a passenger.'

'So? Do you think any truly eminent professor writes their own stuff. The most successful professors have research assistants to do it all for them, and others, if they are lucky, are inspired by the muses. Just think of me as your divine inspiration. Your muse, like. So are you coming to the bar?'

'I just want to be alone. I'll see you later.'

Titivillus turned, made his way down the nave, and out into the churchyard. Geroud followed, only stopping when he saw Titivillus disappear down steep moss-covered steps that separated the church from the little country lane. He felt glad to be alone. He sat himself down on the bench under the ancient yew tree in the church yard and toyed with the rope that dropped from the bell in its branches. Looking down at his feet he closed his eyes and began to take in deep breaths of the warm summer air. Had he a more poetic turn of mind he might have said he felt the peace of nature fall upon him.

'Interesting talk,' said a voice. Geroud opened his eyes to find two young women standing in front of him. 'I said it was an interesting talk,' one of the girls repeated.

'Melusine?' mumbled Geroud, seeming almost mesmerised at the sight in front of him.

'Melusine?' repeated the woman, laughing. 'What's does that mean?'

§37 Pretty girls make graves

The other woman let out a short mocking laugh, the kind Geroud remembered from school. He blinked, as though trying to rouse himself from what he presumed was a dream. It was obvious the woman standing in front of him could not be the Melusine. She and her friend both looked little more than twenty years old.

'Melusine?' mumbled Geroud, still confused at the sight. 'Sorry, it doesn't mean anything. I mean, it's a name.'

'It's a weird name. And it's not mine. I'm actually called Nanny.' Maybe it was the emphasis she placed on the word *actually* that made the woman want to qualify herself. 'Well actually I'm called Annette, but everyone called me Nanny. I like the incongruity of it.'

'I don't understand,' mumbled Geroud.

'Well do I look like a Nanny?' said the girl. 'And this is Becky.' Becky said nothing, but let out another short laugh, as if she was expecting the joke of talking to some old bloke to reach its punchline at any moment.

'Are you sisters?' asked Geroud.

'Like sisters,' replied Nanny, turning to Becky. 'Aren't we Beck?'

'That's nice,' said Geroud. Becky snorted a short laugh again. Was that the punchline?

'What about your friend. The one I reminded you of. What was she called? Mel—.'

'Melusine,' Geroud interrupted. 'But she wasn't called that either. Only I called her that.'

'What, is it a lovers' nick-name or something?' asked Nanny. Becky laughed again. Maybe that was the punchline. Talking to an old bloke about love. He must be a dirty bastard.

Geroud found himself blushing, not at the question, but the bluntness of this facsimile of the Melusine. 'No. Not really.'

'A friend then,' said Nanny.

'No. She wasn't really a friend either. She was more like —' He stopped, not knowing how to describe the original Melusine. He just wanted to say she was the Melusine. In his mind that had always been enough of an explanation, as much a description as a name. But he knew it would be meaningless to anyone else.

'More like what?' asked Nanny. 'Did you even know her?' she added, gently mocking his evasion. Becky snorted.

Geroud laughed nervously. 'That's a good question,' he said. 'I suppose she was an idea.'

'An idea! Now you are weird.'

Becky let out a loud laugh. So that was the punchline. 'What!' she exclaimed.

Geroud was shocked for a moment at how the feelings of inadequacy that had characterised his youth could return so easily. He forced himself to laugh. Better to be in on the joke. 'Maybe. I mean. I mean, maybe she was more an ideal. Not an idea. An ideal.'

'Still weird,' said Nanny. 'And I remind you of her?'

'It means he fancies you, Nan,' said Becky. 'He's a dirty old man.'

Geroud looked away.

'Do you think so?' asked Nanny, not expecting an answer. 'Is that what you are? A dirty old man who fancies young girls?'

Geroud felt the old desire to run rising inside him. But his arms and legs felt strangely limp, as though they wouldn't have carried him more than a step or two, let alone in flight through the countryside. 'No. Of course not,' he stuttered. 'It's just — ' Becky tried to fill the momentary silence with her own thought, but ended up no more than an echo of her friend. 'You're weird,' she said. This time Geroud frowned.

'Becky!' said Nanny with fake shock in her voice. 'You can't go around saying things like that. You'll hurt his feelings.' For a moment Becky looked confused. 'Except he's too old to have feelings.' Becky laughed again, pleased she had set up a punchline. 'Old people don't have feelings,' added Nanny, hoping to provoke a response from Geroud. But the ancient man just sat in silence, long trained not to rise to any bait. Nanny tried to change the subject. 'Still I liked your talk. But you don't really sound like a professor.'

'I don't?' asked Geroud, wondering if he had been found out. 'I don't feel like one either.'

'You're not pretending are you?' Nanny asked laughing. 'Is this some hustle?' This time Becky didn't laugh. For a moment she felt as though allegiances had shifted, and somehow Nanny had moved away from her. 'Only joking,' said Nanny. 'Of course you're a professor. Dad says you are anyway.'

'He said a *poncey professor* di'n he?' added Becky.

'Becky! Yeah he did. Something like that. But he says that about everyone. But you do sound different when you speak. When you speak now I mean. Now you sound like you come from round here.'

'I do,' replied Geroud, immediately regretting his admission. 'I mean I went to school near here. A long time ago of course. Anyway, it's different when you lecture. To when you speak.'

'I guess it's a bit like being a singer. You don't sing in your normal voice.'

'Yes,' said Geroud. 'It's like you've been possessed.'

Had Nanny been paying more attention to Geroud she might have found the way he said the word *possessed* almost sinister — or weird, as she might have call it — but her self-obsession was enough to blindside her. Becky stood in silence. She knew she was now outside the conversation, a feeling she had increasingly often since Nanny had told her she was applying to university. 'That's what I want to be,' said Nanny. 'A singer. Or an actor. Or both. I'm going to uni to study theatre and music.'

'That great.'

'My dad doesn't think so.'

'You mean he thinks it's poncey.' Nanny smiled. 'But parents don't always know best,' added Geroud.

'Yeah. But mum's happy with it. She's keen for me to go. They run the pub.'

'The Skinners' pub? You mean you're Skinner's daughter?'

'Skinner? I guess so. Do you always call people by their surname? Is that because you went to a posh school?'

'No, it's just what professors do,' replied Geroud, feeling for the first time that he might have the upper hand.

'Can we go now?' asked Becky, sounding like a bored child.

'Yes,' said Nanny emphatically, but not to answer Becky's question. 'I'm Skinner's daughter, which I guess makes me a Skinner too.' She laughed as she spoke, and in her gentle teasing Geroud felt he was transported back in time and space to a place he'd never really inhabited, but always imagined. A kind of personal utopia, where he and the Melusine might sit outside a pretty church on a beautiful summer evening, and have a conversation like this, her gentle teasing only adding to the sense of warmth, but without the presence of the petulant Becky.

'Are you alright?' asked Nanny.

'Yes. Why?' asked Geroud.

'You look like you're about to cry.'

'Nah! Don't worry,' replied Geroud. 'Don't forget I'm too old to have feelings.'

§38 Used to be a sweet boy

'Where have you been?' asked Titivillus as Geroud entered the Yew Tree Inn.

'Just sitting outside. By the church,' replied Geroud.

'You're not still feeling unwell are you. It's the problem with possession. It can leave you a bit queasy.'

'No, it's not that. Something else. I met — I mean — can I get a drink?'

Without getting up and without saying a word, Titivillus did something. Geroud could not have said exactly what it was, but behind the bar, Skinner, picked up a glass, filled it with a pint of Guinness and walked over to the table, setting it in front of Geroud. For a moment Skinner grunted, as if rousing from a kind of stupor, but he left without a word.

'That's a nice trick,' said Geroud, taking a few sips of the Guinness. 'Can you teach me it?'

'It's hardly worth it,' replied Titivillus dismissively. 'What were you about to say?'

'Nothing really,' said Geroud. 'It's just I met a woman who could have been the Melusine. I mean, the Melusine I knew twenty years ago. Except it wasn't her. She could only have been about twenty.'

'Oh, you mean the delightful young Nanny.' Titivillus began chuckling. 'I wondered when you'd run into her. She is — as you say — the spitting image, like.'

'But she said she was Skinner's daughter. And that this is Skinner's pub.'

'It is,' replied Titivillus taking a sip of the red wine that glinted in the tall-stemmed glass in his hand. 'It used to belong to the Melusine's father. She married Skinner, inherited the pub, and now —.'

'Now, she runs it with Skinner.'

'Not really. It's Skinner's place really. She's just —' Titivillus paused as if trying to find a particularly damning description. 'Decoration,' he said, nodding towards a middle aged woman propping up the end of the bar, a large glass of gin and tonic in front of her.

'Who's that?' asked Geroud.

'You really don't recognise her?' replied Titivillus. 'That's your Melusine. Mind you, she's not quite the image of her daughter any more.'

* * *

I would like to say that a more sensitive man than Geroud would have stifled the thoughts running through his head as he looked at the woman who had once been the Melusine. Or at least have realised their callousness. Do I mean a more sensitive man, or a more educated one? After all, the one thing I might say about Geroud was that he was hyper-sensitive. As for being educated — well, he lacked a serious education, but even had he been to one of the top schools in the country, there is plenty of evidence in human history that education would not have made him any more generous in his thoughts at that moment. There is an unwritten history in almost every university in the land of ageing male professors leaving their loyal wives of thirty years or more to take up with a young female grad student. It's such a cliché one cannot help wondering how higher education escaped the attentions of the 'me too' movement. For me, though, it is not academia that comes to mind at this moment, not least as Geroud was not really an academic. What comes to mind is Charles Dickens and his obsession with the young Maria Beadnell which dissolved instantly on meeting the middle-aged Maria Beadnell. Writing to Dickens in early 1855 Beadnell warned him that she was not the girl he had known when they were young. Instead, she said, she was 'toothless, fat, old and ugly.' I can imagine her meaning that as a joke, perhaps underlain with some genuine fear as how the older Dickens might judge her. She had good reason to worry as Dickens seemed to agree with her description of herself. As Cathy Davidson described is, 'Dickens beat a hasty retreat.'[65]

In a similar vein, I am beginning to think I am the only person who enjoyed watching the 2015 film, *45 Years,* staring Tom Courtenay and Charlotte Rampling. To be fair, it got good reviews, but I have never met

---

[65] Cathy Davidson (ed.), *The Book of Love: Writers and Their Love Letters* (London: Penguin Books, 1996) 253

another person, in the flesh so to speak, who thought it was as good as I did. In the film, on the eve of their wedding anniversary, Courtenay's character, Geoff, receives news that the body of the woman he loved as a young man has been found, having disappeared into an icy crevasse on a trip to Switzerland in the late 1960s. Her body is said to have been preserved perfectly in the ice, just as she was when he last saw her.

Rampling's character, Kate, is disturbed by the re-emergence of this frozen memory of Geoff's first love, precipitating a crisis in their marriage. But the almost comically gothic idea of the frozen body of the former lover encapsulates precisely the way Geroud thought about his Melusine. And like Dickens, he found himself face to face with reality, and the effect was equally unedifying. It was not simply that Karen no longer looked like the Melusine he remembered, it felt like a theft had taken place, and the effect of that theft disgusted him. Maybe a more sensitive man, or a more educated one, would at least have been horrified as much by his own feelings as by the revelation that time changes everything, but I have my doubts. It makes me want to suggest that all men are bastards, even nice men (if Geroud is a nice man, which is open to question). But not all men are bastards and in the specific case of Geroud we should remember he is only human. He was forced into a fantasy world early on as the real world was too savage for him, and so maybe we should not judge him too harshly when he finds the loss of his reconciling image, the Melusine, is too much to bear.

* * *

Titivillus was laughing. 'What's so funny?' asked Geroud, realising he was the butt of the joke.

'I'm sorry, Lonely Heart, but you are. I can see into your soul, you cannot hide your thoughts from me.'

'She's changed.' There was a bluntness in the way Geroud spoke that surprised even Titivillus. He expected at least some sense of mourning for what was lost. But there was such a disconnect between the girl Geroud had once idolised and the woman now sat at the corner of the bar that it made Geroud sound cruel. 'What happened to her?'

'She was never beautiful, Lonely Heart. I told you that years ago. How can anyone be beautiful if they're such a nasty piece of work. Or have you forgotten?' Titivillus was lighting a cigarette, another of his gold-tipped black Sobranies, which quickly filled the corner of the room with its incense-scented smoke, but no one seemed to mind or notice. Even Geroud didn't notice. He was thinking. No, he hadn't forgotten.

'Any minute now you're going to feel guilty for being so shallow,' said Titivillus. 'I've seen it a thousand times. But always remember, that woman tried to kill you. She's an attempted murderer. She tried to drown you in a roadside ditch and when that didn't work she led you to the top of a gasometer and tried to push you off. She's pure evil. As one of the diabolical hoard I should really be talking to her. If you get what I mean, like. I only hang around with you because I'm so fond of you, my dear deluded Lonely Heart.'

Feeling peeved at his own response to seeing the older Karen, Geroud lashed out. 'Well no one's forcing you,' he said.

'Of course they are,' replied Titivillus. Geroud could not tell if he was joking when he added, 'I'm a creature of passion, just like you. And I am led by my desires, just like you. Our only difference is that after twenty years my passions and desires are still strong. Because they are real. Yours, for that girl, were an illusion. A fantasy. A myth. Even the name you gave her, the Melusine, it was a fantasy. There's no such thing, unless it's carved on a church wall. You were strangely shallow when it came to her. And your love was shallow too. But she is loved, and deeply. When the man who slept with her twenty years ago, after saying some silly magic spell in this very room, sees her its still the image of that pretty young girl that appears in his eye. You see she was always Karen to him, never Melusine. And she still is.'

Geroud stayed silent. Titivillus had rebuked him and it stung. The doggy little devil was a good moralist. Eventually Geroud said, 'But that wasn't Skinner.'

'No. It wasn't. I said the man who loves her, not the man she married. Life can be cruel even for cruel people like her. She loved Scatson, but she married Skinner. And maybe that was her punishment for trying to kill you.'

As Geroud looked at the woman who had been the Melusine he saw only a woman called Karen sitting there, with the large glass of gin in her hand. And yet, for a moment — *perhaps only a second or two* — he thought he saw the Melusine once again, looking sad at her own lost love. For the first and only time in their overlapping lives, he felt there was a kind of bond between them, even if she was unaware of his gaze.

'Karen!' shouted Skinner from behind the bar, breaking Geroud's thoughts. 'Karen! Can you come and help? Do I have to do every fucking thing myself.' The Melusine dissolved and turned back into Skinner's Karen. 'Learn some fucking manners,' she shouted.

§39 Good times for a change

For once Geroud didn't mind Titivillus coming out with strange sentences. Sometimes it felt as though the doggy little devil was in two or three places at once, having conversations in each of them, and that he forgot Geroud could only ever occupy one of them. It was a habit that usually annoyed Geroud, but for some reason, that morning, Geroud felt at ease with the doggy little devil's annoying little ways. The sight of the Melusine the night before, and Titivillus's gentle but damning assessment of Geroud's feelings, seemed to have cleared the air, so that for the first time since they met Geroud felt understood. It was true, that understanding was not pretty, but perhaps that was the point. To be understood and still liked, assuming the doggy little devil really did like Geroud, felt almost soothing, even if in a matter of weeks, or maybe days, that same doggy little devil might torturing him with red hot irons or something equally diabolical.

'You're probably still a little drunk,' suggested Titivillus. 'Alcohol is good. Like cigarettes. Cigarettes are good. They make everything seem better.' Geroud smiled. 'Big day today!' continued Titivillus. 'Your second lecture. The real thing this time. In front of other professors. The one that will make you a real professor!'

'I'm not sure it will,' mumbled Geared.

'Will what?' asked Titivillus.

'Make me a real professor.'

'Ah, I see,' said Titivillus. 'Still got that imposter syndrome. Well, if it helps, there's no such thing.'

'You told me there was,' protested Geroud.

'I think you'll find I said you need to act as if you feel like an imposter. More precisely, if you are going to be a real professor you need to resemble an arrogant bastard in public whilst droning on about how you feel like an imposter in private. It pisses everyone off, but they feign sympathy, all of which will work in your favour.'

As he spoke, a raised voice came from the kitchen. It was Nanny. 'I'm not staying,' she shouted.

'She has a temper on her doesn't she?' said Titivillus. 'I think she's talking about your breakfast.'

'What are you talking about?'

'What?'

'You've lost me.'

'Of course it might not be,' said Titivillus, taking the cigarette case from his pocket, pulling a Sobranie from it and lighting the black tip with a Lucifer. The smoke filled the air, making Geroud cough, although no one else in the room seemed to notice or mind. 'But at the moment she still hates you for trying to seduce her outside the church last night. Or did you pour glue in her hair?'

'What! I didn't!'

'What did you say?' asked Skinner as he loomed menacingly over the table, bringing Geroud his breakfast. 'You didn't what?'

'No,' stuttered Geroud. 'Nothing.' Skinner grunted and walked away.

'And to think you used to be such a nice boy,' said Titivillus, smiling as he leaned back in his chair, puffing on the Sobranie. 'God knows why you'd want to sleep with someone who hates you so much. First the old Melusine, but now she's past it, you move on to the young one. And the young one is seething with real animus.'

'But I didn't do anything. You're making it all up.'

'Yes, of course, if you say so. You can blame me for anything you want to. I'm quite used to it my dear boy. You know, when I started out every incompetent scribe used to blame me for their bad spelling. *It wasn't me, your grace, Titivillus made me do it*. I got my revenge though by drawing penises in the margins of their manuscripts. I thought I might as well be hanged for a sheep as a lamb. Incompetent carvers were the worst. Always blaming me when they misjudged a cut. Why do you think the gate to Canterbury Cathedral has a woman having an orgasm on it? I did that. Put it up there as revenge, like.'

'I didn't know it did.'

'Oh yes. They always tell you some rubbish about it being a leftover from paganism, but these things are usually me. The man sucking himself off at West Knoyle, the big dick gargoyle at Wiggenhall and the arsehole waterspout at Laxton. And all those *sheela na gigs* showing off their you-know-whats. All done by me. All as revenge for one thing or another.'

Geroud found himself laughing, which made Titivillus smile with a sense of satisfaction. 'Yes, she really hates you for something. I almost believe if you walked into that kitchen right now, she'd stick a breadknife in your back while that father of hers would drown you in the washing up bowl.'

'You might be right, judging by this breakfast,' agreed Geroud, looking down at the plate Skinner had set in front of him, wondering if included a dusting of rat poison.

'If you're not going to eat that, I'll have it,' said Titivillus, grabbing the plate and pulling towards him.

'Sure,' said Geroud. 'Go ahead. Kill yourself.'

But before Titivillus had chance to eat any of the rat poison, Geroud's former idol walked in. Karen was smoking, a foul-smelling chemical plume seemed to come from the cigarette in her hand, causing several diners to cough theatrically. 'I'm going out,' she said tersely, possibly in the direction of Skinner.

'No you're not,' barked Skinner. 'Not today. Not with this crowd. I've already got that daughter of yours saying she's going today.'

'Yeah, she's my daughter alright. She's off and I'm off.'

'No you're not,' repeated Skinner. 'I need you.'

'Ha!' scoffed the former Melusine. 'Since when?'

'You're staying here and that's the end of it.'

'Oh piss off,' snarled Karen, before taking a deep drag on her cigarette, blowing the smoke across the room, and stubbing the butt out in Geroud's breakfast. 'Here,' she said, picking up the plate and handing it to Skinner. 'This breakfast seems to have something in it.'

§40 Heaven knows I'm miserable now

Breakfast over, Geroud and Titivillus set out to walk to the little church where Geroud was due to give his second professorial lecture. As they passed the impromptu camp site of the students they saw only a few of its residents were up, their tents resembling Vanessa Bell's painting 'Summer Camp', of 1913, which I believe was formerly in the collection of the writer Henrietta Garnett. Garnett was, of course, the granddaughter of Bell. That said, at least one of the students, sitting outside her tent, resembled more the figure in another of Bell's paintings of that same year, known as 'Girl by a Tent', which sold at Christies London in 2018 for what sounds like a very reasonable £75,000. Another student, scratching her head as she reclined in the orange shade of her open tent, even resembled the figure in Max Pechstein's 1911 painting, 'Nude in a Tent'. This work is often cited in comparison to Bell's campsite paintings as evidence for the relative timidity of British modernism, compared to the full-blooded modernism of continental Europe. At least that's how I use it in my teaching as they make an interesting juxtaposition, even though I do not agree with that reading of British modernism.

But I digress. Geroud and Titivillus were walking from the Yew Tree Inn to the little church, where, as I have said, Geroud would, in a hour's time, give his second inaugural professorial lecture. Despite having the church in their sights, they decided to take a long walk around the village, to kill time, and reaching the edge of the village they found a temporary car park had been set up in a field. A small number of drivers had already parked up and were milling around, wondering which way to go. They could also see the coach that had brought Geroud and his students to Barfrestone, and a second coach reversing slowly into a space beside it. Soon a large number of mature men and women, mostly men, dressed in tweed suits, each with a set of leather elbows sewn neatly into place, began emerging from the second coach. 'It looks like your peers have arrived,' said Titivillus breezily. 'Goodo!'

'My what?' asked Geroud, but Titivillus was distracted at the sight of a woman walking straight towards them. 'Titi! Titi! My little Titi,' she called repeatedly as she approached. It was Professor Fortnum. 'My darling little Titi,' she said in her most theatrical voice as she arrived in front of them, before clasping her arms around Titivillus in an embrace.

'Is it you!' exclaimed Titivillus. 'Is it really you? Out here? Today?'

'How can I know if it is me, or some robotic doll made up to look like me. I am so uncertain as to who I am these days. I might as well be Marilyn Monroe for all the difference it makes.' She turned to Geroud. 'But whoever I am, I am here to see this young man. Look at him! Barely more than a baby, fresh from his mother's arms. Our star of the day. But why do you get them so young, Titi. He had his whole life ahead of him. You naughty boy!'

'He had his whole life ahead of him,' replied Titivillus. 'And now he has eternity. An eternity of fame after today, which is not a bad exchange.'

'So true, Titi! So true! Which is why I have brought the university's finest minds here to — *wherever we are* — to hear him speak. That's them getting off the coach over there. Fusty fellows, and rather poor on the personal hygiene front if I might say so, but rich in intellect. They have minds as sharp as broken glass young man, so be good. Make sure you are very good.'

Geroud looked pale. It was bad enough having Professor Fortnum and Titi — *I mean Titivillus* — mention his impending eternity in such an off-hand way, but the prospect of lecturing to the fusty old men — and a few fusty old women — of the university, with minds as sharp as broken glass, made him feel sick. Fusty and old they might have been, but in Geroud's eyes their arrival was like seeing the Mongol hoard bearing down on Baghdad. 'And if you're not good,' said Professor Fortnum, running her finger down his cheek again, 'they'll let you know it.' She smiled mischievously, as though hinting this was her preferred outcome. Her grin made Geroud wonder if this was in fact the pact Titivillus had made with her when they disappeared into her office all those weeks ago. 'But fear not,' continued Professor Fortnum. 'I have brought my little helper, the one you cruelly seduced with your claims of love, and then abandoned. I cannot say she will forgive you, but if she does I am sure you will find comfort in her arms. Now, my dear Titi, will you lead me to my seat?'

Titivillus held out his arm and Professor Fortnum hooked hers through it. Arm in arm, with wandering steps and slow, through Barfrestone they took their solitary way towards the church, leaving Geroud behind. He was now surrounded by the hoard of academics disgorged from the coach. It was clear none of them had a clue who he was, and each seemed intent on pointing out, with gleeful bad temper, that he was blocking the path from the car park even though it was wide enough to drive a bus through.

§41 Southpaw

Karen had waited a long time for this. It wasn't fear that had prevented her leaving Skinner years earlier, although he had a temper. But he was not violent. That would be too easy a cliché to latch on to, so we'll leave that lazy plot device to the run-of-the-mill British TV script writers. No, Skinner was not violent. In fact, he and Karen were very alike in many ways, and always had been, at least since they started going out together at school. In that respect they should have made the perfect couple. It was just that Karen had fallen in love with someone else, some twenty-odd years ago. She had fallen for a man who had entered her parents' pub on a wintry night and spoken those fateful words, *issy-wizzy-let's-get-busy.* She had long forgotten Scatson saying those words, and neither of them had any sense that their night of passion was the result of anything other than natural attraction.

After that night Karen had expected Scatson to tell Skinner he had slept with her, breaking the boyhood friendship of course, but sorting out the mess of it all.

Inevitably there would have been a fight, but things would work themselves out. Except Scatson had done nothing. They slept together a few more times, until Scatson decided to join the army and was shipped off to Cyprus for a few years. In his absence Karen had remained with Skinner, married Skinner, and had a child with Skinner, and she and Skinner had taken over her parents' pub. That should have been the end it it, except when Scatson returned he found himself still welcome in the bed of his old school friend's wife. Or at least welcome in a bed with her at Baker's Hotel in nearby Canterbury every now and then. Or, for a bit of variety, in a bed with her at a London hotel once in a while. All quite shocking of course, but despite what Miss Dashwood might say, there is no morality when it comes to love. Except, even that is not true in this case. A *kind of* morality did work its way through Karen's veins, stopping her from leaving Skinner even when Scatson started to suggest it. It was a morality tied to her daughter, and an insistence that she wouldn't leave Skinner until Nanny left home.

The arrival of that moment was a long time coming, but all the rehearsals that had played out in Karen's head, detailing what she would say, what she would do and when she would do it, meant nothing in the end. In turns out you cannot plan for a blind leap of faith. All you can do is act, like jumping off a gasometer for a bet, unsure whether you'll break your neck or walk away a little dusted. For Karen there was a growing fear Skinner suspected something, and that he had set a private detective to follow her. The private detective had even spoken to her on the train on her last trip to London, which felt like a subtle warning from Skinner. Everything said it was time to act, and act today, even though the carving festival was the worst time, at least as far as the pub was concerned. It would cause chaos. But that also made it the best time. Karen felt there would be safety in a crowd.

§42 Panic

In time to kill before Geroud's second lecture, most of the gathering congregation headed for the field on the opposite side of the road to the Yew Tree Inn where the student carvers were setting up to show off their skills. The Interim Guild for the Implementation of Visual Acuity (Readian Affiliation) had agreed by democratic vote that the demonstration carving would be undertaken with more speed than finesse, to give visitors sight of something tangible, rather than barely-carved blocks of stone. Alongside this, the democratic mandate dictated, they would also set up an exhibition of more complete works to demonstrate what they were really capable of doing. This exhibition marquee was set by several others, large and small, including a tea tent, a beer tent and food stalls. There was also an outdoor set of quoits, a children's face painter and a Victorian merry-go-round, so that the whole scene resembled a pleasant village fête, complete with the requisite perambulating vicar and a bevy of squires, squiresses and simple countryfolk from Barfrestone and its neighbourhood. The outsiders, almost entirely composed of the Fortnum professors and student masons, mixed causally among them, so that the only thing an omniscient observer might think was missing from the scene was Joan Hickson and a BBC film crew.

Unsurprisingly for a bright early summer day, the busiest marquee was the beer tent, where Skinner was serving. To his satisfaction it was packed out, despite the still early hour. Had he been able to see a simultaneous view inside the Yew Tree Inn itself, located on the other side of the road, he would have found that packed out too, not chaotic, as a management consultant might assume in the circumstances, but running smoothly as an impromptu syndicate, forced to run itself in the absence of an ogre giving orders. That missing ogre was, of course, Karen, who was nowhere to be seen. Nanny had tried to step into her mother's shoes, but lacked both the experience and authority to pull off that confidence trick, and to her credit even she realised it was better to leave the experienced bar and kitchen staff to rule themselves while she carried on with her own plans to leave, first for a week's holiday in Ibiza with Becky and then on to university to start her course in music, *or was it drama?* Whatever.

'How's it going?' called Skinner as he looked up and saw Nanny entering the beer tent a little while later .

'Fucking awful,' Nanny replied, causing two elderly ladies waiting for their port and lemons to glare and tut.

'What?' barked Skinner.

'Where's mum?' replied Nanny, ignoring her father's question in her typical way.

'Isn't she with you?'

'No. I'm on my own.' Nanny ability to ignore the contribution of the three bar staff and two cooks in the kitchen was not noted by Skinner, who was not inclined towards anarcho-syndicalism, but it did suggest Nanny possessed a natural egomania that would probably hold her in good stead in the world of dramatic art.

'But where's your mother?' repeated Skinner.

'I don't know,' replied Nanny petulantly. 'I haven't seen her. I've been on my own in there.'

Skinner frowned while reaching into an icebox to find a bottle of bitter lemon. The frown soon became a deep scowl so that Signore Lombroso, had he been present, might have noted the way it made Skinner's eyebrows protrude, as though the gammon-faced publican was devolving into an earlier phase of humanity. Perhaps even pre-humanity. It was a sight that told Nanny it was time to change the subject and leave if she could.

'Do you know that man?' she asked. 'The one in the church.'

'What?' asked Skinner, distracted by the slow emergence of disturbing thoughts. 'No, why should I?'

'No reason. Just he said he's from round here. He must be your age.' But Skinner barely noticed what his daughter was saying. He barely heard her say she was staying with Becky that night and that she'd see them when she got back from Ibiza. He just grunted something that might have been the fond farewell of a father seeing his young daughter go out into the world on her own for the first time, or might have been some brute clearing his throat. Whatever the case, Nanny turned and left.

Despite the crowd in the marquee bar, Skinner might as well have stood alone as he scowled for two or three minutes more, his nostrils flaring, like an angry bull sizing up an unseen target. He grunted again, took a deep draught of air through his nose and spat, before walking briskly out of the tent, the crowd before him, sensing his mood, parting like the Red Sea. He headed towards the pub. Some instinct told him Karen was up to something.

Karen was in the bedroom. Two unfeasibly large suitcases, one Barbie pink the other canary yellow, lay open on the king size bed in front of her. The sliding mirror doors of the fitted wardrobe were open and between the wardrobe and suitcases stood Karen, removing clothes from the hangers in one, folding them carefully, and placing them neatly in the other. She might have been packing for a fortnight in the Azores rather than a surreptitious flit with her longstanding lover. Except, even by Karen's standards, the volume of clothing being packed was more than needed for any

Voyage Privé package break, and included as much winter wear as summer dresses.

She worked with speed, rather than haste, determined to get the job done properly, and had even found time to write a *Dear John* letter to Skinner. It sat, leaning against the mirror of the dressing table, like the prop in an Agatha Christie film, placed, *as Miss Marple might have said,* almost too deliberately where it would be found.

The lack of haste might not have mattered had Nanny not inadvertently tipped Skinner off that something was happening. As far as Karen was concerned, Skinner would be hours yet, clearing up the beer tent after the morning service, and preparing it for the rest of the day. She and Scatson planned to be far away by then. It came as a surprise to see Skinner standing at the door of the bedroom, his huge body filling the frame, clearly an immoveable object.

For a moment both Karen and Skinner looked at each other as if frozen in time, lost together in amazement, in what would be their last collaborative act. When Skinner came into the room, he looked at the cases on the bed, frowning deeper than ever. Regaining his voice, he asked almost stammering, 'What — what's going on?'

Karen said nothing and kept packing. Skinner saw the note on the dressing table. It seemed to restore some of the strength momentarily drained from his limbs. 'I said, what's going on?'

'I'm leaving.'

'Leaving? What d'you mean? You can't go, I need you in the bar.'

'I'm leaving,' repeated Karen. 'I'm leaving you. I don't give a fuck about the bar. This place, or you. I'm leaving. And now.'

Even Karen was surprised by the hardness in her voice and the violence of the words she spoke, but they grew instinctively from the knot of fear she felt in her stomach. She felt she had to push hard or she would not get away. She needed to reach some kind of exit velocity, or Skinner would have her stay.

'Don't be stupid,' said Skinner, trying his best to sound reasonable. 'You're not going anywhere.' Karen ignored him, and began packing her clothes from the wardrobe again, this time more quickly, fear feeding a sense of urgency. Being watched by Skinner made her feel self-conscious, and soon the folding became perfunctory, as though she was acting a scene. As she pulled out a black dress from the wardrobe, Skinner made a grab for it, and as they struggled, the dress ripped. Skinner grabbed one of Karen's arms. Karen began to struggle. Skinner grabbed her other arm and when this failed to stop her increasingly desperate attempts to get away, he pushed her hard against one of the wardrobe's mirrored door. The mirror cracked from side to side as Karen's body hit it. Winded, she fell to the floor. Skinner knelt down and grabbed her arm again. All pretence of reason now gone, he pressed his face close to hers. 'You're not going anywhere.' Skinner looked confused when Karen just laughed.

'We are,' she said. 'Do you think I'd stay a moment longer than I have to with a pig like you?' Skinner slapped Karen across the face with the back of his hand, lifted her up and threw her onto the bed. She let out a scream as she landed on one of the suitcases.

'Who's this we?' asked Skinner.

'No one,' mumbled Karen. She knew she'd made a mistake. 'Just me. I'm going.'

'No,' said Skinner ominously, moving towards her. 'Who is it?' He grabbed her again. Maybe some mysterious communication passed between their bodies as he grabbed hold of her, or maybe an indistinct suspicion he'd harboured for years finally gained shape. Whatever the cause, for some reason he said the name of his old school friend, his only friend. 'Scatson.'

'No, it's not Scatson,' Karen began to say, more terrified of what Skinner would do to Scatson, than what he was doing to her. He'd surely kill Scatson. 'It's not Scatson. It's not.' Skinner had already loosened his hold of her and was starting to stand up. She knew that somewhere in the impromptu car park, at the edge of the village, Scatson was waiting for her and that Skinner would find him there and beat him to death. After years in the army, Scatson was strong, but Skinner was a like a fully grown Miura bull. Nothing could survive him. 'It's not Scatson,' screamed Karen, grabbing hold of Skinner's arm. It was a brave act she knew would enflame the bull's anger. With little more than a jerk of his arm she flew off him.

'Oh no, who then?' asked Skinner with venomous civility.

'That bloke in the church.'

'Do you think I'm fucking stupid? He's only just arrived.'

'No, he hasn't. Don't you remember him. At school. The boy in the swimming pool. You stole his trunks. And we saw him on the road. You pushed him into a ditch. You remember. It's him. He's called Geroud. You remember.' Skinner looked unconvinced. 'It's him,' Karen repeated, her voice sounding now cold and heartless. It had to be. She knew she was sentencing an innocent man to a beating or worse. 'It's him.'

'Geroud?' said Skinner. Part of him almost wanted to laugh at what seemed so ridiculous. Dusty memories of the boy he had spent so much of his school life bullying started to return. 'Him?' repeated Skinner mechanically. 'He's the one speaking in the church.'

'Yes,' said Karen

'No you're lying. Why would you want to? With him?'

'I felt sorry for him. He came into the pub. One night, twenty years ago. I felt sorry for him and we got drunk. Downstairs. We got drunk and we came up here and we made love. Here in this room.' Karen realised the calm that had descended on Skinner was working against her. She felt she needed to rouse him again if she was going to make her escape with Scatson. 'I was very young and we were drunk, but we came up here and we fucked on that bed. We fucked. And we kept on fucking, again and again. Are you listening? We kept on fucking. But I married you. He disappeared, so I married you. Then he came back. about a year ago. Those trips to London. It was to see him.'

'This is a joke. You're lying, I don't believe you. This is fucking stupid.' Skinner was growing angry again, but even he couldn't tell whether it was at his wife for telling such an obvious lie, or at Geroud for sleeping with her. Except, he knew he couldn't have slept with her. It was a bad joke.

Reeling, he grabbed Karen's arms again and began shaking her hard. 'You're lying. Why are you lying?'

They say if you want someone to believe a lie, tell a big one. It doesn't matter if it's an implausible lie, just make it a big one, and someone will be stupid enough to believe it. Maybe if he had been less stupid Skinner would have realised how big a lie this was, or maybe he couldn't see through his anger once it was raised. When the Miura bull gets angry, just point it at a target and it will charge. Karen was pointing Skinner at Geroud and he was about to charge.

'It's not a lie,' repeated Karen. 'We fucked on this bed and I got pregnant.'

'You got pregnant?' asked Skinner, taking the bait.

'Yes.'

'With Nanny?'

'Yes.'

'Nanny is his?'

'Yes. She's his daughter and now she's gone to find him. He's taking us both away from here. Away from you. You can have this pub, I don't care any more. We're gone. You stay here.'

Pushing Karen back onto the bed, Skinner flew from the room, down the stairs and out of the pub, towards the church. A light smile played across Karen's now bruised face as she realised she had succeeded. Standing, she picked up the torn little black dress and used it to wipe the blood from her arm where she had landed on the shards of broken glass on the floor. Had she more time she might have gone to the bathroom to wash and clean the wounds, and to find a change of clothes. Instead, she closed the canary yellow suitcase, dragged it from the bed and out of the room, leaving the Barbie pink case behind. It felt like carrying a dead weight, as if a body was inside, but somehow she made her way down the stairs, out of the pub door and through the village to the car park where Scatson was waiting.

§43 I don't mind if you forget me

I thought we were going to leave the cliché of white male violence to BBC scriptwriters.

**You're right, we were.
It's just an easy formula to reach for,
when the clock upbraids me with the waste of time.**

Too easy and wrong. The truth is nebulous, so we need options. Maybe it happened this way, or maybe it happened that. I agree with Read when he says, 'Personally I find it hard to accept any ontology or theory of life which insists on a single and exclusive reaction to experience. There are various modes of understanding and various constructions to express this understanding. Why must we assume that life, which has evolved into such a diversity of creatures, should be expressed in a single category of understanding? The way of art and the way of religion, and equally the way of science or dialectical materialism, are equally valid alternatives.'[66] As we preach so should we practise.

* * *

Karen was in the bedroom. Two unfeasibly large suitcases, one Barbie pink the other canary yellow, lay open on the king size bed in front of her. The sliding mirrored doors of the fitted wardrobe were open and between the wardrobe and suitcases stood Karen, removing clothes from the hangers in one, folding them carefully, and placing them neatly in the other. She might have been packing for a fortnight in the Azores rather than a surreptitious flit with her longstanding lover. Except, even by Karen's standards, the volume of clothing was more than needed for any Voyage Privé package break, and included as much winter wear as summer dresses.

Her packing done, she closed first the canary yellow suitcase, and then the one in Barbie pink.

---

[66] Herbert Read, *The Philosophy of Modern Art* (London: Faber, 1952) 97

Inexplicably she felt the need for more haste, as though the chance to escape was in danger of passing her by. She dragged the two cases from the bed, and set them upright on the floor. They felt like dead weights, as though each contained a body. The short distance from the bedroom to the top of the stairs was easy, the wheels on the cases talking the strain. But getting her luggage downstairs looked like an impossible task. Had she really been packing for a holiday she would have called Skinner to help. This time she had to fend for herself, but immediately she tried to lift the first case it slipped from her grip and trundled down the stairs on its own. She expected the noise to bring someone running, perhaps even Skinner, to ask what was she doing, was she alright, what are the cases for. But the busy bar must have drowned out any noise she could make. Or people were too busy to care. Without even trying to lift the second case, she pushed it over the edge of the top step, and it followed its canary-yellow brother to the ground. Karen smiled with satisfaction. She walked slowly down the staircase, picking her way carefully past the two dead cases at the bottom, and once safely on the ground herself, she straightened them onto their wheels. Moving quickly out of the back door and across the car park, she reached the narrow village lane and turned left, to where Scatson was waiting

* * *

Had he been a little quicker, Skinner might have arrived at the Yew Tree Inn at precisely the moment his erstwhile wife was leaving. With Karen nowhere to be seen in the bar downstairs, he started climbing the same staircase his wife had thrown her cases down only minutes earlier.

    It was unusually silent upstairs as though something had died. Only the murmur of voices and the clatter of plates from the bar below provided any sign of life. Skinner found himself walking gingerly, possibly for the first time in his life, as though wary of what he might find in the bedroom. What he did find there was nothing. Just the bed, the mirrored wardrobes, and the fake Louis XIV dressing table and chair, all in their usual place. Except the dressing table seemed emptier than usual, as though some of Karen's things were missing. In their place was an envelope, his name written in Karen's small handwriting on the front. He opened it and read that Karen was leaving him. She said she hadn't loved him for a long time. Maybe never. She said she loved someone else, and that his return had made her realise she must go. She said she had to go with him. She said she was sorry.

Skinner stared out of his face almost blankly, unreadable whether he was reeling from the news he had just been given, or was about to explode. The truth was somewhere in between. He wondered who had returned. And from where. He remembered his daughter saying something about that poncy professor speaking at the church. Something about him being from around there. He had looked familiar. Storm lines started to play across Skinner's face. *Et confestim ceciderunt ab oculis eius tamquam squamæ et visum recepit.*[67]

---

[67] 'Immediately something like scales fell from Saul's eyes, and he regained his sight.' (Acts 9:18)

§44 You just haven't earned it yet, baby

The congregation assembled, and the creature inside him, Geroud began.

* * *

'In Devon, in the parish church of St George at Dean Prior, there is a remarkable carved object. It is a twelfth-century font, made from red sandstone, carved with a band of saltire-like crosses standing proud around the rim and below a series of inscribed arabesques. The arabesques have clearly confused people. The great architectural historian Nikolaus Pevsner described them as being stylised dragons, but this seems a perverse description, albeit one often repeated. The arabesques do not look like dragons. I think the clue to what they might be lies in that generic description of them being arabesques, because the patterning on this romanesque Devon font is very clearly Arabic writing. Or rather, it is Arabic writing written by someone who does not write Arabic. Paradoxically, this was a form of writing not uncommon in the mediæval and early Renaissance period, known as pseudo-Arabic or pseudo-Kufic. Pseudo-Arabic can be found on diverse fine and decorative arts objects, most notably in paintings such as Ugolino di Nerio's *Virgin and Child* of 1315 and seemingly numerous works by Bellini. It also appears on coins, textiles, pottery and crucially on sculpture. This includes the sculpted doors to Seville Cathedral, dating from the late fourteenth century, a wristband on Donatello's Prophet, dating from the 1420s, and on the relief panels representing SS Peter and Paul on the mid-fifteenth-century Filarete door, at St Peter's Basilica in Rome. These are much later examples than the romanesque font from Devon, but earlier examples are known, usually coming from periods when there was particular connection between Western Europe and the eastern Mediterranean.

'Interesting though the font at Dean Prior in Devon is, you might be wondering what has it to do with Barfrestone. Although the font is of a similar date to the carvings at Barfrestone, I am not wanting to suggest there is a direct link between the carvers or their work at the two churches. Rather it is the function of the pseudo-Arabic that matters to me, because what I want to suggest is that we should look at the carved elements at St Nicholas Church, Barfrestone, through a lens coloured by how we understand pseudo-Arabic scripts elsewhere in the mediæval world, even though the carvings at Barfrestone are not scripts.

'Silvia Pedone and Valentina Cantone have offered three categories of explanation for the appearance of pseudo-Arabic texts in the mediæval period, which they label the exotic, the archaic and the apotropaic.[68] The first two of these suggest an othering of the presumed source cultures for the pseudo-Arabic texts, either in the 'orient' or the past. In relation to St Nicholas at Barfrestone we can clearly see how the sacred space of the chancel is pushed away from the

---

[68] Silvia Pedone and Valentina Cantone, 'The Pseudo-Kufic Ornament and the Problem of Cross-Cultural Relationships Between Byzantium and Islam' in I Foletti and Z Frantová (eds.), *Byzantium, Russia and Europe: Meeting and Construction of Worlds,* a special issue of *Opuscula historiae artium.* 2013, vol. 62, 120f

more mundane space of the nave using various architectural devices that survive, including the chancel step and the arches, and this distancing would have been accentuated in the original layout of the church, with a rood screen, complete with a *vema,* literally cordoning off the sacred space. This division is itself an exoticisation of the chancel, and I think it is extremely significant that the most prominent carved course that runs around the walls of the chancel is not figurative, as in the nave, but takes on the archaicising form of a Greek key meander. Just as the Virgin Mary is delineated as not being like ordinary people in a Campin or Bellini painting, partly through the use of pseudo-Arabic script, so the space of the chancel is not like the space we inhabit, partly through the use of exotic and archaic carved form of the Greek key meander, which here seems to be operating as a stand-in for pseudo-Arabic script. The meander almost becomes a *kind of* pseudo-pseudo-Arabic!

'Yet Pedone and Cantone also write about the possibility of an apotropaic understanding of the use of pseudo-Arabic and other fabricated scripts.[69] That is, its use for the presumed magic protection it gave. Clare Vernon offers a brief history of this idea in her 2018 article examining the possible use of pseudo-Arabic script in Greek and Norman Italy from the tenth to twelfth centuries, which raises surprising parallels with the possible use of apotropaic carving in Norman and early Angevin England.[70] In both Greek and Norman Bari, Vernon identifies the use of pseudo-Arabic script on the city's cathedral, evidenced from the Greek period by its appearance on a carved voussoir from the Bitonto Cathedral, and from the Norman period in the apsidal mosaic of St Nicholas Basilica. In both cases, the highly stylised Arabic script, possibly derived from the word Allah,[71] is either combined with classical

---

[69] See Alexander Nagel, 'Twenty-five notes on pseudoscript in Italian art' in Res: Anthropology and Aesthetics, vol.59/60, Spring/Autumn 2011, 228-248

[70] Clare Vernon, 'Pseudo-Arabic and the Material Culture of the First Crusade in Norman Italy: The Sanctuary Mosaic at San Nicola in Bari', *Open Library of Humanities* 4(1) 2018, 36f

[71] Richard Ettinghausen, 'Kufesque in Byzantine Greece, the Latin West and the Muslim world', in A Colloquium in Memory of George Carpenter Miles (1904–1975) (New York: American Numismatic Society, 1976) 28–47

foliate forms, or becomes foliated in its rendering. As I have said, there is clearly no pseudo-Arabic script used in the chancel at Barfrestone, but the Greek key meander is paired with a second carved course, only visible in this part of the church, that certainly resembles the foliate stylisations that can be seen in Vernon's Byzantine and Norman examples in Bari. More tenuously, the rhythm of the stylisation in the carved foliate band at Barfrestone echoes the rhythms of Arabic calligraphy, although I accept that might be a speculation too far. So too might be the suggestion that there is a direct familial link between the Norman buildings in Italy and those erected by their cousins, the Normans and Angevins, in Kent, but those direct links are not necessary. The differentiation of the chancel from the nave by means of a modification to the carved stone course, from a figurative to an abstract form, can legitimately be interpreted in the same light as the presumed apotropaic function of pseudo-Arabic scripts in Norman Italy and elsewhere. At Barfrestone, it is a Greek key meander, a form equally exotic, archaic and therefore potentially apotropaic as any script. The meander is, in this context, effectively operating as a protective ring around the sacred space, or even being used for its enixibility in conjuring a sacred otherness. With this in mind, we might again think of that font from Devon, with its pseudo-Arabic text running around the outside of the bowl, almost as though the space inside is being defined as magical by virtue of being surrounded by an inscription seen as apotropaic. Certainly a belief in the talismanic value of carved inscriptions, even when unintelligible, appears to have been common amongst both Byzantine Greeks and muslims in the eastern Mediterranean, from whom we can surmise it was taken up by Western pilgrims and crusaders.[72]

'If we can accept that the Greek key meander in the chancel of Barfrestone church is operating in the same way as is suggested for pseudo-Arabic script, or as a kind of pseudo-spolia in which a form, but not the material, is taken from the ancient eastern Mediterranean, then can we extend this to the other

---

[72] See Scott Redford, 'The Seljuks of Rum and the Antique' in *Auqarnas*, 10:1993, 148–56

carved elements of the church at Barfrestone? Is there a sense in which those carvings too are standing in for something else, possibly talismanic spolia or apotropaic pseudo-scripts?

'At Barfrestone, the carved course around the chancel is in some ways an extension to the carved course that runs around the walls of the nave, and it is in relation to the version in the nave that we see it is significantly different. The nave course is largely figurative, and comprises the kind of images that delight so many of us when we see mediæval carving — heraldic beasts, mythical creatures straight from the pages of illuminated bestiaries and monkeys and other animals performing human acts. It is all very charming, but does it too have a symbolic or even talismanic function? I have already suggested these carvings might be an indication of the church being a thanksgiving church, for departing or returning crusaders, with at least some of the figurative elements, such as the lions, arguably having Levantine connotations. The Greek key motif in the chancel could, of course, operate exactly the same way, but the presence of the lions in the carved course of the nave could also have apotropaic intention. There is no reason to presume that mediæval symbolism only ever had one meaning of function, so could the lions also be apotropaic is the sense suggested by Clare Vernon in relation to St Nicholas Basilica in Bari? There the decorative scheme, Vernon suggests, reinforces a sense of the building's 'liminality', existing at the meeting point of the material and spiritual worlds of earth and heaven. As we have heard, in the Norman decoration at Bari there is pseudo-Arabic script, but Vernon also highlights the presence of two carved lions:

> Crouching at the back of the (episcopal) throne are two lionesses, violently devouring their human prey. Pairs of lions are often to be found guarding doorways in southern Italian churches (including at San Nicola) so their protection of liminal zones is well-established. The pseudo-Arabic mosaic needs to be read in conjunction

with the lionesses, as part of an apotropaic programme of imagery.[73]

'While we might be willing to accept Vernon's analysis of a major building such as St Nicholas Basilica at Bari, we might be tempted to discount the idea of a similar sophisticated symbolic intent in relation to a minor provincial structure like St Nicholas at Barfrestone, but I think that would be a mistake. What makes Barfrestone so interesting is not simply the level and quality of the carving, but the way it seems to draw on sources far beyond the confines of a tiny Kent village. There is no doubt the quality of the artisanship at Bari is far in advance of anything at Barfrestone, but the iconographic language and the symbolic cultural meanings the artisans drew upon appears to be the same.

'I want to take this idea a little further, to think about the decorative forms that can be seen in the tympanum above the external door to St Nicholas at

---

[73] Clare Vernon, 'Pseudo-Arabic and the Material Culture of the First Crusade in Norman Italy: The Sanctuary Mosaic at San Nicola in Bari', *Open Library of Humanities* 4(1) 2018, 36f

Barfrestone. In this we can see Christ seated in a mandorla, surrounded by foliate tendrils, amongst which are various figures, ranging from human heads to mythical beasts. Although the meaning of the imagery surrounding Christ is not fully decipherable, the tympanum itself can easily be read in terms of standard decorative forms in the mediæval world. In short, lovely though it is, the decoration on the tympanum is not so very different from other carved decorations from the twelfth century, or manuscript illumination. And yet, the idea the carving is merely decorative is difficult to accept forcing us to speculate *ex silentio* as to what it might mean. I cannot prove my speculation, but I wonder if the presence of the archbishop keystone on one of the stepped arches offers a clue. As I mentioned yesterday, there has long been speculation it is a representation of St Thomas Becket, although this identification is not without its problems. Leaving those problems aside, is it possible the curving forms of foliage surrounding Christ in the tympanum are not simply generic romanesque forms, but a reference to one of the relics of St Thomas

Becket, a chasuble now in the cathedral at Fermo in Italy. The chasuble — *a kind of* cloak worn by higher clergy — is believed to have been constructed from an ornate muslim tent, probably made in Cordoba in the mid-eleventh century. As was common with high-status tents in both the Byzantine and muslim worlds at the time, the Cordoba tent was made of silk and decorated with 'medallions and stars containing figurative images and animals.' As described by Annabelle Simon-Cahn, the garment contains:

> images of peacocks, winged lion griffins (two), eagle griffins (four), frontalised eagles with spread wings, confronted birds, con fronted winged lions, some rapacious birds atop gazelles, a winged sphinx, and fragments of other animals. In addition, there are elephants with howdahs, one containing women, turbaned hunters holding falcons seated on horses with rabbits below (four groups), and two enthroned

men flanked by musicians and other attendants.[74]

The exact sequence of events that led to part of the tent being cut up — assuming the tradition is correct — and reworked into a chasuble for Becket, is not known, but assuming the chasuble was used by Becket during his time as Archbishop of Canterbury is it possible it was associated closely with him at the time of the carving of Barfrestone in the late 1100s? Certainly its translation to Fermo as a relic would indicate it was a well-known and highly regarded cult object, and if this is the case can we not read the similar foliate forms used in the Barfrestone tympanum, beneath what is possibly an image of Becket, as a deliberate echo of the chasuble at Fermo?

'As I have said, an objection to this speculation might be that the forms of the chasuble are not replicated exactly, but in the context of a small parish

---

[74] Annabelle Simon-Cahn, 'The Fermo Chasuble of St. Thomas Becket and Hispano-Mauresque Cosmological Silks: Some Speculations on the Adaptive Reuse of Textiles' in *Muqarnas* Vol. 10, 'Essays in Honor of Oleg Grabar' , 1993, 1f

church in southern England I do not think they have to be exact. The Greek key meander inside Barfrestone church is charmingly crude compared to its antecedents in the Mediterranean, but it is still a Greek key meander. The tympanum might be more removed still from the chasuble at Fermo, but that would not necessarily negate the intention to evoke it, and, as with the presumed representation of the saint himself in the keystone, seek apotropaic protection through it, almost as though St Thomas's stone chasuble in the tympanum is operating like the carved and painted mantle of the Virgin Mary in the numerous *Madonna della Misericordia* images.

'With that in mind, let's move our speculations further east, again to Jerusalem, this time to the primary site of veneration for Christians in Jerusalem, the Church of the Holy Sepulchre.

'The Church of the Holy Sepulchre is a curious structure, comprising a central shrine, once a tomb cut into the side of a hill, where Christ's body is believed by Christians to have been laid following the crucifixion. The rock of the hill surrounding Christ's tomb has been cut away, and the remaining tomb encased in a circular building. This is, in turn, surrounded by a series of later buildings, in a mishmash of styles from Byzantine to romanesque and gothic. The reason for this medley of styles lies partly in the history of Jerusalem as a contested space. A particularly problematic period for the building occurred just before the call, by Pope Urban II, for a crusade against the muslims ruling Jerusalem, in 1095, the event we know as the First Crusade. This event segues with another, almost a century earlier, in 1009, when the Fatimid muslim ruler of Jerusalem, Al-Hakim, ordered the destruction of the Church of the Holy Sepulchre. That destruction was undoubtedly used by proponents of the Crusades to justify the attack on muslim-rule in the Holy Lands, although the Church of the Holy Sepulchre was already largely rebuilt by the time the First Crusade was called. Nonetheless, when the Christians retook Jerusalem in 1099 they set about restoring the Church of the Holy Sepulchre, adding romanesque and, later, gothic, elements to the surviving Byzantine structures.

'Bearing this in mind, I have suggested that St Nicholas Church at Barfrestone might have had a particular connection to pilgrimage and possibly crusading, evident through some of the carved imagery. But perhaps that suggestion can be made even stronger. In attempting to show this, I want to concentrate on just one, relatively small, feature of the Church of the Holy Sepulchre, namely the carved lintel that once sat above the eastern door to the church on the southern facade, and is now in the Rockefeller Archæological Museum in Jerusalem. The lintel depicts the swirling tendril of a plant, in which human figures and fantastical beasts appear. Describing the tendril and beasts, the Israeli archæologist Levi Yizhaq Rahmani suggested the source of the imagery might be English manuscripts,[75] with them being carved possibly at precisely the time the Barfrestone carvings were made. Like most other authorities, the assumption has is made that the lintel over the eastern door is meant to be contrasted with another carved lintel, over the

---

[75] Levi Yizhaq Rahman, 'The Eastern Lintel of the Holy Sepulchre' in *The Israel Exploration Journal,* vol. 26, no. 2/3, 1976: 128

western door, which depicts scenes from the life of Christ in a far more naturalistic style. These double doors have been linked to similar portals at Santiago de Compostela Cathedral, known as the Platerías of Santiago de Compostela Cathedral. Avital Heyman has indicated the parallel would have been intentional, setting up in the mind of any mediæval pilgrim who had travelled from Santiago to Jerusalem, the idea of a single thread of being, binding the Christian world together.[76] Is it feasible to see the tympanum and other carvings at Barfrestone, both inside and out, as part of this same world view with the imagery at the Holy Sepulchre being so similar to that at Barfrestone? Again, as with the suggested connection to Thomas Becket's chasuble, the sophistication of the carving at sites like Santiago and the Holy Sepulchre, is far greater than anything at Barfrestone, but similarly that does not negate a connection. Certainly Rahmani identified something distinctly English in the forms used on the eastern door lintel in Jerusalem, but perhaps we

---

[76] A Heyman, 'Fulcher's Bestiary at the Door of the Holy Sepulcher' in *Ad Limina*, mol. 6, 2015, 108

need also to reverse this connection and think about the possibility that the tympanum and other carvings at Barfrestone were meant to evoke the idea of the Holy Sepulchre itself.

'This would certainly fit in with my suggestion Barfrestone is a kind of pilgrimage church, or thanksgiving chapel, but I think the suggested symbolic meanings of the images at Barfrestone might also fit in with this. Among the most frequent of images at Barfrestone and in the eastern door lintel at the Church of the Holy Sepulchre are chimærical mythical beasts. Rahmani identifies the creatures from the Holy Sepulchre as a centaur, complete with bow and arrow, a harpy, sharp-taloned birds and dragons,[77] most of which can also be found in one form or another at Barfrestone. This would seem to provide any viewer with a typical vision of the torments of hell, especially when set against the neighbouring lintel showing the life of Christ, but as Lucy Hunt has suggested it is difficult to read the imagery on the lintel as a *kind of*

---

[77] Levi Yizhaq Rahman, 'The Eastern Lintel of the Holy Sepulchre' in *The Israel Exploration Journal,* vol. 26, no. 2/3, 1976: 123

stand in for Last Judgement. If that was the intention, why not choose the Last Judgement as the subject?[78] More fruitful appears to be the idea put forward by Heyman that it was the chimerical quality of the fantastical beasts shown in Jerusalem that was being held up as evil, as she quotes Jacques Le Goff assertion that Christian belief at the time identified goodness with unity and evil with diversity.[79] The beasts entwined in the plant tendrils on the eastern door lintel are frequently 'cut and shut' creatures, with some parts from one animal and other parts from another. At Barfrestone too we see numerous examples of these cut and shut creatures, evoking both the eastern door lintel of the Church of the Holy Sepulchre, and its same symbolic message. That the lintel shows these creatures entwined, and therefore controlled, by the vine is surely evidence too that for Christians the forces of evil will be controlled, again finding an echo in

---

[78] L.A. Hunt, "Artistic and Cultural Inter-Relations between the Christian Communities at the Holy Sepulchre in the Twelfth Century", in *The Christian Heritage in the Holy Land,* ed. O'MAHONY, A., London, 1995, p.78

[79] A Heyman, 'Fulcher's Bestiary at the Door of the Holy Sepulcher' in *Ad Limina,* mol. 6, 2015, 114

Barfrestone where the cut and shut creatures are evident in the lower section of the tympanum, but also in the course running around the nave of the church. It is only when we reach the geometric order of the most sacred space, the chancel, that the monsters are finally left behind.

'My point in these lectures has never been to offer categoric proofs. That is always the problem with mediæval art history, but it should not really matter. For me, there is no problem with Hussey positing the existence of a semi-built new cathedral for Canterbury at Hackington, it then being dismantled and its parts reused at Barfrestone. That is perfectly legitimate speculation when faced with the silence of the stones. In the end, my speculations on Barfrestone have to face the same level of skepticism, but even if I am wrong in the details, I hope I have indicated that there is enough plausibility in the broader idea, namely that this little parish church, with its remarkable decorative scheme, was not quite the isolated backwater it appears to be today. That somehow, St Nicholas Church at Barfrestone was always connected to a widely-spread network of beliefs, stretching from Jerusalem in the east, to the Kingdom of Sicily in the south and Santiago de Compostela in the west.'

§45 Suedehead

I have a weird liking for pseudo-kufic. It stems from my teenage years. As well as running the *Michael 100 Share Index* to measure whether my stock amongst my school peers had gone up or down each day, I started to keep a diary. Looking back I suspect it was another kind of coping mechanism for someone who wasn't really coping. A *kind of* temporary stay of execution.

      Although I began to keep a diary I didn't want my thoughts to be seen by anyone so I wrote it in the most impractical way possible. Into an exercise book each night I would write on the day's events and my thoughts and feelings about them, but I sought to avoid writing down the full words. Instead I would only use the first letter of each word. Consequently that last sentence would have looked something like this: I I W O U T F L O E W. I suppose that got it out of my system, externalising my experience of life as if speaking out into the air to an exercise-book-psychotherapist, but it meant reading the diary entries back was impossible. I would have to remember the exact sentence to reconstruct what I I W O U T F L O E W once meant. Do that with the long entries written over many weeks, and you see the impossibility of it all.

Maybe that is how written languages evolve, the practicalities of them being refined into something ever more useful, the Egyptian hieroglyphs evolving into Hieratic, and Hieratic evolving into Demotic Egyptian. So my method of keeping a diary evolved into my own alphabet, written right to left, in which each character of the Latin alphabet became a new character, some derived from Greek and Arabic letters, some made up by me. I named my script Linear C, before I realised there was already an ancient Cypriot script known to academics as Linear C.

I only have one of my diaries of this time left, written in Linear C. I don't know what happened to the rest. They were probably lost during one of my many house moves, as I don't remember actively destroying them. But I still do write in Linear C occasionally, usually in a meeting when I don't want the other inmates to know what I am writing.

Only one other person ever learned Linear C — my now dead friend Ben taught himself the script after I told him about it. He would even write me occasional letters in it. A *kind of* private joke between us, I suppose, and an act of love.

§46 Reel around the fountain

Death is never peaceful. No body wants to die. It struggles. It writhes in agony against the moment of its extinction. It knows there is nothing after life. Death is always a violent affair and for Geroud the moment of death was both violent and puzzling.

Before that, he and Titivillus stood on the step leading into the chancel beneath the arch that separated it from the nave. They watched as the congregation, who had just listened to Geroud's second talk, left the building, both smiling contentedly at the sound of chatter.

Titivillus reached into his pocket for his red cigarette case. From it he took a black Sobranie, placed the end in his mouth and lit the tip. 'Didn't I say I'd make you a famous art historian?' he said as he lit the cigarette.

'What?' asked Geroud.

'Famous,' repeated Titivillus, exhaling a long plume of sweetly scented smoke as he spoke. 'I said I'd make you a famous art historian. Can you hear that crowd. Today Barfrestone parish church, next year, Wembley!'

Geroud laughed. 'I'm surprised you've even heard of Wembley.'

'Of course I've heard of Wembley,' replied Titivillus with mock indignation. 'It's where the Wombles live.'

Geroud laughed again. 'Now I know you know that's wrong.'

'Yes,' agreed Titivillus, 'but I might make some hack write it by mistake. The Wombles of Wembley Common. Something they won't live down.'

The congregation gone, Geroud and Titivillus stood alone in the building, savouring the sense of triumph before it inevitably dissipated to leave them feeling deflated. 'That will come I'm afraid,' said Titivillus ruefully.

'What will?' asked Geroud.

'The feeling of being deflated. It always does after a triumph like this. It's why you have to have more triumphs and more and more. It's why you can never be satisfied.'

'I didn't say I wasn't satisfied.'

'I don't mean you. I mean people. Most people. Hardly anyone says, I have had my moment in the sun, I'm lucky to have had that, now I'm satisfied. It's what keeps me in business.'

'You mean the fifteen minutes of fame thing.'

'Exactly. Give someone fifteen minutes of fame and they'll want another fifteen minutes, and then an hour and then a lifetime. And they'll give more and more to get it.'

'Like Professor Fortnum you mean?'

'I'll have nothing said against Professor Fortnum. What a woman! Except, yes. Like Professor Fortnum. She's your Vice Chancellor now. Just what she wanted. This time at least. It's not bad for someone I found working as a waitress is a cocktail bar.'

'Now you really are making it up.'

'Okay, she was a part-time geography teacher, but you know what I mean. God only knows what she'll want next. Maybe she'll want to be God!'

'Are you trying to tell me not to want Wembley?'

Titivillus looked away. 'It's not that I don't want you to have ambition, like. It's just not everything is in my hands.'

'I thought you could do anything. I've always had faith in you.'

'Did you?' asked Titivillus, sounding sad. 'That's nice. Thank you. It's a kind thing to say. But it's not really true.'

Almost without thinking Geroud and Titivillus had walked the length of the nave as they spoke and they were now standing by the door, next to the carved font. Maybe Titivillus had planned for them to end up there or maybe a higher force was working its own magic, but as they stood in that spot the church door flew open with such violence that even Titivillus seemed startled. Skinner stood silhouetted in the doorway, fists clenched and snorting like some terrifying dæmon. Before Geroud could react, Skinner moved forward, grabbed hold of him with one hand and began to land punch after punch on Geroud's head with the other. Geroud fell to the floor, but soon found himself on his feet again, not by choice, but lifted up by

Skinner's clenched fist holding him by the throat. Skinner hit him again, this time on the side of his head, sending Geroud crashing into the basin of the stone font. Skinner began shouting, something about she's not coming and calling Geroud a bastard. As he tried to right himself from the font, Geroud felt Skinner's hand grab him again, this time hard on the back of the neck, almost as though he wanted to crush the bones inside. But instead Geroud found himself being tipped forward, into the font, his head held under the water. For a moment Skinner, pulled him up, shouting at him again that someone wasn't coming to meet him, and that he was going to teach him a lesson. If this didn't puzzle Geroud enough, he couldn't understand why Titivillus, didn't intervene. He was leaning against the west wall of the church looking at the fight, not even trying to help, a black Sobranie cigarette in his mouth about to be lit wlth a Lucifer match. For a moment Geroud thought the doggy little devil might even be smiling, although he had only a fleeting glance. Geroud tried to speak, but as the words formed in his mouth, Skinner pushed him under the water again.

* * *

When Geroud's body fell limp, Skinner let go. At first Geroud remained face down in the water, but as gravity took hold of his body, he slipped backwards from the font, and his head fell onto the flag stone floor with a deadly thud. In the calm that followed, Skinner sat on a nearby pew. Even a creature like him could not maintain the energy needed for anger indefinitely, and for a moment he rubbed his head in what might have been taken as remorse. Remorse over, Skinner stood again and gave a halfhearted kick to Geroud's body to make certain there was no life left in it. Assured, he stepped to the nearby little cupboard in the western wall and opened the door. In a methodical fashion, as though rearranging the barrels in the beer cellar on delivery day, he returned to Geroud's body, pulled it along the floor by its feet, and pushed it through the little door into the darkness of the Devil's Nook inside.

'Serves you right, you bent bastard,' said Skinner calmly. 'Dirty wop.'

§47 There's a place in hell for me and my friends

Inside the Devil's Nook, Titivillus sat in silence, almost as though he was savouring being alone in the darkness. Perhaps one of the torments of hell is that one is never alone. Except even here Titivillus was not alone. Not really alone. Beside him, in a heap, was the body of Geroud.

      Titivillus reached into his pocket and pulled out a box of Lucifer matches. He pushed the inner draw of the box forward, fumbled with his thumb and forefinger for a match, and removed it from the box. Closing the drawer, he struck the match along the rough side of the box. Sparks seemed to fly in all directions, but the match lit and illuminated the doggy little devil's face with a soft orange glow, so he might almost have been painted by Georges de La Tour. He looked around the cupboard for a moment, then down to the soaking body of Geroud and smiled. It was not a malevolent smile, or even triumphant at finally having harvested a long-bought soul. It was an indulgent, almost loving, smile.

Geroud coughed, tried to take a deep breath, coughed again and sat bolt upright. 'What happened?' he asked. 'Where am I?'

'We,' said Titivillus pointedly, 'are in a cupboard in the church.'

'You mean he got you too?' asked Geroud.

'Who?' asked Titivillus.

'Skinner. He got you too.'

'No, I came in here on my own. That pig drowned you in the font, and threw your body in here. I just came in to keep you company, like.'

'You mean he tried to drown me,' Geroud corrected him. 'It's weird, I've never felt better. Must be all that holy water.'

Titivillus laughed. He liked the way Geroud seemed to have developed a sense of humour, and also that he seemed so lively. It was a pity he was dead and a bigger pity Titivillus would have to break the news to him.

'Actually,' said Titivillus. 'He did drown you. I mean, well, as I say. He did. Like.'

'You mean this is another one of your miracles,' suggested Geroud. 'You brought me back to life.'

Titivillus paused again. 'Not exactly, my dear Lonely Heart. You're not another Lazarus. Obviously you are alive in a certain sense. I mean I couldn't talk to you if you were just dead, like. Or I could, but you wouldn't say much back. Nothing in fact. Mind you, there was a time when you didn't say much. But now, you'd be, well, dead. Like a sculpture even. Although, is a sculpture really dead, like?'

'What are you talking about?' asked Geroud impatiently. 'Let's get out here.' Geroud tried to push at the cupboard door, but it wouldn't move. 'Shit! He's locked it. But I can hear them out there. They must be coming to find us.' He began to hammer on the door, shouting for help.

'It's not locked and they cannot hear you,' said Titivillus quietly. 'Sit down, I want you to listen carefully.'

'I can't even stand up in here! How long's that match been burning?' As Geroud spoke the match burned itself out, as though Geroud had reminded the little stick of its short life. Titivillus struck another.

'I need you to understand something, Lonely Heart,' said Titivillus sounding ominously serious. 'I need you to understand— what I mean is—'

'Oh get on with it,' snapped Geroud.

'What I mean is, you are dead. You did drown in that font. Skinner did hold you under the water and you did die.'

Geroud let out a short laugh. 'So how am I alive now?'

'You're not,' said Titivillus bluntly. 'I mean, you're not alive in the normal bodily sense, like. You're not in the land of the living. So to speak.'

Geroud scowled, but the serious look on Titivillus's face told him this wasn't just another of the doggy little devil's silly jokes. 'You mean this is hell?'

'Well, yes and no. Technically speaking this is a cupboard in the west wall of Barfrestone church, but now you're dead — '

'So to speak.'

'Yes, so to speak. Now you're dead, this is also the start of a new world for you. You can call it hell if you like. You could call it heaven if you prefer. Valhalla,

Hades, the Elysian Fields. It's all a matter of perspective really.'

Geroud looked deflated. 'So the bastard got me in the end.'

'What bastard?' asked Titivillus, unsure if Geroud was referring to him.

'Skinner,' said Geroud. 'The bastard got me. But why? After all these years, why now?'

'You could say you are a hero. You could say, that you saved his wife, the lovely Melusine, from living the rest of her life with that pig. While you were taking a swim, head down in a font, she was making her escape, like. From him.'

'Escape?'

'Yes, escape. That pig thought she was having an affair you see. And she was. But not with you. But he didn't know that. Thick as shit you see. She told him it was you and he believed her, like.'

'She said that?' asked Geroud.

'In one version of the story. So it is almost real.'

'Yes. Almost real. But it doesn't justify him drowning me in a font full of baby piss.'

Titivillus laughed.

'What's so funny?' asked Geroud.

'A font full of holy water and you call it baby piss. You might be right. I wonder how often the clean it out, like.'

Now both of them began laughing. When they stopped, the match between Titivllus's fingers burned itself out again. He struck a third. 'I must say, you are taking your demise extremely well.'

'Yes, I suppose I am,' replied Geroud. 'Maybe I'm in shock. Or maybe it's a relief after so many years of waiting for it.'

'Very Zen,' said Titivillus.

'So is this where my torment begins?' asked Geroud.

'What torment?' asked Titivillus.

'You know, my eternal torment for selling my soul to the devil.'

'You really are a drama queen,' said Titivillus. 'I said you're dead, not that it's the end of the world. Almost the opposite. It's the beginning of eternity. When one door closes — *literally in this case* — another one opens, like.'

'So this is my fate? To be stuck in a cupboard with you until the end of time.'

'You don't have to make it sound so bad,' replied Titivillus, sounding hurt.

'I don't mean it like that,' Geroud corrected himself. 'It's just a very small space. I mean to spend eternity in.'

Titivillus let out a short 'ha!' Let's forget the matches. Behind you, next to the door, you'll find the light switch.'

Geroud turned, mumbling that Titiviluus could have asked sooner instead of filling the air with the sulphurous smell of the matches.

For a moment the tiny cupboard fell into darkness as the third and final match went out. Titivillus could her Geroud struggling to turn in the small space and find the light switch. When he did, the light coming from the 40 watt incandescent bulb flickered, before it seemed to become a physical force. Geroud might have said he felt the light brush past him, like feeling a breath of wind on his face, except the light seemed more powerful, as though it could blow the walls of the tiny cupboard apart. And in a way it did. As the room lit up, the cupboard walls around them appeared to expand away from the door through which they entered, and off into the distance. Soon, far from being in a tiny nook in a tiny church wall, the room resembled a vast library, with a ground floor of glass-fronted mahogany bookcases lining the side walls, as far as the eye could see. A mezzanine had appeared, the balconies supported on dark mahogany columns, each fluted and capped with beautifully-carved ionic capitals. It too was filled with glass-fronted mahogany bookcases along the side walls, stretching into the far distance. All the bookcases were filled with books, some modern, with brightly coloured spines, others ancient and faded. In the middle of the ground floor there was row upon row of simply carved, but elegantly beautiful, desks, each with a rich green leather blotter set into the top, and a personal reading lamp topped with a green glass shade.

'What is this place?' asked Geroud in little more than a whisper. 'How?'

'Welcome to my library,' replied Titivillus. 'Or hell's library, like.'

'But what are all these books?' asked Geroud.

'Almost every book that's ever been written. At least every book that has ever been banned by some bigoted prig, or destroyed by an ignorant mob. And that covers most books really, so we have the collections from the Library of Alexandria, the Imperial Library of Constantinople, the Imperial Library of Luoyang, the National Library of Cambodia, all those kinds of things. Then all the monastic libraries destroyed during the Reformations, and the books burned during the bonfire of vanities, and the Nazi book burnings, and, well, everything that is wilfully destroyed by ignorance. It all comes down here to my little library.'

'Every book?'

'There's not a book been published that someone doesn't object to. And, if we don't have something we can get it on interlibrary loan.'

Geroud looked behind him. The door to the Devil's Nook they had come through was still there, still permanently shut to him. But the tiny cupboard was now a vast, seemingly eternal space. 'How is it —' Geroud began to ask.

'Bigger on the inside?' Titivillus interrupted. 'I love that Doctor Who moment. It's all about perspective, as the good Doctor might say, like. Except here the explanation is slightly different. Now you're dead, dear Lonely Heart, you have entered into a new space. Or should that be a new kind of space. It's what is meant by eternity. Time and space as you have known them no longer apply. Like in a painting, so to speak. The canvas is five-by-four but it can contain an entire universe. And this cupboard is five feet by four, but it too could be infinite. Perspective you see.'

'But where are all the eternal torments and pits of hell?'

'Do you mean the section of Susan Hill books?' asked Titivillus. Geroud didn't answer. It's possible he didn't hear as he began peering at the nearest book shelves. 'I was really hoping you'd help me out here.'

continued Titivillus. 'You know, a bit of cataloguing, some filing, a little shelving, that kind of thing. Plenty of time to read too of course. All of these to read.'

'That's a lot of books,' said Geroud looking up at the mezzanine.

'Eternity is a long time. A long time to read books. Or not. It's not really time. Still it's a long not-really-time. A lot of not-really-time to read a lot of books. And for other things you might feel like doing. It's up to you, like. We have eternity to fill.'

Geroud frowned. Eventually he said, 'I suppose. I mean, I suppose, had this been some romantic novel, or a film, then this would be the moment I'd walk up to you, put my arms around your neck and say something like, forget all that, all I really want is you.'

'I'm not sure,' replied Titivillus. 'I guess that sort of thing might be alright in the writings of Jill Tomlinson, but I don't think it's really appropriate here, do you?'

'I suppose not,' agreed Geroud. 'But what is appropriate?'

'I suppose you could turn your mind to revenge. If you want to, like. You could have a *kind of* revenge on the Skinners. I can easily turn myself into Skinner every so often so you can subject him, or rather me, to unspeakable sexual terrors! You know, get it out of your system, like. Or I could be the Melusine. Either the old or the new one. Or both together.'

'In your dreams! After the day I've had I don't want to see anyone from that family ever again even if I do get to stick red hot pokers in their backsides. But I suppose they'll all arrive here one day and I'll have to, face them.'

'Not necessarily. I could have a word in the Almighty's ear, like, and we'll send them to the other place.'

Geroud laughed. 'You really do have a perverse sense of punishment. I get murdered and he goes to heaven. Why am I the one being punished?'

'Rumour has it you were having an affair with his wife.'

'Only in my dreams. Long lost dreams.'

'And I was only joking. But you're the one with perverse ideas. A perverse idea of heaven and hell. Even if heaven is like you think it is, do you think an eternity spent singing *Gloria Deo* sounds fun? Especially for Skinner. He prefers Phil Collins.'

'Really? Tasteless knob. When you put it like that, it's a deal. If you condemn both the Skinners to heaven, I'll stay here. In fact send all three of them.'

§48 A song from under the floorboards

'I never expected to see this place again,' said Geroud cheerily as he sat beside Titivillus on the pew at the front of the nave of Barfrestone parish church.

Titivillus looked even more pleased with himself than usual, as though he really was placing the final cherry on a well-iced cake.

'I'm not sure I ever wanted to,' continued Geroud. 'Except that it is lovely.'

'True,' agreed Titivillus, pulling the red cigarette case given to him by the last Tzar of Russia from his breast pocket. Opening it he took a black Sobranie cigarette from inside, closed the case and placed the cigarette in his mouth. Replacing the cigarette case in his pocket, he deftly swapped it in his hand for a box of Lucifers, struck one and lit the cigarette. 'One day we'll have to visit it in its heyday, like. When the walls were all painted and the carving fresh.'

'Sounds nice. But why are we here?'

'Really dear Lonely Heart, I do worry for your memory. As I told you only last week, it's time for the final lecture.'

'No you didn't,' replied Geroud, so calmly it might have been a different Geroud to the one who, in life, would have been driven into panic and despair at the doggy little devil's casual indifference to time.

'I'm sure I did, but never mind. You'll manage.'

'With help from that handsome devil you used to send? What happened to him? Or it? I've not seen him once since I entered the abyss.'

'Good grief!' exclaimed Titivillus, sounding suspiciously like he wanted to change the subject. 'It would be an insult to your intelligence, trotting out other people's ideas like some bog standard art historian. The sorcerer's apprenticeship is well and truly over. It's time for you to speak. Your own words, like. In hell everything has the right to speak in its own words.'

'Everyone,' Geroud corrected him.

'I know what I said,' replied Titivillus.

The empty church looked different to how Geroud remembered it, plainer, as though Hussey had returned to finish his brutal restoration, but at last he realised the difference. The band of carving running midway up the nave wall was missing. A course of grey stone still ran laterally, but it lacked the carved rabbits, foxes and sea-lions that it once held. Even the decorative florets were missing. 'What's happened to —' Geroud began to say, but Titivillus was caught up in such a reverie smoking his Sobranie, he stopped.

At last, the Sobranie finished, Titivillus turned to look at Geroud. 'You have to have an audience, dear Lonely Heart' he said. 'And a more receptive audience this time.'

'I don't understand. Where are they? What audience?'

'Titivillus let out a short laugh, almost a childish giggle. 'They're waiting to come in. At the door. You need to let them in.'

'We didn't pass anyone outside,' said Geroud, sounding confused.

'Not that door. The door to the Devil's Nook. You need to go and open it and let them in.'

Geroud gave Titivillus a quizzical look, before standing to walk to the back of the church where he knelt down by the door to the Devil's Nook. It was true, from the other side he could hear the sound of excited voices. It reminded him of the sound of the students he used to teach at the art school, as they waited for his lectures to start, and a warm glow of nostalgia entered his stomach. For the first time he realised how much he had missed his students after an eternity in the library of hell.

Geroud reached out to turn the oversize iron handle on the door, deciding consciously to move slowly and theatrically, as though he was been watched on a stage and needed to play up the drama. The handle turned easily enough, but Geroud pulled and opened the door with equal deliberation. From inside the sound of the excited crowd grew louder as the door opened and through the growing gap the audience began to flow, almost like a troop of *Commedia dell'arte* tumblers entering the ring. Except this was the strangest audience Geroud had ever seen, comprising not the people of the village, but Christ in a mandorla, a man in a bishop's mitre, a knight on horseback, a fox and a rabbit carrying a donkey in what could have been a primitive sedan chair, or could have been a cooking pot. More figures followed, and strange abstract shapes too, florets and Greek key motifs, all eager to get into the church and find a seat on one of the pews. Most surprising of all was a group of bricks, one set laid in English bond, the other in Flemish bond, some red roof tiles, a family of knapped flints and a group of galleted stones set in lime mortar.

The audience welcomed, Geroud made his way to the pulpit from which he would speak and looked at the unorthodox congregation. It was only now, seeing the stone figures that once stood on the building's walls, all massed before him that Geroud realised that what he had always taken to be their grey stone was in fact a feint green shade, not quite the colour of duck egg, but heading in that direction. The rounded forms of the human figures were particularly striking, with their egg-shaped heads and faces without perceptible eyebrows, all enlivened with tiny eyes, bright, like those of a ferret.[80]

For a moment Geroud expected the handsome creature to appear as it always had before when he lectured at the art school and for the final two talks he had given in this church. But this time nothing appeared at his side. For the first time he stood alone at the lectern, about to lecture.

---

[80] A paraphrase of Herbert Read, *The Green Child* (New York: New Directions, 1948) 165

§49 Sheila take a bow

'Thank you all for coming here today. When I finished the second of my professorial lectures I thought that was it, and in a way it was. That was it for me anyway. But in those lectures I never quite got to say what I wanted to say. And I do mean what I wanted to say. Except, I don't think I really knew what I wanted to say. Not then. That's the thing with being a lecturer. You are thrown into teaching the next generation without really knowing what you want to say. That's my experience anyway. The experience that says it takes time to have something to say, and it takes time to know what it is. Sometimes a long time. A spell in eternity in my case. So being given the opportunity to give a final lecture in the land of the dead is an unexpected prize. I've never really won any prizes, except for that book back in primary school, so this is particularly special to me.

'It is special too to have this particular audience of the dead. What some would call the dead. The creatures of the walls, the niches and the plinths, treated as so much dead matter, felled wood, shaped

clay and carved stone. Dead to modern eyes and ears
in a way you never were to our ancestors. It seems so
unfair it makes me want to cry. If I still lived, in the land
of the living, in an act of solidarity with you I would ask
people to stop calling me by the pronoun *he*. I would
ask them to call me *it,* just as they call you *its*. That
would seem strange at first, and people would make
mistakes and sometimes I too would make mistakes.
But it wouldn't matter. Over time it would get easier and
it would show my radical solidarity with you, the beings
labelled *its* by a patriarchal world in which the human
he, she, they and *ze* is set above the non-human *its*. I
would do this as an act of radical levelling, an act of
solidarity with you and all of nature, so we become as
one, *matrixial in our being.*

    Except I could not do this. It would be
forbidden. It is is too radical. It is too open to wilful
misinterpretation.

    I do not digress. This is all relevant to my talk
today. My final talk is about the distinction between
those who set themselves up as subjects and the those
they lay down as objects. The things they consider

beings, and the things they consider non-beings. I suppose I am reworking a talk I once gave to my students at the art school, except now I think I know what I want to say in a way I didn't back then. Of course, next week, or next year, I might want to say things differently. But this week, today, I want to say it like this.

'To do that I am going to begin with something deeply unfashionable — *at least unfashionable in the land of the living.* I am going to begin with some religious education or R.E. as we used to call it in school. Which is to say, I am going to begin with something that I was taught in one of my religious education classes that was, to put it quite simply, false. I don't mean we were taught the falsehood that there is a god. It should be obvious God does not exist. I know that because I know someone who has met Him. I am talking about a falsehood in the retelling of one of the stories from the Bible about God.

'Now, I probably shouldn't be surprised that I was taught a falsehood at school. Schools are full of people telling falsehoods. And I am not saying I was told a lie, because I cannot know if it was a deliberate falsehood. But it was false nonetheless. And yet, it is a falsehood that has stayed with me, as one of those curious moments in one's personal history, that seem to underpin our whole system of knowledge and understanding of the world for the rest of our lives. Or rather, *my* system of knowledge and *my* understanding of the world.

'In R.E. I remember being told by the visiting teacher, who was the local vicar, that the reason Moses was forbidden by God from entering the Promised Land was because he had committed murder during his time in Egypt. It all sounded plausible and, of course, in keeping with Moses's own laws, so why wouldn't I believe it.

'I even continued to believe it long after I became an art historian, long after I had read the Bible in full, which is something every art historian does, suggesting I might have skimmed over some bits of that book, maybe glazing over every now and then in the face of its beautifully-written, but undeniably dense, text.

'But if that was the falsehood, then what was the truth?

'Recently I heard a rabbi talking about this same story and that's when I realised that I'd got it all wrong. Moses was not forbidden from entering the Promised Land because he was a murderer; he was forbidden from entering the Promised Land because he broke a much more unexpected instruction from God — one that you will not find in the Ten Commandments. In Numbers, chapter 20, verses 4 to 12, we find the Israelites, led by Moses, are dying of thirst, and so Moses asks God for help. God tells Moses to go and find a rock. Moses was used to this instruction as it was similar to one he had been given by God earlier in the story. Go and find a rock, strike it and it will give you water, he had been told. But this time God says something quite different and quite extraordinary. God says to Moses, "Speak to the rock... and it will pour out its water." Let me just repeat that, God says to Moses, *"Speak to the rock...* and it will pour out its water."

'Now that is a god clearly after my own heart. But Moses clearly has a problem with this instruction and instead of speaking to the rock, he takes his staff and hits it, just as he did before. He hits it hard, and water does indeed gush from it, saving the Israelites. But Moses has broken God's instruction and it is because of this that God forbids him from entering the Promised Land. He was told to talk to the rock, not to strike it.

'So why did that vicar teach my school class something false, when he could have taught us something truly extraordinary? Rather than the obvious, and arguably mundane, lesson of *Thou shall not kill,* why did he not go for the unexpected and other-worldly lesson that God wants us to speak to rocks?

'Maybe that vicar suspected we children might grow up to be murderers — *it was that sort of school* — and so felt compelled to give us a reason not to commit homicide. I just don't know. But I cannot help wondering if that vicar, a rather silly little man who was too easily roused to anger to be let loose on children, was afraid that we would not take religion seriously if he told us the real story. Afraid at what we might think of a God who wants us to talk to rocks. Now that was a lack of faith.

'But, let's turn this all around for a moment and ask ourselves, why did Moses disobey God, and ask why, instead of talking to the rock, he hit it.

'For me, there is a temptation to see this as a deliberate echo of the story of the Fall from the Garden of Eden, also brought about by humankind, in the form of Adam and Eve, failing to obey God's command. They ate the fruit from the Tree of Knowledge, the so-called apple. That act of disobedience, which seems so inconsequential, like a child scrumping in the orchards of Kent and annoying the farmer, but doing no real harm, can be seen as a kind of metaphorical fork in the road for humankind. With Adam and Eve we have representatives of humanity, and as a species we can either go one way and be obedient, or we can go another way and disobey. That decision changes the course of history.

'And, in the same way the story of Adam and Eve is a fork in the road for humankind, so is the story of Moses and the rock. Moses can obey God and talk to the rock, setting humankind on one path, or Moses can disobey God and strike the rock, setting humankind on another path. Moses chooses the latter, striking the rock, and in that act it is not just Moses who is metaphorically exiled from the new Eden, the Promised Land, but all of us.

'Now we live, in the West at least, in a post-religious age, so maybe you are thinking it was a good thing not to obey God. But remember these are metaphors and allegories. They represent not only humanity's relationship to a mythical divine being, but its relationship to nature. So let's think of God in the Moses story, not as a elderly white man with a grey beard floating on a cloud, but as Nature. In that act of disobedience Moses set up a specific relationship with nature, and the objects in nature such as the rock. He set up a relationship based not on communication and collaboration, but on acts of patriarchal violence. Instead of talking to rocks, and other aspects of nature, such as trees, animals and even each other, we are set on a path where we seek to dominate the world around us, and see ourselves as so fundamentally different to rocks, trees, animals and each other, that we define ourselves as beings, and those other things as non-beings.

'Maybe that is all still too religious for you and you are thinking I wouldn't have come if I had known it was going to be a talk about religion. Well, unfortunately, if you don't want to talk about religion then art is probably not the subject for you. The story of art is predominantly a story of religion — *get over it.* However, let me help you out on this by moving my focus onto the social relationships of Capitalism.

'You may be familiar with an illustration from the early twentieth century, which depicts the hierarchy of the patriarchal system of Capitalism. That hierarchy is represented as a triangle or pyramid, shown in the illustration as looking like the tiers of a wedding cake. On each tier are representatives of each social class, with the smallest section at the top of society inhabited by the wealthiest classes, and the largest section at the bottom of society, inhabited by the poorest classes. Capitalism is seen as a patriarchal system because of this hierarchical inequality – *because all hierarchies are inescapably patriarchal* — and the situation is the same today as it was a century ago when the wedding cake illustration was published.

'But this is not simply a question of wealth. It is also one of power. And with power comes agency. The wealthiest top 1% in society are economically and politically more powerful than the bottom 50% and that power gives them more agency. They have greater clout when it comes to dictating who, or what, matters and can be considered a being, and who or what does not matter and should be considered a non-being.

'What we see in that story about Moses striking the rock is part of the process of codifying, and therefore normalising, the division between being and non-being. Moses is a being, he has power and agency and so he can strike the rock. The rock is a non-being, it lacks power and agency, and so it cannot object to being struck. Similarly as a human being Moses can strike the rock but as a rock non-being — *avalanches in the Alps notwithstanding* — the rock cannot choose to strike Moses. This forms a basic hierarchy, like the tiers of the wedding cake, at the top of which we place ourselves as fully human, then on the next tier those beings most like us, then those beings not like us and finally the non-human, the non-beings. At that point we even change the nature of the noun. We call the non-human non-beings 'its'. This category of non-beings, the 'its', is a category that includes most animals and plants and rocks, but it has, historically at least, also included some people. People who have been categorised, not as human beings with agency, but as objects, as chattels, and things to be bought and sold, and disposed of as the powerful might wish.

'I have to stress I can only speak for myself in these matters. I make no claim for their universality. So let me return to talking about myself.

'As my inability to get the story of Moses being forbidden from entering the Promised Land out of my thoughts shows, I find myself constantly haunted by the past. When I wrote my masters thesis on English Expressioninism some twenty years ago I included in it a short statement written by the German expressionist artist Paula Modersohn-Becker. This too has haunted me as I have never felt I did Modersohn-Becker justice.

I just saw her as an example of how expressionist art can be seen as an extension of romanticism, which was fine in the context of my thesis, but still an injustice. What should have interested me in what Modersohn-Becker was saying was the idea of listening, which is to say I should have listened more carefully to what she had to say, because Paula Modersohn-Becker was an artist very much interested in listening, and specifically listening to nature. Go and talk to the rock Moses was told, and go and listen to the rock Modersohn-Becker effectively says. Actually, what Paula Modersohn-Becker says is, "How happy I would be if I could give figurative expression to the unconscious feeling that often murmurs so softly and sweetly within me."[81]

'I only wish I had enough sense at the time to realise how closely this really aligned with the thinking of Herbert Read, who has been a guiding figure in my research for some time now. But even academic thought is an evolving process. Had mine evolved far

---

[81] Quoted in Werner Haftmann, *Painting in the Twentieth Century*, vol. 2 (New York: Praeger, 1965) 82

enough back then I might have asked the question I am asking now, namely the question, what are the voices that speak — *or murmur* — to artists? And, if I had asked that question I might have wondered whether, in the process of making the things we call works of art, we have the right to silence any of those voices in favour of our own voice and our own expression.

When I was writing my PhD thesis, on Herbert Read, a few years later I returned to this theme and saw it as a romantic phenomenon, linking it to William Wordsworth's poem 'The Prelude' and Emily Brontë's 'The Night Wind'. I was not wrong on that, but I am less certain that I was right to link it to the emergence of Surrealism. With its obsession with the self and the ego, I feel there is a fundamental difference, the difference between the internal ego, and the idea of and external voice. In short, I have been too crass in my approach to all of this and as a result I have repeatedly failed to recognise the difference between the inner and the outer voice, and I have repeatedly failed to realise that many of the expressionist artists of the early twentieth century were not really concerned with expressing themselves in the way we tend to think. Instead they sought to be a channel, or conduit, for something other than themselves. Wassily Kandinsky's inner voice, his *Innerer Klang,* was really an *Außenklang,* an outer voice.

'Maybe I should go further and suggest that, while Moses did not talk to the rocks, and was forbidden entry into the Promised Land, Modersohn-Becker, Kandinsky and others did talk and listen to the rocks, and so did enter the promised land of creative art. But in saying that I might be going further than the evidence really allows. So let's try to pin this down more formally, more academically if you like.

'I would suggest that in order to accept the notion of artists talking and listening to rocks there are two prerequisites. I will keep with the example of rocks to save having to list a range of things, but I mean it to stand in for all non-beings. The first prerequisite is that the rocks we wish to talk and listen to possess a state of beingness. And the second is that we identify some mechanism that allows us to talk and listen to those rocks.

'These might appear ridiculous statements, but the idea that seemingly inanimate or inert objects have their own sense of existence is relatively commonplace in art and literature. Indeed, I have lectured on this before. To recap, as Kenneth Gross suggested in his 1992 book, *The Dream of the Moving Statue,* there is a long history of viewing carvings and other sculptures as sentient.[82] It is there in Shakespeare's *The Winter's Tale,* in Molière's Dom Juan, Pushkin's *The Bronze Horseman,* Meyrink's *Der Golem,* and Oscar Wilde's *The Happy Prince*. But the most famous example is perhaps Ovid's retelling of the Greek myth of Pygmalion and Galatea, which I discussed in my contribution to the conference and book *Sculpture and Touch,* organised by Peter Dent.[83]

'As Deborah Steiner has shown in her book *Images in Mind,* in pre-Christian Europe, amongst the Greeks and Romans, a sculpture of a god or goddess

---

[82] Kenneth Gross, *The Dream of the Moving Statue* (Ithaca: Cornell University Press, 1992) 7 and *passim*

[83] Michael Paraskos, 'Bringing into being: vivifying sculpture through touch' in Peter Dent (ed.), *Sculpture and Touch* (London: Ashgate, 2014)

in a temple or sacred grove was not seen as a signifier of that god or goddess, it was that god or goddess, living in the stone or wood.[84] David Freedberg makes a similar point in relation to Christian sculptures in western Europe in the middle ages, in his book *The Power of Images*.[85]

'In the twentieth century the same idea manifested itself in both Jean Cocteau's film *The Poet's Blood*, made in 1930, in which a sculpture comes alive and, more obliquely, Herbert Read's 1934 novel *The Green Child*, in which the green child of the title not only comes from under the ground, like a rock, but is clearly a living Henry Moore sculpture.

'Of course, we might argue that these are either primitive superstitions or artistic conceits, that exist in the alternative realities of myth, art and literature. But as artists the alternative realities of myth, art and literature are our world. We are not philosophers or scientists, even if we sometimes draw

---

[84] Deborah Steiner, *Images in Mind* (Princeton: Princeton University Press, 2002)

[85] David Freedberg, *The Power of Images* (Chicago: University of Chicago Press, 1991)

on, and respond to, philosophy and science, just as we might draw on and respond to religious, political or social conceptions of reality. As artists we exist inevitably in the discourse of art and it is within that discourse, or space if you prefer, that we find nature, rocks and sculpture seemingly sentient. In that discourse, nature, rocks and sculpture possess being. They do not need the human gaze just to be.

'It is with that in mind that the work of the artist Bracha Ettinger has become important to me, albeit only within the last few months. It is fair to say, discovering her work has been a curious piece of serendipity for me. As I say, I am only just discovering her work and her writings, and if I am honest not all of it is comprehensible to me. Rooted in Lacanian psychoanalysis — *a body of knowledge in which I am out of my depth* — it is even probable that not all of it will be useful to me. But I find within it a resonance with what I have already mentioned, and my wider interests.

'My introduction to Ettinger came accidentally, via Dr Diana Georgiou, an artist and writer who teaches at Goldsmiths' College in London, who contacted me on another matter. Dr Georgiou's brilliant PhD thesis includes sections on Ettinger, all of which has been useful to me.[86] But my introduction to some of the ideas I see in Ettinger came much earlier. Like Dr Georgiou I have Cypriot ancestry, and my interest in the relationship between the understanding of art in the Orthodox Church and aspects of contemporary art goes back over a decade. In 2012 I gave a talk at the Anarchist Studies Conference, held at Loughborough University, and later published in the Turkish art magazine *Sanat Dunyamiz,* which was an early and rather naïve attempt to present these ideas, focusing on the idea of what I called hypostatic space.[87] That is a space that is simultaneously here and elsewhere, such as the space occupied by a saint in a painted Orthodox religious icon. For Orthodox Christians, the saint in the icon is simultaneously in our space on earth and in the divine space of heaven. This dual position,

---

[86] Diana Georgiou, *Erotic Responsiveness: An Ethics of Auto/biographical Art-Writing,* unpublished PhD (London: Goldsmiths's College, University of London, 2019)

[87] Michael Paraskos "Anarsist Bir Rembrandt Nasil Olurdu? / What Does an Anarchist Rembrandt Look Like?', in *Sanat Dünyamiz,* (131), Kasım-Aralık 2012;

here and there, is hypostatic space, which means that the theory of hypostatic space is a theory in which objects like painted icons, or the eucharistic bread and wine, which are both bread and wine and human flesh and blood, exist as a distinct category, each with multiple natures. They are here and there.

'Ettinger talks about the artistic need to "self-fragilise", which is to say, the artistic need to make oneself "vulnerable in accessing the other and the cosmos, to join as I differ, to witness what I give witness to."[88] So let me try to self-fragilise myself, and make myself vulnerable to access the other. From the moment I presented my ideas in my talk to the anarchist conference, and in subsequent talks elsewhere, I felt underpowered in presenting my ideas. In fact I dislike intensely the last third of my essay in *Sanat Dünyamiz* and I have being actively trying to work out the problem with it for much of the last decade. The focus of this has been a book I have been working on for some time. This book.

---

[88] Annie Godfrey Larmon, Interview with Bracha Ettinger in *Artforum* 2 July, 2018

'This book didn't begin with a clear plan. It began as a kind of metamorphic flux. That's a pretentious way of saying it was chaotic. It refused to take form, ideas emerging, merging and disappearing, like watching globules of oil rising and falling in a lava lamp. At first my assumption was that I would publish the chaotic version of the book, and maybe I still shall. I like the idea of multiple editions of the same book, all with the same title and cover, but each a different thing. I like too that readers might not know which version they will receive until it arrives in the post, possibly provoking delight or disappointment, if not indifference.

'The book is not what most people would consider standard art history. But it is art history, even if it does not follow the standard academic model. It is more like a kind of story – as though I have taken the idea that art history is just another narrative very literally. In the space of that story we are in a hypostatic space – here and somewhere else. One thing, and also another. The standard model of academic discourse does not usually accept the legitimacy of this methodology. Not usually and maybe not now. Despite half a century of feminism informing the subject, art history remains stubbornly patriarchal, not simply in terms of who or what is discussed, but more especially in terms of how we discuss. We still look for the definitive facts, for proof for what we say, for the ability to assert IT IS. And that's the point. We search for an absolute IT IS, rather than embracing the fluvial WE COULD BE. This is where, in a very short space of time, Ettinger, and specifically the exegesis on Ettinger by my former tutor Griselda Pollock, has been important for me. It enabled me to finish this book.

'Ettinger wrote:

> For thinking of the coemerging I and non-I in terms of the feminine/prenatal encounter, I rotate the idea of connectivity within autopolesis toward metramorphosis in what I term co-polesis, borderlinking to the in/out- side: to the "extimate" with-in-side and the intimate with-out-side, to the transgressive withness of I and non-I.[89]

---

[89] Quoted in Anna Louise Johnson, *Bracha Ettinger's Theory of the Matrix* (Leeds: University of Leeds Unpublished PhD thesis, 2006) 45

As I said, not necessarily easy to grasp, but what I think Ettinger is elucidating is the existence of things in a state of duality. No, I mean more than duality, I mean mutuality, a state of existence in which the 'I AM' and the 'IT IS' are not differentiated or separated, just as the Orthodox Christian icons' physical and divine presences are not separated. They are mutual. In my mind, at least, this mutuality is very clearly an anarchist philosophical position to take, predicated on the existence of a special kind of space, of the kind I discussed so clumsily at Loughborough and in my *Sanat Dünyamiz* article. It is a psychological space – a dream space if you prefer – but it is also an artistic space. Drawing on my Greek Orthodox heritage, I called this space in the past *hypostatic space,* but maybe the name used by Ettinger is better. She calls it *matrixial space.*[90]

'Ettinger is not alone, either in contemporary or historic thought, in delineating these ideas, although her clear feminist understanding that this is an anti-

---

[90] Griselda Pollock, 'Thinking the Feminine' in *Thinking the Feminine: Theory, Culture & Society* 2004 21:1, 5-65

patriarchal space is an important and welcome development. As I have suggested, I think a basic outline of the theory was present in the ideas of many expressionist artists from the early twentieth century, but I think something similar was also in the work of European philosophers at that time, such as Henri Bergson and Alfred North Whitehead. Whitehead is of particular interest as he seems to have literally believed there is a kind of sub-atomic interaction between the physical stuff of an object that we might perceive of as distinct and the other objects it interacts with. It was the essential separateness of things, inherent in the doctrine of *scientific materialism,* that Whitehead was explicit in stating he rejected:

> This is the grand doctrine of Nature as a self-sufficient, meaningless complex of facts. It is the doctrine of the autonomy of physical science.[91]

---

[91] A.N. Whitehead, *Modes of Thought* (New York: Free Press, 1938) 132. For further explanation and commentary on this see Olav Bryant Smith, 'The Social Self of Whitehead's Organic Philosophy' in *The European Journal of Pragmatism and American Philosophy,* vol. 2, no. 1: 2010, 50-64.

Whitehead also brings me back to Herbert Read, with Whitehead's ideas peppering Read's writings throughout his life, not least his novel *The Green Child.* Read said he saw in Whitehead an attack on Cartesian dualism, which is to say the tendency of post-enlightenment Western culture to cut off the human mind from the rest of existence.[92] In Cartesian thought objects outside the human mind, such as our Mosaic rock, can have no autonomy, they can exist only as inactive things being perceived by an active human mind. In short, they lack being. In light of this, it is surely significant that in *The Green Child* the ultimate state of fulfilment for the green-skinned people is the distinctly anti-dualist desire for physical union with the rock in which they live. This also seems to tie into Whitehead's belief that all objects are communities, or societies. A group of people might be described as a community, but each person in that group is composed of living cells, which are also a community. In turn, those cells are composed of a community of atoms,

---

[92] Herbert Read, *Essays in Literary Criticism* (London: Faber, 1969) 53f

and so on, and for Whitehead each of these communities exists as a collective, different only in form, not in hierarchical kind. As Whitehead noted:

> A rock is nothing else than a society of molecules, indulging in every species of activity open to molecules.'[93]

'From this perspective, maybe the rock struck by Moses should be seen as a community or society. It might differ from other communities or societies, such as the community of humans to which Moses belonged, but it does so only in form, not in hierarchical kind. As someone who has been labelled by others as an anarchist writer, I will say that it is hard for me to see this concept as anything other than a radical anarchistic levelling-up of the status of the rock, in which the rock's existence is posited as a parallel equivalence — *an equivalent community* — to the existence of Moses. Both possess being, or perhaps we should say social

---

[93] A.N. Whitehead, *Symbolism* (New York: Fordham University Press, 1927) 64

being, each different in form but not in principle, and it is this shared beingness that modifies the power relationship between them. Or, to put it another way, Moses becomes an *it,* just as the rock is an *it,* and this *it-ness* must necessarily extend to all of us. It is why my preferred pronoun to you, this audience, is *it,* as we are fundamentally alike, even in our difference, all of us *its.*

'The rock and Moses were both communities, and the only difference between those communities was one of form, not principle. It is only an act of intellectual egotism that says a community of cells, family or society matters more than a community of molecules, atoms and minerals. The kind of egotism that led Moses to disobey God, and strike the rock instead of talking to it. If we accept the rock now has beingness, then our relationship to it necessarily changes and the Cartesian differentiation between me with being and it without being no longer holds.

'In an age when we have realised the disaster to the ecology of our planet, stemming from the power imbalance between human beings and non-human non-beings, this seems to be both relevant and radical, not least because it suggests there is a higher community that sits on top of all of our sub-group communities, the community of Earth. In that community, we human beings, non-human animals, plants, fungi, bacteria and viruses, rocks, rivers and the air around us become a single collective, interacting in a kind of hypostatic, *or matrixial,* space for the common good. It is a community in which we talk to the rock, rather than blithely blasting it into oblivion in order to build a new motorway or a shopping mall. In which we talk to the rock, or do I mean commune with the rock, I am not entirely sure.

'If this starts to address the first prerequisite, that we need to establish that the rock we wish to talk and listen to possesses a state of beingness, then what about the second prerequisite, that we identify some kind of mechanism to commune with the rock?

'Sometimes, when I write, I find have answered questions that I have not yet asked. It is a mysterious experience, almost mystical, and I think it happened to me back in 2008 when I gave a talk at the Courtauld Institute of Art in London, entitled 'Bringing into being:

vivifying sculpture through touch'. In that talk I argued for the importance of touch as a key component in visual art, particularly sculpture, taking as my starting point the story of Pygmalion and Galatea, where life comes through the act of touch. I connected it to the story of Echo and Narcissus, where the refusal to touch leads to death, as well as Herbert Read's introduction to his book *The Art of Sculpture,* where he suggested sculpture is essentially a tactile art form, not only for the maker, but the viewer.[94] I was happier with that lecture than the one I would give at Loughborough, but now I wonder if it was really a lecture in which I was answering a question I had not yet asked. The question, how do we talk to rocks?

'I have long thought visual artists have an advantage in all of this, at least over we writers, in that most artists are used to handling and touching materials, responding to a material's tactile properties and, if an artist is sensitive, listening through her fingers to what the material says she can and cannot do. This

---

[94] Herbert Read, *The Art of Sculpture* (Princeton: Princeton University Press, 1956)

is a kind of tactile communication. Suddenly those artists, like Modershohn-Becker, make a new kind of sense when they write of listening to nature, rather than imposing upon her. Rather than mute objects available for our use and abuse, animals, plants, oceans and rocks become loquacious, and perhaps over time, eloquent.

'That said, it is possible that the type of information we glean, or should I say experience, from tactile communication will be very different to that we gain from verbal communication, but that does not make it any less valid or valuable. We will never know what Moses would have said to, or heard from, the rock had he only followed God's instruction, but I cannot see why it should have resembled a conversation with one of his human companions. Indeed, I would hope for a profoundly different experience communicating with a rock than a simple replication of communication between humans. And, flowing on from this train of thought, if Moses had followed God's instruction, I wonder whether the world might have been a very different place. Perhaps the destruction of our poor beautiful planet in the name of greed might not have happened. In that Bible story Moses chose not to allow the rock to communicate, he chose instead to hit it with his staff, and in that choice a whole new perspective on reality and existence was lost.

'When Moses struck the rock he did not simply disobey God. That was not his sin — *not his real sin*. His real sin was to steal beingness from the rock, to take away her agency, and through that theft, to divide the human being from the non-human non-being. Moses turned the rock from a "ME" into an "IT" and the rest is, in a metaphorical sense, history. Which is where I came in, asking whether art and artists today can revisit that decision, as a radical and revolutionary act of contrition. In asking that question I hope I have set out my stall, not with all the answers, but with the questions and my thoughts on them. My hope is that this has enough merit to bring others into the conversation. Thank you very much.'

* * *

Geroud stepped away from the lectern and was about to sit down next to Titivillus, except it was stopped at the unexpected sight of the stone beings in front of it rise to their feet — at least those that had feet on which to rise. Once stood, they began to applaud rapturously. It could hear them shouting words like bravo and brilliant; a triumph and incredible.

'You see,' said Titivillus. 'I promised I'd make you a famous art historian, and I always deliver on my promises.'

'Always?'

'Mostly always. Either way, you'll agree I was right when I said being an art historian is better than sex.'

'I don't think you did say that. You said art historians are sexy. You never said if art historians have sex.'

§50 The teachers are afraid of the pupils

'Boy! Boy! What are you doing boy?'

'What?'

'I said what are you doing boy?'

'Nuffin sir.'

'I can see that boy. But what are you meant to be doing?'

'Gardnin' sir. Gardnin' in hell, sir.'

'Hell? What do you mean gardening in hell?'

'What I say, sir. I'm gardnin'. Here in hell sir. Birdy said I had to separate the plants from the weeds.'

'Do you mean Mr Partridge, boy?'

'Yes, sir. Mr Partridge, sir. Birdy.'

'Then call him Mr Partridge. But why do you keep saying you are in hell, boy? This isn't hell. This is a school. A centre for learning and ambition. A place full of joy. It isn't hell.'

'Looks like hell to me sir.'

'Oh, you stupid boy.'

✣ The Art-Art History Manifesto

1. We hold that Western art history has its origins not in the instructional universities but in the original Western art schools, the art academies of the Italian Renaissance. As such it stands to reason Western art history has more in common with the creative practise of art than with instructional history.

2. As Western art history has more in common with the creative practise of Western art than instructional history we hold that Western art history is always, at some level, a creative act and should be seen as such. The knowledge it reveals is a living knowledge, akin to the creative knowledge made manifest by the artist.

3. To differentiate adherents of this living art history from those of instructional art history we call this branch of knowledge Art-Art History.

4. Art-Art History is concerned with investigation, the gathering of facts and speculation, but this concern is set on a belief that the form of investigation always dictates the outcome. Consequently, a staid intellectual form, borrowed from other instructional disciplines, will lead to a staid intellectual outcome. A creative intellectual form will similarly lead to a creative intellectual outcome.

5. Art-Art History should happen within a creative framework that is capable of imaginative leaps of faith, original ways in which to engage with material and ideas, and pioneering forms for the presentation of our investigative experiences.

6. The experience of the investigations we undertake should be considered primary and above the presentation of fully coherent outcomes, to the point that the outcomes might be arbitrary or irrelevant.

7. Just as for the artist, for the Art-Art Historian the process of engaging with visual phenomena should be

fluvial and matrixial, without predetermined outcomes or expectations, as this is the only way in which human knowledge and understanding can evolve.

8. The position of the Art-Art Historian is ideally within the art school, alongside and equal to the artist. In effect the Art-Art Historian is an artist as both the Art-Art Historian and the Artist have simultaneous origin in the ancient art academies. We are twins born of one egg.

9. The Art-Art Historian is never hidden in their work. The Art-Art Historian is an explicit presence, evidenced through use of the first person pronoun, a rejection of the fallacy of objective language and a disdain for the monarchical we. I am my writing.

10 The writings of the Art-Art Historian are infused with life. Our lives. Our writings should be full of our lived experiences no matter how seemingly inconsequential or mundane, as well as our success and failings, our hopes, histories and fears. We reject the

depersonalisation inherent in instructional art history as a falsification of art history and life.

Acknowledgements

With special thanks to Vanessa Corby and her colleagues and students at York St John University for allowing me to test some of the material on them, and also to Richard Barnes, Emma Hardy, Richard Hull, Sarah James and Ronnie McGrath.

Also thanks to Harriet Lam, Matthew Rowe and colleagues, both students and staff, at City and Guilds of London Art School, for your inspiration, encouragement and support.

I have dedicated this book to Ben Read. Much missed, he would understand why.

www.ingramcontent.com/pod-product-compliance
Lightning Source LLC
Chambersburg PA
CBHW031602210526
45464CB00004B/1400